JUDAS ISCARIOT
AND THE MYTH OF
JEWISH EVIL

JUDAS ISCARIOT
AND THE MYTH OF
JEWISH EVIL

HYAM MACCOBY

THE FREE PRESS
A Division of Macmillan, Inc.
New York

Maxwell Macmillan Canada
Toronto

Maxwell Macmillan International
New York   Oxford   Singapore   Sydney

Library of Congress Cataloging-in-Publication Data

Maccoby, Hyam.
  Judas Iscariot and the myth of Jewish evil/Hyam Maccoby.
    p. cm.
  Includes bibliographical references and index.
  ISBN 0-02-919555-1
  1. Judas Iscariot. 2. Antisemitism—History. I. Title.
BS2460.J8M33 1992
226'.092—dc20   92-7574
                                                              CIP

The Free Press
A Division of Macmillan, Inc.
866 Third Avenue, New York, N.Y. 10022

Maxwell Macmillan Canada, Inc.
1200 Eglinton Avenue East
Suite 200
Don Mills, Ontario M3C 3N1

Macmillan, Inc. is part of the Maxwell Communication
Group of Companies.

First American Edition 1992

Printed in the United States of America

printing number
1 2 3 4 5 6 7 8 9 10

For Cynthia

batah bah lev ba'alah

Contents

Preface and
Acknowledgments

It may seem a strange coincidence that of all Jesus's twelve disciples, the one whom the Gospel story singles out as traitor bears the name of the Jewish people. The coincidence was not overlooked by Christian commentators, who saw it as a mysterious sign, by which the Judas-role of the Jews was divinely hinted at. I have taken this as the starting-point of a consideration of the part played by the character of Judas Iscariot in the history of Christian antisemitism. As the argument develops, the element of coincidence will tend to disappear, and it will become reasonably clear that Judas was chosen for a baleful but necessary mythological role precisely because of his name.

I have received invaluable help from many people in the course of writing this book. On the subject of the treatment of Judas in art, I must thank my friends Professor Moshe Lazar of the University of South California, and Professor Michael Podro, of the University of Essex, for the trouble they took to provide me with information about sources. I must also thank the staff of the London Library and of the Warburg Institute for their courteous help. Peter Halban has been a source of unfailing encouragement and understanding. Adam Bellow, of the Free Press, New York, has been the best of editors, both through his sensitivity to style and his informed and creative criticism of the subject-matter. Most of all, however, I have benefited from the constant help, criticism and co-operation of Cynthia, my wife, who has contributed so much to this book that it is only to her that it could be dedicated.

❖ 1 ❖

Judas in the
Western Imagination

How important is Judas Iscariot in the history of Christianity? A simple answer might be that he is not important at all. He does not figure in any Christian system of theology, nor is he mentioned in any of the creeds. Yet such an answer would be superficial. Christianity is not just a theological system, or a list of definable beliefs. It is also a structure of the imagination; its most striking feature, by which it has gained its hold on a great portion of humanity, is its narrative. The central story of Christianity, embodied in the Gospels, and especially in the Passion episodes, is the chief instiller of the emotions of horror, sympathy, mourning and joy (and, one might add, hate) that bind the Christian believer to his religion, and set the tone of his religious and moral life. In this story Judas Iscariot has an essential part to play, that of the betrayer, and as such he is the focus of emotions that are integral to the Christian religious attitude.

All religions are concerned with the clash between universal good and evil. In Christianity, this conflict is resolved not by a picture of unremitting struggle, in which the good eventually wins, but by a story of the apparent sudden defeat of the good, which meekly surrenders to evil. But goodness thereby gains a greater victory, since this very abnegation and defeat is what was needed to nullify evil. In this story, there is need of a figure that somehow acts as intermediary between good and evil: someone who belongs to the party of good, but acts as an agent of evil, so that the temporary defeat can be achieved. Why exactly there is need of such a figure is a matter for enquiry.

It may be noticed already that the Christian story is being treated here on the level of myth, rather than of history or fact. Judas Iscariot appears in it not because there actually was such a person,

1

but because such a person is needed for the story to have its maximum psychological and spiritual impact. We will be showing that the story of Judas Iscariot is almost entirely fictional. But this does not reduce the story to triviality by any means; its status as myth is unaffected. It is the task of the enquirer to explore both the power and purpose of the myth, and to reconstruct the historical reality on which it was based. The contrast between reality and myth may itself become the subject of useful reflection.

Let us first have before us the familiar story of Judas's betrayal, as it exists in the minds of lay readers of the Gospels: Judas Iscariot was one of Jesus's disciples. We are not told anything about his family or background, or the meaning of his second name "Iscariot", or how he came to follow Jesus. He is not to be confused with another disciple of Jesus, also called Judas, but not "Iscariot", who remained loyal. Judas Iscariot was appointed by Jesus to be the treasurer of the group of disciples, and held the communal purse; but he had an avaricious nature, and used his position both to cheat for his own advantage, and to adopt a niggardly attitude towards charitable expenditure. Finally, his avarice led him into treachery, to which he was tempted by Satan. He approached the chief enemies of Jesus, the leaders of the priests, and offered to betray Jesus to them for money. The sum of thirty pieces of silver was agreed, and paid to him, and Judas awaited a suitable opportunity for betrayal. Judas was present at the Last Supper with the other disciples. Jesus, however, was aware that Judas Iscariot intended to betray him, and showed this awareness at the Last Supper by handing Judas a sop of bread dipped in wine, saying that the person receiving this would betray him. Judas then left the table and went to meet the priests. After the meal, Jesus, with the other disciples, went to the Garden of Gethsemane, where he spent the night in prayer. Here Judas came, leading Jesus's enemies, and identified Jesus by giving him a kiss. Thereupon, Jesus was arrested and led away to his imprisonment, trial and execution. Judas Iscariot, however, was overcome with remorse, returned the money to the priests in the Temple, and hanged himself; alternatively, he burst asunder in a field that he bought with the thirty pieces of silver.

The above account is arrived at by an unconscious amalgamation of the accounts found in the various Gospels. Actually, these accounts are inconsistent with each other in many respects, but the non-expert reader does not therefore regard the Gospels as being at variance or as contradicting each other. Instead, he fills in the lacunae of one Gospel from another, and adopts harmonizing interpretations where contradictions appear to exist. The only aspect of the story where harmonization is so difficult that any reader may become aware of contradiction is that of Judas's death. The reader would not be worried by the fact that there is no account at all of Judas's death in Mark and John,[1] since he would simply take the accounts found in Matthew and Acts as filling the gap. But he might well be puzzled that Matthew and Acts give such different accounts of Judas's death (Matthew describing the suicide of a penitent, and Acts the Heaven-inflicted death of an unrepentant villain). It took the ingeniousness of medieval scholars to arrive at some solution (such as that Judas's suicide attempt having failed, he abandoned his penitence, and finally perished by act of God). It was not until modern times, when the New Testament ceased to be regarded as an infallible document free of all contradictions, that harmonizing methods were abandoned by scholars (though not by ordinary believers), and it was acknowledged that different and incompatible features existed in the various and differently-dated Gospel accounts. It thus became possible to consider the question (to which the next four chapters in this book are devoted), "By what stages did the Judas story change and develop through the course of the writing of the four Gospels?"

Even the non-expert reader, however, may not rely entirely on the evidence presented in the New Testament. He may be aware of certain widely diffused scholarly theories about Judas Iscariot, though he will probably think vaguely that they are to be found somewhere in the New Testament texts. Such scholarly theories often reach the public through films or novels about the life of Jesus, which necessarily include a presentation of Jesus's relationship with Judas. For example, there is a widely diffused idea that Judas Iscariot was a Judaean, unlike the other disciples, who were Galileans. Many people would be surprised to learn that the Gospels contain nothing explicitly supporting this theory, which depends entirely on a questionable scholarly derivation of the name "Iscariot". There is also a popular theory that Judas Iscariot was motivated by patriotism and Zealotism in his betrayal of Jesus; in some versions of this theory, Judas Iscariot did not really wish to

3

bring about Jesus's death, but rather to force him into decisive and miraculous action to overthrow the Romans. Again, this is not in the New Testament. It was suggested first in the nineteenth century, in an effort to provide Judas Iscariot with a credible motivation.

However arrived at, the average person's idea of the Judas story is that it is a historical record of something that actually happened: Jesus was betrayed by one of his disciples. It is only when a more critical approach is adopted, discerning the growth of the story from a narrative kernel into a more elaborate form, that the mythical character of the story emerges.

Indeed the fascination of the Judas story throughout its career has been precisely because of its unhistorical aspects, and particularly its portrayal of motiveless evil. Judas, in the classical version of the story, is in the grip of the Devil; and the Devil himself is the embodiment of motiveless evil. The motive of avarice hardly seems adequate to the dimensions of the crime. The philosophy and theology behind the story is nakedly dualistic: there is a cosmic force of evil that is eternally opposed to good. The modern versions that seek to humanize the Judas story by giving Judas a sympathetic role, and endowing him with credible motives, are missing the point.[2] In a novel or play or film, every character has to have a motivation; but in a myth, this is not so. On the contrary, every character stands for an element of existence, which is what it is and no other. Lévi-Strauss, in his studies of myth, stresses correctly that myth is not a literary phenomenon, and that it exists independently of any particular telling of it. Once it is elaborated in literary form, it tends to lose its mythical power and status, though some forms of literature consciously preserve the aura of myth. The Gospels are not novels, but the enactment of a myth and a ritual; they have far more in common with early Greek drama, with the Passion Plays of Attis, and with the medieval Christian Passion Plays than with modern secular literature.

Yet the power of the Judas myth is shown by the role it has played even in the Western secular imagination. Judas Iscariot has been the archetypal traitor in legend, art and literature. Wherever the charge of betrayal has been raised, in order to account for inexplicable disaster, the name "Judas" has surfaced. He is the symbol of motiveless evil that is always ready to destroy the good. The kiss of Judas is the seal of this insidious threat; the kiss that shows the intimacy and

4

the kinship between the highest good and the blackest evil. Even where the name "Judas" does not appear explicitly, the Western imagination seems fascinated by this theme of the kinship, friendship and even love between the hero and the force that destroys him. Arthur must have his close kinsman, Mordred—actually his bastard son—who is fated to bring him down. Othello cannot be overcome by external enemies, whom he triumphantly overcomes, but his intimate friend and adviser Iago is his downfall. Brutus and Cassius, conceived as archetypal conspirators plotting the death of their benefactor Julius Caesar, are placed alongside Judas in Dante's Hell. Behind all images of betrayal stands Judas, one of the chosen Twelve, lying on a couch beside his master, coalescing disturbingly with the figure of the "disciple whom Jesus loved", but accepting the bread dipped in wine, proffered by Jesus himself, that designates him as the Enemy, imbued with the principle of evil.

Intertwined with Judas as both intimate and enemy is the position of the Jews in the Christian imagination. The Jews are Jesus's people, with whom he has the closest ties. He speaks of them with love, and also sorrow and reproof: "O Jerusalem, Jerusalem, the city that murders the prophets and stones the messengers sent to her! How often have I longed to gather your children, as a hen gathers her brood under her wings; but you would not let me." (Matthew 23:37.) Yet this very people, in the Christian story, are destined to betray him; like Judas, they do not kill him in a straightforward murder, as allegedly with previous prophets, but stealthily betray him to his enemies, strangers against whom they ought to protect him. Nowhere in the Gospels is Judas said to be a representative of the Jewish people as a whole; yet there is an extraordinary thematic echo between the story of individual betrayal by a close disciple, and the story of communal betrayal by Jesus's blood-relatives the Jews. This resonance affects every reader of the Gospels, whether he is conscious of it or not. In medieval and even in modern times, as we shall see, the parallel is elaborated further, although usually with a kind of reticence, as if there were some inhibition about saying explicitly, "Judas and the Jews are one". Judas is not an allegory, but a symbol, which must be allowed to work its magic in darkness. In times of stress, however, the normal inhibition breaks down. When some disaster has occurred, such as the Great Plague, or a defeat as in the Franco–Prussian War, and World War I—whenever there is a need for a traitor who can be burdened with the guilt of an intolerable disaster—the Jews are chosen for this role and the name "Judas" is openly applied to them. At such times, the symbol is unveiled, and the saying of Pope Gelasius I becomes current wisdom: "In the Bible, the whole is often named after the part: as Judas was called a devil and the devil's workman, he gives his name to the whole race."

A striking illustration not only of the power of myth over fact, but also of the link between the Judas story and the image of the Jews, is the widespread perception of the Jews as mean and miserly. The best-known example in literature is Shylock, but he is only one of a long succession of Jewish literary misers.[3] The Jews, in fact, have never been lacking in generosity. Generosity is one of the most prized qualities in the Jewish ethos. The concept of charity has received more deep consideration and humane elaboration in Jewish tradition than in any other culture, especially in relation to the avoidance of humiliation or condescension in giving charity. The Mishnah, the most authoritative rabbinic work, stresses that charity must be given to Jews and non-Jews alike;[4] a precept that has been followed by a long succession of Jewish philanthropists. Yet this fact has not in the least affected the image of the Jew as miser, because it is not based on observation but on deeply implanted, canonical myth. The traitor who sold his master for money is the underlying archetype, and the money of which every Jew is regarded as desirous is none other than the thirty pieces of silver which were the price of Judas's treachery. In the Passion Plays of the Middle Ages, the audiences delighted in a scene in which Judas bargained with the Jewish elders for his blood-money, each trying to outdo the other in avarice. It was in this kind of vivid dramatization that the image of the Jewish miser was indelibly forged.

In the ancient world, even the most virulent of Hellenistic antisemites, such as Apion and Manetho, never accused the Jews of being money-hungry. On the contrary, they dismissed them as uncouth agriculturists who were unversed in trade, a charge from which Josephus, the Jewish historian, tried to defend them. And outside the Western world, in areas where the Christian myth, with its Judas-component, has no hold, the Jews have never had to endure this charge.[5]

Jews were of course the prominent middle-men and moneylenders of Christian Europe, and this fact has been pointed to as the historical basis for the antisemitic slander. But this argument reverses the order of events. In fact, it could be argued that the Christian world sought to mould the Jews into conformity with their negative image by excluding the Jews from all trades and professions, and by forbidding them to own or cultivate land. Christendom thus ensured that the Jews would be transformed into a nation of usurers. Only a rare Christian thinker, such as Peter Abelard, was enlightened enough to remark that the Jews could hardly be blamed for being usurers when they were not allowed to be anything else. Meanwhile the function of the Jews as professional usurers was of the greatest utility to Christian society; without the Jewish usurers (or as we would say today, "bankers") many of the magnificent churches of Christian Europe would never have been built.[6] A prudent Christian king would regard the Jews (legally his *servi* or slaves) as his most treasured possession, for they loaned him money, and often collected his taxes, coincidentally deflecting the resentment of the populace. Meanwhile, the Jews could be sacrificed by massacre or expulsion if some emergency demanded their wholesale expropriation. The sin of usury was denounced in every pulpit; but every wise ruler understood that without charging interest, money would not be lent and great enterprises would remain unrealized. How fortunate then that the necessary sin could be committed by a people already damned. This damnation had been incurred by an even more necessary crime, the betrayal of Jesus, without which salvation would never have come to the world. The Jews could therefore function as the Untouchables of Christian society, performing in this case not the physical, but the moral dirty work. And the more they were vilified and loathed, the better they performed their function, since every curse dissociated the curser from participation in their necessary but evil tasks. A perfect illustration of this function is the fact that in many areas the Jewish communities were compelled to supply a hangman for public executions.

In a previous book, *Revolution in Judaea*, I sought to disentangle the historical Jesus from the sacrificial myth that formed the Pauline Christian Church. In *The Mythmaker*, I tried to show how this myth had sprung from a Hellenistic background of Gnosticism and

7

mystery-religion, how it developed in the Middle Ages, and how it gave rise inescapably to antisemitism. In *The Sacred Executioner*, I argued that sacrificial myths of the Christian type were the rule rather than the exception in ancient times, and that all the salvation-religions involved the dark figure of the betrayer, without whose co-operative evil there could be no salvation from evil. In earlier religion, the salvation sought through human sacrifice was from tangible evils, such as famine, plague or military defeat. The salvation-cults ("mystery-religions") of the Greco-Roman world, however, sought salvation from the evil of death itself, through the death and resurrection of a man-god (Osiris, Adonis, Attis, Dionysus), an idealized form of human sacrifice. Christianity too believed that the death of Jesus brought immortality to his devotees, but stressed that death was caused by sin, which was the chief evil exorcised by the salvation-sacrifice. Only Judaism rejected the god-man sacrifice as a means of coping with the problem of evil. Judaism, like Christianity, centred its concern on moral evil, but held that man was capable of handling the "evil inclination" by his own efforts, helped by his innate "good inclination" and by the guidance of the Torah.

In *The Sacred Executioner* I touched on the subject of Judas Iscariot, but my main concern there was still the role allotted to the Jewish people as the ritual betrayers in the Christian cult of sacrifice. In the present book, I turn to Judas Iscariot as the central topic of attention. I am mainly concerned with the myth of Judas Iscariot, rather than with any historical reality that lies behind it, though this too will receive attention. First, I will trace the development of the myth in the Gospels themselves, changing and growing from one to the next from a bare idea of the betrayer to a burgeoning saga; I will then review the post-Gospel period and the Middle Ages when a full-blown Judas-saga developed, covering the whole of Judas's life from cradle to grave; and I will consider the deadly part played by the figure of Judas Iscariot and the semantic charge of the word "Judas", meaning "traitor", in modern antisemitic post-Christian movements.

The Christian myth is about a sacrifice. Jesus, the incarnate God, suffers death in order to redeem mankind, and to procure eternal life for those who accept him as their saviour. But this description of the myth is not quite accurate. There are really two sacrificial figures in the myth, one of whom loses his life, and the other his soul. These two figures, who may be called the White Christ and the Black Christ, are both essential to the Christian myth, as to many similar myths.

For example, we may compare the Christian story with that of Balder, in Scandinavian mythology. The story, as found in the prose *Edda*, is as follows. Balder was a good and beautiful god, the son of Odin, the greatest god. Once Balder dreamt that his death was at hand. He told the other gods, who were dismayed and decided to protect him. They arranged with the goddess Frigg that she would take an oath from all beings and substances on earth, animal, vegetable and mineral, that they would not harm Balder. They all gave this undertaking, so the gods now regarded Balder as invulnerable. Consequently, they amused themselves by putting him in their midst and throwing and shooting all kinds of substances at him, to see how nothing could harm him. The evil god, Loki, however, sought to bring harm to Balder. To this end, he went to Frigg in the guise of an old woman and asked her whether there was anything in the world from which Frigg had not bothered to require an oath not to harm Balder. Frigg revealed that there was one thing so insignificant that she had not troubled to require an oath from it: the mistletoe. Loki went and plucked the mistletoe and went back to the assembly of the gods, where the game of hurling and shooting things at Balder was still going on. Standing on the edge of the circle was the blind god Hother. Loki asked Hother why he too did not join in doing honour to Balder by shooting at him. Hother replied that he could not join in as he was blind and had no weapon. Loki then put a bow into his hand, and inserting the mistletoe as an arrow, directed Hother where to shoot. Hother shot the mistletoe, which struck Balder and killed him. Balder's body was then burned on a great funeral pyre, together with his wife and his horse, amid scenes of great sorrow.

Frazer has proved with a wealth of examples that the myth of Balder's death was derived from an actual ritual in which an effigy of Balder (earlier, a human victim representing the god) was burned at a fire festival to promote the fertility of the crops.[7]

Here too a god is brought to his death, and no one is to blame

9

except the wicked plotter, Loki, the god of mischief and evil. Even the blind Hother is not to blame, because he has been tricked by Loki into thinking that the arrow will be harmless. All the gods throw stones at Balder, but their stones are really harmless, and they are only throwing them in play. The wicked Loki, whom everyone regards with horror, is alone responsible and therefore is banished and cursed for his deed.

Yet the death of Balder is a salvific event, for without it the crops will fail. The wicked Loki takes the blame, but gods and men all benefit by it. Clearly Loki has his place and function, which is to perform a deed of inexpressible wickedness, and bear the resultant hatred and curses. In the Christian myth it is Judas Iscariot who performs this function. The role of the blind Hother is played by Pontius Pilate, who actually crucifies Jesus, but bears no blame for this deed, since he has been tricked into it (the mechanism of the trick has different versions). When Pontius Pilate washes his hands, while the massed Jewish Judases accept responsibility by chanting, "Crucify him!", he symbolizes the innocence of Roman power, exonerated from complicity in the death of Jesus, so that the blame can fall wholly on the Jews. It is no wonder that in the Ethiopian Church, Pontius Pilate was a saint, though his canonization did not receive confirmation from the mainstream Church because of a new theory, supported by Eusebius, that Pilate was partly to blame after all.[8] In any case, the common view of Pilate as guilty of weakness in acceding to Jewish murderousness is not part of the Gospel narrative, which exonerates Pilate from blame.

It is interesting that the central scene of the Christian myth pictures a guilty crowd and an innocent individual, while the Balder myth pictures the opposite, an innocent crowd and a guilty individual, Loki. Hother does parallel Pilate, but the participating crowd of gods share Hother's innocence. In the Christian myth, there is only one Hother and a crowd of Lokis, or Judases. This difference shows that the Christian myth (unlike the Scandinavian version) aims to elect a whole people, the Jews, to the Judas role. This is partly because the Scandinavian myth remains on the supernatural level; all its participants are gods, whereas the Christian myth has a mixture of gods and human beings. Satan, an evil god like Loki, is present, having taken possession of Judas and (by implication) the Jewish crowd; and Jesus, a good god like Balder, is the central

10

victim. But the sacrificial tragedy takes place on earth, to which the good god has descended. And, most importantly, the evil god acts through human representatives, who remain as earthly bearers of the guilt; "His blood be on us and on our children." (Matthew 27:25.)

What is the meaning of these sacrificial dramas? Both versions of the myth clearly arise from an ancient blood-ritual. Both are removed from the actual practice of human sacrifice—the Scandinavian myth by exalting the whole procedure to the abode of the gods, the Christian myth by adapting a historical death to a sacrificial purpose. But the spiritualizing of human sacrifice is the normal strategy of mystery-religion. The psychological mechanism is the same, whether in actual or in spiritualized human sacrifice: the community wants the sacrifice to occur, because otherwise there will be no salvation, but it shifts the responsibility to some evil figure. The death of the victim is mourned with every appearance of heartfelt grief, for the deeper the grief the more complete the dissociation of the community from the death which they desired. The means by which the death came about is disowned, either by banishing, ostracizing or humiliating the executioner, or even, as in the case of the Athenian Bouphonia, holding a trial of the knife with which the sacrifice was performed.[9] Restitution is made by adoring the victim's spirit; he becomes a god, or is already a god when executed. Thus the resurrection of the victim is a necessary part of the process, and can even become the whole point, when the ritual involves initiation into a mystery that promises immortality. But the essence of the ritual is to be able to perform it without guilt, and that means to repress deeply the responsibility of the community for the ritual death. In the Balder myth (if we strip it of what Freud called "secondary elaboration") we have a picture of the whole community stoning a victim; this is the reality of communal responsibility for the death. But the myth tells us that this is only appearance: the stones are harmless, and the death does not occur because of them, but through the machinations of an individual whom the community disowns.[10] In the Christian myth, a guilty community is carefully distinguished from the Christian community for whose benefit the death occurs. This community of Jews is shortly to be outlawed, branded and dispossessed: the real community is represented by the handful of sorrowing Christians present, and by the innocent Roman Governor. The very people who most ardently desire the death,

11

because they believe with perfect faith that it brings them salvation, are stricken by grief and horror when it occurs, and hence entirely absolved from the guilt of bringing it about.[11]

The Mapuche Indians, who live beside Lake Titicaca in Peru, have been investigated recently by Patrick Tierney.[12] He found that they performed a grisly human sacrifice, about once every ten years, when their community was threatened by a huge periodical influx of sea-water. The sacrifice was that of a boy, placed in the sea with his arms and legs chopped off; and it was believed that he became a tutelary deity for the tribe. A woman of the tribe, Machi Juana, was the performer of the sacrifice. She was ostracized and treated by the whole tribe with loathing; every misfortune that occurred to any member of the tribe was blamed on her. Yet whenever an important feast took place, she was given an honoured place at the table. She is thus a good example of what I have called "the sacred executioner"; the performer of the sacrifice who is hated and outlawed, but who still retains an awesome quality because his wicked deed has brought salvation. A disguised example of this is the biblical Cain, who killed his brother, yet received divine protection in his wanderings, and was the founder of a city and the ancestor of the founders of the arts (Genesis 4:17–22); what the Bible calls a murder, was, in the Kenite saga from which the Bible derives the story,[13] a salvific sacrifice. The Jews too, despite the loathing inspired by their alleged cosmic crime, have also been regarded with a certain awe. Even at their lowest ebb of powerlessness, they have been viewed as the possessors of magical power. The legend of the Wandering Jew (which has sometimes coalesced with the legend of Judas Iscariot) expresses this Christian awe of the Sacred Executioner, condemned to suffer for the act that brought salvation to mankind. In the New Testament, Judas Iscariot does not, like Cain or the Wandering Jew, receive the dubious gift of prolonged life; he dies by suicide in one version, by heavenly destruction in another. But in some later versions of the story, his charisma is enhanced. He becomes a prince, and a formidable person, with an awesome destiny. However much the aim of the myth is to foster detestation, it can never be quite forgotten that he is after all the Black Christ, an agent of salvation.

The Christian myth is a powerful version of a means of exorcising guilt that has been practised by mankind since Neolithic times.[14] Judaism is a revolutionary religion that attempted to eschew both human and divine sacrifice,[15] and sought to lay moral responsibility on the community itself and on the individuals who compose it. It is ironic that the Jews were saddled with the very role that they had tried to banish from religion—the performer of the human-divine sacrifice.

The Hebrew Bible wages a campaign against human sacrifice. Psalm 106:37 indicts those who "sacrificed their sons and their daughters to demons, and shed innocent blood, the blood of their sons and of their daughters". The Torah (Deuteronomy 12:31) solemnly bans human sacrifice: "Thou shalt not do so unto the Lord thy God; for every abomination to the Lord, which he hateth, have they [the Canaanites] done unto their gods; for even their sons and their daughters do they burn in the fire to their gods." The prophets too inveigh against human sacrifice: "They have built the high places of Topheth, which is in the valley of Hinnom, to burn their sons and their daughters in the fire; which I commanded not, neither came it into My mind" (Jeremiah 7:31). The sacrificial Phoenician cult of Moloch is denounced time and again. The vehemence of the Hebrew Bible shows that it was combating a very real threat. Human sacrifice was endemic in the ancient world, and it exercised a strong appeal as a means of salvation. There is evidence that it had played a part in the early history of the Israelites themselves. The story of the Binding of Isaac (Genesis 22) shows God demanding a child-sacrifice. But He relents, and instead institutes animal sacrifice. Even animal sacrifice, however, lost its atoning significance in biblical and rabbinic thought. The model of sacrifice is the "peace-offering" which is a meal of friendship shared with God. Even the "sin-offerings" acquired this character; they no longer brought atonement, which could be procured only by repentance and reparation, but marked a final celebration of reconciliation between the repentant sinner and God.[16]

Thus the whole Jewish sacrificial system had moved in the direction of seeing sacrifices as gifts to God, rather than as vicarious sufferers for the sacrificer's sins. This being so, it was no great shock to the Jewish system of atonement when the Temple was destroyed and all sacrifices ceased. However, the Christian theory of the atoning power of the death of Jesus based itself on a primitive model of the Jewish animal sacrifices as vicarious.[17]

In modern times, the Christian myth is all the more powerful because of the illusion that it has been outgrown. Post-Christian movements have arisen, both of the Right and of the Left, in which the Judas-myth has flourished, and the Jews have remained the people of the Devil, no longer portrayed with horns, tail and hooves, but in a rationalist guise as the biological menace, the alien threat to the nation, or the capitalist, imperialist or Zionist conspiracy. The Jews continue to act the role of traitor, but it is no longer a Christ-figure whom they betray to a redeeming death; instead they betray the nation, or the race, or the rightful Tsar—as "Jewish Bolsheviks" were said to do—or the true Revolution, as in Stalin's attacks on Judas-Trotsky. In this modern mythic role, the Jews have no positive aspect; they are no longer the unwitting causers of salvation, as in the Christian myth. They no longer represent necessary evil, but unmitigated evil; they are therefore dispensable and can be totally annihilated.

Notice the *optimism* of this destroying attitude: evil can be expunged from the world. Once the Jews have been destroyed, a new world will begin, cleansed of evil, because *Judenrein*. This new optimism produced greater danger to the Jews than the old-style pogroms and massacres. Oddly enough, the ferocity of modern antisemitism might be explained as arising from the rationalism of the Enlightenment. The eighteenth-century rationalists themselves did not put the Jews into a Judas role. When they were antisemitic (as in the case of Voltaire), they portrayed the Jews not as dangerous, but as stupid, ignorant and backward. Sometimes their attacks on the Jews were indirect criticisms of Christianity, which was based on the "superstition" of Judaism. Even though Voltaire declared the Jews too backward to be reclaimed, it was the Enlightenment that actually emancipated the Jews. This led eventually to complaints that the Jews were monopolizing the arts, sciences and professions and were acquiring frightening power. When the Jews could no longer be despised or patronized as backward, atavistic fears made them into the enemy required by the ideological movements that had inherited the Enlightenment's conviction that the world was to be made anew and that the problem of evil was soluble by human reason. The *hubris* of unbounded Utopianism revivified ancient stereotypes operating all the more powerfully because their origin could not be admitted—since they belonged to an age of irrationalism that had been officially transcended.

But though the influence of Enlightenment rationalistic optimism on modern movements, certainly on Communism but even on Nazism,[18] cannot be denied, this is not the whole story. There is also an influence from the Christian myth; for that myth provided not just a Suffering Christ, but also a Christ Triumphant. The millenarian movements of the Middle Ages, though often falling foul of established papal and secular authority, built their dreams on respectable Christian tradition, beginning with the Book of Revelation.[19] This apocalyptic tradition foretold that one day the imperfect world would cease, and a new world would begin. It would be inaugurated by the return of Christ, who would lead an army of the faithful against the Antichrist.[20] In some versions, the Antichrist would be a Jew leading a powerful Jewish army. The Antichrist, before the final battle, would have great success: he would rebuild the Jewish Temple, and be accepted by the Jews as their promised Messiah. But in the final battle, the army of Christ Triumphant would annihilate the Jews unto the last man, woman and child. In this myth, evil is ultimately subject to obliteration; and this means that a time will come when the role of the Jews can be terminated. When the sufferings of Christ are no longer needed, because sin has been abolished, then the Jews can be dispensed with. They can disappear or be wiped out, either by physical annihilation or by wholesale conversion. Whenever waves of millenarian fervour swept through Christendom, there were periodic attempts to put the more savage alternative into effect. The worst massacres of Jews, before the Nazi era, were at the time of the Crusades, when popular millenarianism was at its height. In more normal times, the Jews were tolerated, because both the inevitability and the usefulness of evil were accepted.

Thus in attempting to detach itself from mythical patterns of thought, the modern world has often only reinforced them. Instead of relegating evil to the realm of unsupported superstition, Enlightenment succeeded only in supplanting one version of the Christian myth with another, leaving the Jews firmly in the Judas-role. We may ask, "What is in common between the two Christian scenarios of the Suffering and the Triumphant Christ?" The answer is that both see the problem of evil as insuperable on an individual level. Both the attempt to shift the solution to a divine figure, for whose sacrifice someone has to pay, and the attempt to abolish evil altogether, imply a despair about coping with evil on the everyday level. This despair is expressed in the very elevation of evil to cosmic status, as proceeding from a supernatural source, the Devil.

Judaism has a very different philosophy of evil, although it has never been considered seriously as an alternative to the Christian scheme. Satan has no role to play in the Hebrew Bible, except in the book of Job as a divinely sanctioned *provocateur*. In the Pseude-pigrapha, Satan does achieve independence, and this promotion is carried even further in Christianity; but normative Judaism never accepted these works into the canon and refused to give Satan more exalted status than he had enjoyed in the Hebrew Bible. He remains simply a symbol of what the rabbis called "the evil inclination", which they viewed as a constituent of human moral structure, and not an independent cosmic principle. Evil, they claimed, was capable of control by human will; its energies could even be harnessed for good. But the corollary was that evil could not be got rid of. It was part of the human condition for ever.[21] This fact could only be borne because it was believed that evil was controllable; indeed learning to control it was precisely the human task. More optimistic than Christianity in one way, Judaism was more pessimistic in another. But its acceptance of evil in man meant that Judaism did not require a supernatural rescue-operation, did not have to recruit the power of evil in a violent salvation-drama, and did not look forward to a genocidal Final Solution.

Books and articles have been written on Judas Iscariot, but they all concentrate on historical or literary questions such as, "What were Judas's real motives?" or "What kind of person was Judas?" Recently, Frank Kermode has written about the Judas story from an aesthetic standpoint, asking such questions as, "How did the story develop from Gospel to Gospel?" and "How did the inner narrative logic of the story of an Opposer lead to imaginative elaborations?"[22] Drawing on the work of Vladimir Propp on folk-tales, Kermode shows that the Judas story conforms to a narrative pattern in which the Opposer's function is more important than his personal char-acteristics, which only appear at a later stage in the transmission of the story in response to the narrative urge of the teller and the curiosity of his audience. Kermode's work displays clearly the large element of fiction in the Judas saga. But his purely aesthetic interest divests the story of its mythic status. The Gospel-writers who generated this story, and their successors who developed it further, were not novelists or poets in our modern sense. They were pondering on a tale on which their whole salvation rested. If they added some detail it was not to gratify their literary taste, but rather because the change seemed to promote salvation. The story was a weapon in the fight against the devil and his servants. Every time the story was told it re-enacted a cosmic drama of betrayal and submission, agonized death and glorious resurrection which the teller and his audience must personally undergo. The story also had political significance, showing why the Church was destined to prosper at the expense of the Synagogue, why the Jews were damned and the Christians were to take their place as the People of God. It explained why the Church had to be in Rome, and why Rome had to be in the Church. It was a myth that also validated the upstart Church in jettisoning Jewish tradition, and in usurping the patriarchal covenants. To consider such a story in terms of folk-tale or novel is either to trivialize it, or to promote what is essentially a piece of propaganda to the status of literature.

Rudolf Bultmann popularized the idea that every myth is a repository of deep, unquestionable wisdom, which needs only to be translated into modern terms in order to become available to us. Applied to the Christian myth, this idea restored the fundamentalist position that had been shattered by textual criticism of the New Testament. Instead of a fundamentalism that insisted on the total historical truth and consistency of the New Testament, the new fundamentalism claimed for it total truth on the symbolic level. Jung too influenced a school of writers, including Joseph Campbell, to treat mythology of every kind with a new reverence, though the Christian myth always seems to benefit most, as the purported apex of mythological thought. This over-reverent approach precludes the sort of careful moral examination to which every myth should be submitted. We no longer feel that a myth has been "exploded" just because its lack of historical content has been exposed; but that does not mean that it cannot be exploded in another way. A myth must be tested by its social effects.

Indeed, it is possible to deal with antisemitism only on the mythic level. The need to exorcize the Judas Iscariot image, and restore the name "Judas" to honour, is part of a confrontation with the imaginative, mythic basis of antisemitism. Such a confrontation, involving a

17

descent into the myth-world of Western culture, is far more important than rationalistic discourse on the causes or evils of anti-semitism. Certain non-mythical explanations of antisemitism, however, are so widely accepted that it is as well to clear them out of the way before proceeding further.

Xenophobia   It is widely believed that the Jews are hated simply because they are different. This is certainly a factor at times (as when Yiddish-speaking Jews fled from the Russian pogroms to Europe and America), but never a very important one. The Jews of Germany were fully assimilated, and were hated all the more for that. The insidious threat of the Jew who is so cunning that he cannot be distinguished from the non-Jew is particularly frightening to the antisemite. On the other hand, when Jews are easily distinguishable (Hasidic Jews, for example), they appear eerie and threatening. No such reaction is aroused by say, the Amish, whose distinctiveness, in dress, food and endogamy, is seen as quaint and charming. In India and China, where no antisemitic myth exists in Hindu, Buddhist, Taoist or Confucian religion, the Jews have never been hated for their distinctiveness, but rather respected as a dedicated community. One variety of the "xenophobia" theory is that propounded by early Zionists: that the Jews are hated because they are landless. The rise of Israel disproved this theory, for antisemitism has shown no sign of disappearing, and "anti-Zionism" has become a cover-word for antisemitism.[23] The existence of a flourishing antisemitism in areas where there are no Jews is sufficient disproof of the "xenophobia" theory, except as a contributory factor.

Economic factors   It is the favourite theory of "hard-headed" people that antisemitism is purely economic in origin. Concentration of Jews on trade, or money-lending or property-owning, for example, are blamed. This ignores the fact that Jews are hated just as much when they desert these professions. Jews can be hated for being doctors, or lawyers, or farmers, or even for being Nobel Prize winners. When one considers that some of this economic concentration was actually *caused* by antisemitism, the inadequacy of this kind of theory is apparent. When the "economic" explanation becomes itself a form of diabolization, as in Marxism, or in the antisemitism of Ezra Pound,[24] we return to the medieval concept of the Jew as usurer, an outcrop, as we have argued, of the Judas-myth. More

18

usually, however, the economic explanation is used to show that there is nothing extraordinary about antisemitism: it is simply an instance of hostility to minorities. Even the Holocaust, it is often said, was not unusual, but is paralleled by exterminations of Armenians, Gypsies, and other hated minorities. On examination, however, we find that in the other cases there were always "rational", even though amoral, political or economic motivations for massacre. The Armenians were pressing for an independent Anatolian enclave in the heart of Turkey, which would have caused serious economic and political problems for the Turks, while the German extermination of the Jews was anti-economic and detrimental to their own war-effort. Only in the case of the Jews was massacre based on pure paranoia, i.e. on a nightmare mythology in which the Jews figured as Satanic figures.

The severity of Jewish morality   An explanation of antisemitism put forward by Freud,[25] and more recently revived by George Steiner,[26] is that it arises from resentment at the moral demands of Judaism. In this theory, Christians wish to revert to the moral liberty of paganism, but see as preventing this the Judaism-derived elements of Christianity, notably the demand to transcend "property, rank and worldly comfort" (Steiner).

According to this theory, when Christians face severe moral demands from Christian saints such as St. Francis or St. Dominic, they feel resentful and blame the Jews for having been the first to set such a standard through the Mosaic Covenant. This is most implausible. It ignores the whole history of the diabolization of the Jews as having a moral standard far *lower* than that of other people; as being thieves, poisoners, murderers of children, and plotters against humanity. Steiner's theory of antisemitism is only a variant of the commonly held idea that strong criticism of Jewish behaviour arises from an expectation that Jews will behave better than other people. The real explanation of the "double standard" is that behaviour condoned in other people as a moral lapse is regarded, in a Jew, as evidence of his basic depravity. When Israel, for example, is condemned harshly for political conduct regarded as normal in other countries, this is not because Israel is expected to be a paragon; such criticism comes especially from those who have the lowest opinion of Israel and Zionism.

There is, however, a certain element of confused truth in the Steiner theory. This is that somewhere in the Christian psyche the Jews are regarded as the censorious superego. The figures who embody this image are the Pharisees of the Gospels, who are portrayed as severe, reprimanding father-figures. This does not make them into revered moral teachers, however. On the contrary, they are portrayed as hypocrites and cruel villains, who do not understand that anyone who claims to have fulfilled God's moral demands can only be a hypocrite. The only true response to guilt is is to say "Have mercy on me, a sinner," and throw oneself on the protection of the sacrificial atonement of the Crucifixion. The Pharisees do not stand for a severe moral standard; they stand for a total moral failure arising from complacency. But by making moral demands that neither they nor anyone else can fulfil, they are insisting cruelly on the continuance of an impossible moral struggle, which God the Father, in his mercy, has discontinued by sending his son to suffer on the Cross. Christians do resent this continuance of moral demands by the Jews, but this is a very different thing from regarding the Jews as moral exemplars; in the Christian mind, such moral demands go together with cruelty, hypocrisy and every kind of moral failing.

The deicide of Jesus is brought about not only by his treacherous brother-Jews, symbolized by Judas, but also by these father-Jews. On an unconscious level, the Pharisees symbolize God the Father himself, who, in Christianity is seen as a very cruel figure. He insists on the death of his Son in expiation of sins committed in disobedience to his cruel moral demands—sins which would otherwise receive ferocious punishment. This aspect is hidden by the Christian myth, which instead speaks only about the Father's love for the world in giving up his only son in order to provide a merciful escape for humanity from eternal damnation. But the unconscious hatred felt by Christians towards this Father-God is diverted into hatred of his alleged devotees, the Jews.

Of course, the Jews see this matter quite differently. To them the demands of the Law are not an expression of God's cruelty, but of his love.[27] For Jews, the essence of God's message to them is that morality is possible: "it is not too hard for thee, neither is it far off" (Deut. 30:11). In Judaism, God has never condemned humanity to damnation, and so does not have to engineer a rescue through the torture of a divine victim. It is not because Judaism preaches an

20

impossibly severe morality that it is hated (such a morality is more characteristic of Christianity, whose saints make the ordinary person feel incapable of goodness, thus reinforcing the central message that morality is something to be escaped). Rather Judaism is hated because it preaches, contrary to the Christian doctrine of Original Sin, that ordinary people are capable of moral responsibility, decency and loving behaviour by their own efforts, though with the guidance of the Law. By insisting on the possibility of morality for all, Judaism threatens the Christian mode of escape. George Steiner, in his elaboration of the Freudian theory of antisemitism, fails to see any essential difference between Judaism and Christianity. He sees Christianity as merely continuing the Jewish moral demands, though in a rather less severe form, and antisemitism as arising through resentment of the residual Judaism left in Christianity. But this view entirely ignores the distinctive Christian approach to justification, and the way in which this is threatened by Judaism.

The Gospel image of the Pharisees is important in antisemitism, because it caricatures the Judaism which Jesus allegedly came to overthrow. But even more important is the means by which Judaism was overthrown: the drama of divine sacrifice, by which the Law was made unnecessary for salvation, and the role of the Jews as opposers, yet unwitting promoters, of the sacrifice. What we have to deal with is a deep-seated myth, inculcated over many centuries, and having the force of psychological necessity for a whole society. The image of Judas Iscariot has formed an important part of this myth. What we need to know is how the Judas story developed, and what special needs it served.

❖ 2 ❖

The Enigma
of the Early Sources

B
y any account, one of the dramatic highpoints of the crucifixion story is the betrayal of Jesus to his enemies. This moment
is one of the most vivid elements in the Gospel narrative and
has played a role in the Christian imagination for nearly 2000 years.
Yet when we turn to the origins of the story of Judas Iscariot in the
four Gospels, we are struck immediately by the fact that the story
changes and develops from Gospel to Gospel. Important elements of
the story which finally emerged and became implanted in the imagination of ordinary Christians are absent in the earliest version, that of
Mark. For example, the theme of avarice, as Judas's motive for his
betrayal, is missing, and it is not until the latest Gospel account that
Judas is described as being the treasurer of the group of disciples.
Even the famous sum of "thirty pieces of silver", the price of Judas's
betrayal, is unmentioned in Mark, which also lacks any description
of the death of Judas. This is a story that begins as a bare kernel of
narrative, but responds to growing emotional need, by which it is
moulded to the purposes of a religious community. We will consider
the progress of the Judas myth through the successive Gospels in
later chapters. Here we will focus on those parts of the New Testament that are earlier than the Gospels, and on those portions of the
Gospels themselves that show traces of a version of the story of Judas
even earlier than that of Mark.

As all scholars agree, the earliest documents in the New Testament
are the Epistles of Paul. Not all of these are authentic. Some (such as
the Epistle to the Hebrews) have long been recognized as having been
spuriously attributed to Paul. Others are still the subject of debate
(Colossians, II Thessalonians, Ephesians, the Pastorals). However,
the Pauline authorship of Romans, I and II Corinthians, Galatians,
Philippians, I Thessalonians and Philemon remains unanimously

accepted. These authentic Epistles may be dated to the years 50–60 CE, whereas the earliest of the Gospels, Mark, was composed around 70 CE (though some scholars date it at about 65 CE).

Thus the New Testament consists of two main sections: the Gospels (plus Acts, written by Luke, one of the Gospel-writers) and the Epistles of Paul. The order in which the Gospels were written, as most scholars agree, was: Mark (about 70 CE), Matthew (about 80 CE), Luke (about 85 CE), John (about 100 CE). The three Gospels Mark, Matthew and Luke are very similar to each other in general layout, and much of the material in Matthew and Luke is almost a repetition of material in Mark. These three Gospels are therefore known as "the Synoptic Gospels" ("Synoptic" meaning "having the same view"). The fourth Gospel, John, however, has a very different layout and is clearly not based on Mark. The book of Acts was written about 90 CE, and it describes the history of the early Church after the death of Jesus. It gives evidence of the tension that existed between Paul and the Jerusalem Church led by James, Peter and John. But Paul's writings, especially Galatians, show that this tension was in historical fact far greater than the book of Acts reveals. The Jerusalem Church was led by figures of great authority, since they were Jesus's immediate followers who had known him personally during his lifetime and knew his teaching at first hand. Paul, on the other hand, never knew Jesus. He joined the movement after Jesus's death as a result of his vision on the road to Damascus. Yet he claimed great authority too, as an Apostle, on the basis of visions in which, he claimed, he received instructions from the heavenly Jesus. The book of Acts aims to show that Paul and the Jerusalem Church became reconciled after initial differences, and that Peter, the leading teacher of the Jerusalem Church, gradually came to accept the Pauline doctrine of the abolition of the Torah. This picture is historically doubtful. The Jerusalem Church continued to regard Jewish observances as essential.[1] Around 60 CE, the followers of Jesus split into two separate bodies, the Jerusalem Church and the Pauline Church. The Gospels and Acts were produced by the Pauline Church, which sought to bolster its authority among its largely Gentile following by the fiction of a reconciliation with the Jerusalem Church, but also regarded the latter as backward in its adherence to Jewish observances. In the second century, the successors of the Jerusalem Church, known as Nazarenes (later

Ebionites), were declared heretical, and their writings were destroyed, only a few fragments remaining. This historical background is important when we come to consider the development of the Judas story.

When we turn to the Epistles of Paul, the earliest documents in the New Testament, we find that Paul does not seem to have heard of the role of Judas in bringing about the death of Jesus. His one allusion to an act of betrayal occurs in the introduction to his account of the Last Supper, where he writes, "... the Lord Jesus, on the night in which he was betrayed took bread ..." (I Corinthians 11:23). But even this is doubtful, since the Greek expression *paredidoto* need not mean "betrayed". It can mean simply "handed over", without any connotation of betrayal.[2] If it were not for the Gospel story of Judas, which biblical translators had in mind, Paul's expression would probably have been regarded as referring to the handing over of Jesus to the High Priest by the arresting troops. But Paul's Epistles should not be read with the Gospel story in mind, since the Gospels did not exist when Paul wrote the Epistles. Accordingly, the New English Bible does not translate the passage as concerned with betrayal, rendering it, "... on the night of his arrest ..."

Even if Paul does mean the verb in the sense of betrayal, this would only show that the idea was already current in the '50s that Jesus had been betrayed to his death; not necessarily that the betrayal was associated with Judas Iscariot. There is, in fact, further, more positive evidence in Paul's writings that this association did not yet exist, namely Paul's assertion that Jesus, immediately after his resurrection, was seen by "the Twelve" (I Corinthians 15:5). When we compare this with the later accounts in the Gospels, we see that the Gospel-writers were careful *not* to say that the resurrected Jesus was seen by the twelve disciples; according to their account, there were only eleven disciples at this time, Judas Iscariot having defected. Matthew says, very distinctly, "Then the eleven disciples went away into Galilee, into a mountain where Jesus had appointed them. And when they saw him, they worshipped him ..." (Matthew 28:16). Mark uses the same precision: "Afterwards, while the Eleven were at table, he appeared to them ..." (Mark 16:14). Luke similarly refers to "the eleven" (Luke 24:33). Only John fails to give a precise number for the remaining disciples. He does indeed refer to Thomas (John 20:24) as "one of the Twelve", in a resurrection-appearance

24

context, but this appears to mean "one of the original Twelve", and does not indicate that they are still twelve in number at this time.

The careful insistence of the Synoptic Gospels (i.e. Mark, Matthew and Luke) that the resurrected Jesus appeared to only eleven disciples suggests that a contrary tradition existed that needed to be undermined. This is the earlier tradition which Paul received and handed on. Our conclusion must be, therefore, that no tradition of the betrayal and defection of Judas existed before 60 CE. Before this date, Judas was regarded as a faithful apostle who mourned the death of Jesus together with the others and shared their experience of his resurrection. The whole story of the betrayal was invented not less than 30 years after Jesus's death, for reasons which we will investigate. We must always bear in mind that the Gospels reflect the struggle of the Pauline Church to define itself in relation to the Jerusalem Church.

Of course, the eleven Apostles, in the later accounts, were soon made up to twelve again. The story of how this was done is told in the book of Acts (1:12–26), which begins with an account of Jesus's post-resurrection appearance to the Apostles. Again, they are meticulously numbered as eleven, not twelve; a list of their names is even given, which omits Judas Iscariot, but includes another Judas, called the son (or brother) of James, who has been previously mentioned only in the Gospel of Luke. Then comes an account of the election of another Apostle to take Judas Iscariot's place. The person finally chosen is Matthias; a parenthetical account of the pitiable death of Judas is given. The interesting thing is that nothing is ever heard of Matthias again. Even in later Church legend he is a null figure. One might conclude from this that he is a non-existent person, created simply to fill the gap left by the defection of Judas Iscariot. The name "Matthias" is merely a double of the already-existing apostle, Matthew, with only a slight variation in the spelling.[3] At any rate, it is clear that he was not present when the resurrection-experience of the Eleven took place, according to Acts. So there is a real contradiction between the accounts given by the Gospels and Acts, and that given by Paul, who says that the resurrection was witnessed by "the Twelve". This contradiction can only be explained by assuming that Paul knew nothing of Judas's defection, while the later accounts were forced to reduce the number of the Apostles in order to avoid an inconsistency with the story about Judas that had arisen in the interval. For it is quite impossible to imagine that Judas, after betraying Jesus, could have rejoined the other eleven Apostles and shared their experience of his resurrection. Such narrative illogic cannot be entertained as an explanation of Paul's account.[4]

What happened between the composition of Paul's Epistles and the composition of the Gospels and Acts to prompt the creation of the story of Judas's betrayal? A fuller answer to this question will be given in due course. Here it may be noted that, in general, a need was felt by the Gospel-writers to fill out the life of Jesus in narrative form in a way that Paul never attempted. To this end, they utilized historical traditions derived from the Jerusalem Church. But they also developed narrative details that stemmed from a new concept unknown to the Nazarene followers of Jesus, or to Jesus himself—namely that Jesus was a divine sacrifice. This concept was first developed by Paul in a somewhat schematic manner; he provided only the outline of a myth consisting of the descent of the divine saviour, his founding of a church by rites of baptism and communion, his violent death at the hand of the forces of evil, his resurrection and resumption of divinity, and his provision of salvation through the atonement effected by his death.[5] Some of these ingredients, such as baptism and resurrection, already existed in the Jerusalem Church, but even such materials were reinterpreted by Paul in a radical way. These factors required further narrative elaboration by his successors, and the materials for such elaboration were ready to hand in pagan deicidal myths. Among such elaborations, derived from pagan myths, are the virgin birth of Jesus, his birth in a manger (or, in another version, a cave), the visit of the Magi, and many other details unthought of by Paul, by which Jesus was made plausible to the Greco-Roman world as a sacrificial divinity through whom salvation was to be obtained. It is in this post-Pauline elaboration that the origin and growth of the Judas-legend must be sought.

We must also ask the question why it was Judas, and not one of the other Apostles, who was chosen for this role. The others are also associated with a certain level of betrayal: all of them "forsook him and fled" (Matthew 16:56) at the time of his arrest, and Peter plumbed a lower depth when he denied Jesus thrice. But Judas alone took the active role of a traitor, not under pressure of fear, as with the others. It is indeed a valid question why treachery is predicated of all the Apostles, as there are good reasons to doubt the plausibility of such weakness on their part. But Judas is a special case; and we may well enquire why he was singled out for the ultimate sin.

The answer may be that Judas was chosen because of his name, which signifies "Jew". During the period leading up to the composition of the Gospels, the incipient antisemitism found in Paul's Epistles[6] developed into a full-blown indictment of the Jewish people as the rejecters, betrayers, and finally murderers of Jesus. Probably belonging to this interim period is a passage included in one of Paul's Epistles, but written, as it appears, not by him but by one of his Gentile disciples, who added it to the text of his master's composition:[7]

> You have fared like the congregations in Judaea, God's people in Christ Jesus. You have been treated by your countrymen as they are treated by the Jews, who killed the Lord Jesus and the prophets and drove us out, the Jews who are heedless of God's will and enemies of their fellow-men, hindering us from speaking to the Gentiles to lead them to salvation. All this time they have been making up the full measure of their guilt, and now retribution has overtaken them for good and all. (I Thessalonians 2:14–16.)

The accusation that the Jews are "enemies of their fellow-men" is typical of Hellenistic antisemitism, as found in Alexandrian writers such as Apion and Manetho, and Roman writers such as Tacitus and Seneca. The assertion that the Jews have been "making up the full measure of their guilt" recalls biblical expressions about the Canaanites (Genesis 15:16), and hints that the Jews are doomed to be expelled from their land as punishment for their sins in killing their own prophets and, as a culminating crime, Jesus himself. The further assertion that "retribution has overtaken them for good and all" suggests that this passage was written either during or after the Jewish War against Rome which ended in military disaster and the destruction of the Temple. As a result of this war the Pauline Church (already separated from the Jerusalem Church) determined to disclaim all Jewish connections, deny that Jesus was in any way a rebel against Rome, and assert instead that he was a rebel against the Jewish religion, thus throwing the entire blame for the crucifixion of

Jesus on the Jews. The Gospels and Acts are the documents in which these Pauline positions were established. The first of the Gospels, Mark, was written, probably in Rome itself, just at the time of the Jewish War. It is the first literary expression of the new Pauline Church, based in Rome. It pours obloquy on the Jews, and ends with the proclamation of Jesus's divinity by a Roman centurion (Mark 15:39), thus contrasting Roman faith with Jewish treachery.[8]

Nowhere else does Paul say that the Jews killed Jesus or their own prophets, though he does upbraid them for rejecting Jesus's claim to be the saviour, and criticizes their blindness. There is in the above-quoted passage a bitterness against the Jews that goes far beyond Paul's attitude. It belongs to a period when the Pauline Church—the communities converted by Paul from paganism or near-paganism—had lost all respect for the Jews as the elected people of God, seeing them only as an evil nation. The expressions used can all be paralleled in the Gospels and Acts, which carry even further the notion that the Jews are entirely rejected by God as a criminal people.[9] The Gospels too contain, for the first time in literary form, the figure of Judas the traitor, whose legend must have arisen during the period immediately preceding the Gospels, along with the developing picture of the Jews as a nation of traitors.

The name "Judas" is a Grecized form of the ancient biblical name Yehudah (Judah), which was first held by the formidable son of Jacob, who became the progenitor of a great tribe. King David belonged to this tribe, as did his dynastic successors, whose kingdom became known as Judah, after the Northern tribes broke away to form the kingdom of Israel around 975 BCE. When the Ten Tribes of the Northern Kingdom were led into captivity by the Assyrians in 740 BCE, the kingdom of Judah became the main remnant of the Israelites who had left Egypt and invaded the Holy Land centuries before. Consequently, the remaining Israelites gradually became known as Judahites, or Jews, though they retained the name Israel for their land and their religious community. The portion of the tribe of Benjamin that had remained loyal to the Davidic royal family at the time of the secession of the Northern tribes joined the tribe of Judah and became indistinguishable from it, being known also as Jews. Even the members of the priestly tribe of Levi, which retained its patrilinear identity (and has done so to this day), became known as Jews, a name which, in earlier times, had meant members of the tribe of Judah only. Thus the name Judah, or Judas, was honoured above all others by the Jews, as their national and royal name. The name acquired even more honour through the fame of the heroic Judas Maccabaeus, who saved the Jews from their Syrian-Hellenistic oppressors in the second century BCE.

That this noble name should have become synonymous with evil and treachery throughout the Western world provides a measure of the obloquy thrown on the Jews by the Christian myth. If there were some English name that combined the aura of "England", "the Church of England", "Queen Elizabeth" and "Nelson" in the English mind, and this name were used for the villain of even a fictional story (let alone a story alleged to be the highest truth), one would readily suppose that some serious disparagement was intended towards the English people and their history. It is therefore not hard to suppose that the name "Judas" was deliberately chosen in preference to the name of any other Apostle for a diabolic role, as part of the antisemitic campaign within the Pauline Church, which had cast the Jews as people of the devil and enemies of the incarnate God.[10]

Thus Judas was chosen to represent the betrayal of Jesus by his fellow-Jews, who refused to recognize him as the Messiah. But, as pointed out above, a certain air of betrayal hangs over all the twelve disciples, not only over Judas Iscariot. Peter, the greatest of the Twelve, chosen by Jesus to be the Rock of his kingdom, has the greatest mark against him. Not only does he deny Jesus thrice on the night of his imprisonment (though he does not desert him as the other disciples do); he has also had a serious quarrel with Jesus at the time of the Salutation (see Mark 8:32–33, Matthew 16:21–23). When Jesus revealed his imminent sacrifice, Peter failed to understand the need for Jesus's crucifixion and "rebuked" him for predicting it. On this occasion, Peter was harshly addressed by Jesus as "Satan" (Mark 8:33, Matthew 16:23).

These negative elements in the tradition concerning Jesus's closest friends and disciples apparently arose from the burgeoning conflict between the Jerusalem Church and the Pauline Church. It is most unlikely that in the Jerusalem Church, where Peter was the chief spiritual guide (though not the titular head), stories were told denigrating his role in the events leading to Jesus's death. At the most, it may have been said that the disciples failed to rise to the heights of prayer required in Gethsemane. But that they, and especially Peter,

29

should have failed to understand the main feature of Jesus's mission, and also showed a lack of faith and courage at the time of Jesus's arrest, would seem to be charges deriving from adversaries, not from the Apostles themselves who formed the Jerusalem Church and assumed the chief authority after Jesus's death. For one thing, Peter's alleged cowardice in denying Jesus contrasts strangely with his steadfast courage at his own Sanhedrin trial (Acts 5), whose main details undoubtedly derive from authentic traditions of the Jerusalem Church.[11]

Moreover, one of the main issues that divided the churches was the very question highlighted in Peter's "quarrel" with Jesus—whether Jesus came into the world to act as a saviour in the Jewish sense (to free his own people from slavery to idolaters) or in the mystery-religion sense (to save the whole world from damnation). It was the contention of the Pauline Church, following the doctrines of Paul himself, that Jesus had intended to die on the cross all along, and that this was his main purpose in descending from above. The Jerusalem Church, on the other hand (as appears from their loyal adherence to the practices of Judaism, including the atoning rites of the Jewish Temple), regarded Jesus as a human figure sent by God to deliver Israel, like Moses and other saviours in the past. They believed that he had been resurrected, not by way of divine ascent, but by a miracle, like Lazarus, and would soon return to complete his human mission of national salvation. This fundamental difference between the churches is obscured in the book of Acts, which presents an unhistorical scenario of reconciliation between Peter and Paul, in which Peter is represented as struggling painfully towards the higher truths advocated by Paul.

This Paulinist picture clearly attributes a measure of stupidity to Peter, and this "Jewish" stupidity is also employed in the Gospels to explain the failure of the Twelve to understand Jesus's alleged aim of immolation as a divine atoning sacrifice. Like the betrayal-syndrome, this notion arises in the Paulinist literature (the Gospels and Acts) in order to cope with the fact that Paul, who never knew Jesus in the flesh, nevertheless claimed to know more about his aims than his closest disciples, to whom Paul's idea of Jesus as a divine sacrifice was unknown. Paul, the late-comer, had to supplant the authentic Twelve, and this was effected by the development of stories portraying them as both stupid and unreliable. However, such was their authority that they could not be supplanted altogether, and had to be represented as belatedly accepting the superior insight of Paul.[12]

Thus the treachery of Judas can be seen as an extreme instance of the alleged general unreliability of the Twelve and of their teachings in the Jerusalem Church.

Some interesting evidence exists to show that there was an earlier, milder stage of the Judas-legend, in which Judas was regarded as having only the same kind of stupidity and unreliability as the other Apostles. This evidence is to be found in the Gospel of John, which, though the latest of the four, does sometimes, because of its independence of the Synoptic Gospels, present traditions not to be found elsewhere. In this Gospel, one of the Apostles rebukes Jesus:

Judas asked him—the other Judas, not Iscariot—"Lord, what can have happened, that you mean to disclose yourself to us alone and not to the world?" (John 14:22.)

We may wonder about the abruptness of this question, coming from the *other* Judas, who is a null character in the Gospels generally. Is there something too insistent about the editorial comment that the Judas meant here is not Judas Iscariot? Such a suspicion is confirmed when we find that there is a variant reading in some manuscripts in which the word "not" is omitted.[13] Also, we may ask, what exactly is the meaning of the question put here to Jesus?

The clue to the meaning of the question is found in another very startling passage in John's Gospel, where the same question is put in the same words:

As the Jewish Feast of Tabernacles was close at hand, his brothers said to him, "You should leave this district and go into Judaea, so that your disciples there may see the great things you are doing. Surely no one can hope to be in the public eye if he works in seclusion. If you are really doing such things as these, show yourself to the world." For even his brothers had no faith in him. Jesus said to them, "The right time for me has not yet come . . ." (John 7:2–6.)

Here the criticism of Jesus is sharper, and the "brothers" are put into a confrontational role, unlike "Judas, not Iscariot" in the other

31

passage. Yet the coincidence of expression is remarkable: both recommend that Jesus "show himself to the world". It is most likely, then, that both passages derive from the same incident, though one passage attributes the criticism to Judas, and the other to Jesus's brothers. But the most surprising thing about the dialogue of Jesus with his brothers is that it took place at all. For we are told elsewhere that Jesus's family dismissed him as a madman (Mark 3:21). Moreover, we are told that Jesus himself refused to have any special relationship with his mother and brothers, or to allow them any special access to him (Matthew 12:46, Mark 3:31, Luke 8:19). Yet here we have a picture of Jesus conferring with his brothers, who give him advice (though the beginnings of a hostile picture of these brothers can already be discerned). In addition, there is the puzzling fact to be explained that, while the Gospels portray Jesus's brothers as unfriendly, indifferent, or, at best carping (in John 7), we know from Acts and other sources that Jesus's brothers were prominent in his movement shortly after his death; indeed his brother James succeeded him as leader of the movement.

Another point to be noted is that one of Jesus's brothers was actually called Judas, a fact revealed in only one of the Gospels (Matthew 13:55). This is usually regarded as a matter of no significance, since Jesus's brothers were not his disciples and regarded him with indifference or hostility. This, at any rate, is the picture given in the Gospels as a whole; but the anomalous passage in John, where Jesus's brothers do not seem indifferent at all, but interest themselves keenly in his career, makes us wonder whether there is after all significance in the fact that the total story contains not just two disciples called Judas (Judas Iscariot and "Judas son of James"), both apparently unrelated to Jesus by blood, but a third Judas, who was his brother. What is the historical truth about Jesus's brothers? Were they more important in his life-story than the Gospels wish to admit? Moreover, this same brother Judas, who apparently played no part in Jesus's own movement, is known to have played a prominent part, like James, in the Jerusalem Church after Jesus's death, being the author of the canonical Epistle of Jude.[14] These matters will be taken up again in a later chapter, when we enquire who exactly Judas Iscariot was (see pp. 141–160), and what was his relationship to the other Judases. For the moment it is sufficient to point out that a Judas, probably Iscariot (though this has been

32

negated by the editor of the most widely disseminated manuscript of John), criticized Jesus from an activist standpoint more usually associated with Peter.

We may conclude from all this evidence that Judas Iscariot did not suddenly spring into existence as the diabolic betrayer of Jesus, but developed gradually through several distinct phases. Certain aspects of the evolution will be examined further in later chapters, especially the meaning of the name "Iscariot". But even the emergence of Judas as betrayer was by no means the end of his development. We turn to an examination of the changes and elaboration which took place in the course of the Gospels in both the character and the role of Judas Iscariot.

$$\text{◆} \quad 3 \quad \text{◆}$$

The Story Develops:
Mark and Matthew

Most scholars, after nearly two centuries of discussion, have concluded that the Gospels were written in the following order: Mark, Matthew, Luke and John. The priority of Mark is shown chiefly by the extent to which Matthew and Luke use material taken from Mark, with slight individual alterations. The lateness of John is shown chiefly by his developed theology, and by his resignation to the prospect of a long delay in the return of Jesus. We shall see that the way the Judas story develops and becomes more elaborate from Gospel to Gospel adds one more confirmation to an order that has been arrived at for many other reasons.

According to Church tradition, Mark's Gospel was written in Rome. The name "Mark" (Marcus) itself is Roman. Whether Mark is to be identified with the character called Mark or John Mark in the New Testament (Acts 12:25, 13:5, 15:38; Colossians 4:10; Philemon 24; II Timothy 4:11) is not clear. If so, he was once a personal assistant to Paul, whom Paul alternately distrusted (Acts 15:38) and trusted (II Timothy 4:11). Tradition also claimed that Mark derived the material of his Gospel from Peter while the latter was in Rome.[1] This claim can probably be dismissed as an attempt to give Mark's Gospel the authority of the Jerusalem Church. It is unlikely that Peter was ever in Rome.

Mark's Gospel is written in a rough, colloquial Greek. It portrays Jesus as a Galilean wonder-worker, who is the Son of God, and knows that he must suffer on the Cross. It gives a graphic and laconic version of the Passion story, portraying the Jews as Jesus's chief enemies, and as blind to the obsolescence of their religion. It ends abruptly with the "empty tomb", and gives no account of resurrection appearances.

In Mark's Gospel, Judas Iscariot is first mentioned in the list of

34

disciples given in 3:14–19. It is noteworthy that this list contains only one Judas. Evidently the division of this character into two, the good Judas and the bad Judas, had not yet taken place. Indeed, throughout Mark there does not appear to be more than one Judas.[2]

The next mention of Judas Iscariot is the abrupt notice of his betrayal (Mark 14:10–11):

> Then Judas Iscariot, one of the Twelve, went to the chief priests to betray him to them. When they heard what he had come for, they were greatly pleased, and promised him money; and he began to look for a good opportunity to betray him.

No motivation is ascribed for this betrayal. The bare fact of his offer is recounted; and though the "chief priests" offer him money, this is not suggested as the motive for his action. Nor is it explained what his betrayal would consist of. Since Jesus was unarmed and had no escort, it is not clear why the "priests" cannot arrest him at any time, or why they should need a betrayer's assistance. The only clue to this mystery occurs in a previous passage, which says that the priests were afraid of "rioting among the people", and therefore determined to "devise some cunning plan" and to wait until after the festival (Mark 14:1–2).

Then comes the account of the Last Supper, in which the betrayal is foreshadowed, though Judas himself is not mentioned:

> As they sat at supper Jesus said, "I tell you this: one of you will betray me—one who is eating with me." At this they were dismayed; and one by one they said to him, "Not I, surely?" "It is one of the Twelve", he said, "who is dipping into the same bowl with me. The son of Man is going the way appointed for him in the scriptures; but alas for that man by whom the Son of Man is betrayed! It would be better for that man if he had never been born." (Mark 14:18–21.)

Presumably Judas, like the other disciples, says to Jesus, "Not I, surely?", while knowing that he himself was the traitor and that Jesus was aware of it. This poignant detail is not exploited. But Jesus's comment puts a profound gloss on the matter; for he indicates that the betrayal is fated and necessary. There is thus a bond of complicity between Jesus and Judas; we feel that Judas is shouldering the terrible sin of betrayal with the consent of Jesus, or at least his acceptance of its inevitability. But none of this is spelt out or even, perhaps, consciously thought of. It remains for the accounts in the later Gospels to make these matters more plain.

There follows the account of the Last Supper with its two themes of Jesus's eucharistic words and his so-called "vow of abstinence".[3] A hymn is sung and then Jesus leads the disciples to the Mount of Olives, where, on the way to Gethsemane, Jesus prophesies the desertion of the disciples and the disloyalty of Peter. At no point is it mentioned that Judas has left the company of Jesus and the disciples.

At Gethsemane, Jesus prays; but the disciples fail him by falling asleep. He awakens and reproves them twice, but when he finds them asleep for the third time, he is resigned, saying: "The hour has come. The Son of Man is betrayed to sinful men. Up, let us go forward! My betrayer is upon us." (Mark 14:41–42.)

> Suddenly, while he was speaking, Judas, one of the Twelve, appeared, and with him was a crowd armed with swords and cudgels, sent by the chief priests, lawyers, and elders. Now the traitor had agreed with them upon a signal: "The one I kiss is your man; seize him and get him safely away." When he reached the spot, he stepped forward at once and said to Jesus, "Rabbi," and kissed him. Then they seized him and held him fast. (Mark 14:43–46.)

Judas suddenly appears, although no indication has been given that he ever left the company of Jesus. This flaw in the narrative engages the attention of the later narrators who attempt to amend it. The clumsiness may indicate that the betrayal theme has been superimposed on an earlier narrative in which there was no such betrayal. It is interesting too that the betrayer is here called "Judas", not "Judas Iscariot", showing that we have here a narrative in which Judas had not yet been differentiated from Judas Iscariot. Moreover, Judas is identified as "one of the Twelve", as if it were necessary to explain who he was; this shows that in some earlier version, which Mark is adapting, this was the first introduction of Judas into the Gospel narrative. This would imply that the previous appearances of Judas in Mark's Gospel were not part of the earliest Judas story.

This verse, indeed, introducing Judas for the first time as traitor in Gethsemane, is the germ from which the Markian stratum of elaborations of the Judas story was developed; there was not originally any section in the Last Supper story about Judas's imminent defection and Jesus's foreknowledge. The story, as we have it here in our earliest source, has already undergone several modifications. The sudden treachery of Judas in Gethsemane (the germ of the story) has already been felt to require some episodes leading up to it, which have been supplied, but without careful attention to the modifications logically required in the way of narrative links.

It is interesting that Mark involves the "lawyers and elders" in Jesus's arrest, contrary to evidence elsewhere (see p. 76). It was important that the whole Jewish establishment should be involved in the betrayal of Jesus, not merely the entourage of the High Priest. The kiss of the traitor is a narrative theme that will require investigation in the light of comparative mythology and biblical precedent. Judas's reverent address of Jesus as "Rabbi" is also a twist of hypocrisy that adds to the treachery of the kiss. Here it is sufficient to point out that the mechanics of the treachery are far from clear. Why did Jesus need to be identified by Judas? Surely Jesus was well enough known after preaching in the Temple before enthusiastic crowds? What exactly did Judas's treachery consist of? Was it his identification of Jesus, or that he led the arresting "crowd" to Jesus's hiding-place? These puzzling questions require investigation in the light of the sum of these accounts. But here it may be remarked that the confusion and clumsiness of the story adds to the impression of an *ad hoc* improvization.

It remains only to note how much of the familiar story of Judas is lacking in Mark's version. There is no mention of a price of thirty pieces of silver being agreed with the high priests, nor is anything said about Judas being actually paid, only that payment was "promised". Nothing is said either about Judas's repentance, or about his death. In fact, after the scene in Gethsemane, we do not hear of Judas again. The character remains bare of individualizing traits. In this earliest surviving version of the Judas-legend, the narrative remains rudimentary, though it has already progressed far beyond its earliest stages.

Matthew's Gospel is a more elaborate composition. While using Mark's material about Jesus's preaching and wonder-working, it also provides a narrative about Jesus's birth and infancy—the virgin birth, the journey of the Magi, and the massacre of the Innocents by Herod. It adds much apocalyptic material to Jesus's teaching, and provides a number of other sayings of Jesus not found in Mark. It follows Mark closely in the Passion narrative, but adds accounts of Jesus's resurrection appearances. Matthew's portrayal of Jesus has many authentically Jewish details, probably deriving from the traditions of the Jerusalem Church; yet this Gospel is virulently anti-Jewish, even including a scene in which the Jews call upon themselves an eternal curse (27:25).

The name "Gospel of Matthew" is a misnomer, as the author was not Jesus's disciple Matthew, despite Church tradition to this effect. The name of the actual author is not known; internal evidence shows that he probably knew no Hebrew, and lived after the destruction of the Temple. The place where he composed the Gospel was probably Antioch, but may have been Alexandria. His Greek is more idiomatic and correct than that of Mark. Some scholars think that he was Jewish, others that he was a Gentile. The theory that this Gospel was written for a Jewish-Christian community is fashionable, but probably incorrect.

In Matthew's Gospel, Judas Iscariot is again first mentioned in the list given of the twelve disciples (Matthew 10:2–4). Here again we note that there is no second Judas in the list. Nowhere in Matthew, as in Mark, do we hear of an apostle called Judas other than Judas Iscariot. As we shall see, it was only when records showing that there was a blameless and loyal Judas had to be taken into the reckoning that a second Judas was introduced.

In other respects, however, Matthew's story receives much greater elaboration than Mark's. Here is Matthew's account of the deal struck between Judas and the high priests:

> Then one of the twelve, the man called Judas Iscariot, went to the chief priests and said, "What will you give me to betray him to you?" They weighed him out (or: agreed to pay him) thirty silver pieces. From that moment he began to look out for an opportunity to betray him. (Matthew 26:14–16.)

Here Judas is given a definite motive for his betrayal—desire for money. Whereas in Mark the question of payment is raised by the

38

priests, in Matthew the question comes from Judas. Moreover, the amount is not left unspecified, as in Mark, but fixed at thirty silver pieces. Further, Judas's motive is no longer mysterious. He acts for money, and this gives him some individuality—he has a personal characteristic of greed. The sum of thirty pieces of silver is not a great one—it was the average price of a slave (Exodus 21:32), and was enough to provide food for one person for about five months.[4] It would not make Judas rich, but would be a sufficient inducement for greed. New questions, however, present themselves: why should Judas, one of the twelve apostles, abandon his ideals in this way? Presumably a man of great qualities (or Jesus would not have chosen him), what made him choose money over loyalty and salvation? Or did Jesus choose him for his vices, rather than for his virtues, knowing that someone would be required to betray him? New details raise new questions, and the way is open for further elaboration. But it should also be said that additional details do not necessarily bring an improvement in narrative quality. The reticence of Mark conveys an impression of an inexplicable eruption of evil in the heart of Jesus's following, and prompts thoughts about the metaphysical status of evil itself. When Judas is given a financial motive in Matthew, we may feel that there has been a descent into triviality.

It is interesting that Judas is *not* given the more understandable motive of disappointment with Jesus's failure to act as a this-worldly Messiah and his insistence on the necessity for his own crucifixion. We have already encountered this motive in incidents where disciples have shown incomprehension of Jesus's intentions. Could not such disappointment have resulted in actual betrayal? Many commentators have thought so, and given this as the reason for Judas's action. This explanation, however, has no support in the texts, which prefer either some version of Mark's absolute evil, or of Matthew's ascription of greed, or some combination. The reason, I suggest, is that the attitude of clinging to a worldly messiah is regarded as typical of the Jerusalem Church, which is not being accused of treachery to Jesus, but only of slowness of comprehension. The Paulinist writers, though in conflict with the Jerusalem Church, do not wish to sever connection with it, as would be the case if they accused it of the ultimate treachery. Consequently, Judas, the ultimate traitor, cannot be characterized in a way that would identify him with the Jerusalem Church. Though he did begin his legendary career as a typical worldly messianist protesting against Jesus's "spiritual" aims, this role was transferred to Peter, so that Judas could make the leap into treachery, where he would be identified not with the Jerusalem Church but with the Jews, the exemplars in Christian mythology of both motiveless evil and greed.

It is important to keep in mind that the Gospels and Acts belong not to the age which they describe but to the succeeding age in which the Pauline Church was at odds with both the Jerusalem Church and the Jewish synagogue. They are writings of the Paulinist camp, and they describe the life of Jesus and the early history of the Christian movement from a partisan perspective. It was not until the middle of the second century that these writings began to be regarded as having scriptural status like the writings of the Hebrew Bible (which now began to be called the "Old Testament"). At their time of composition, the Epistles of Paul and the Gospels and Acts were party literature, written to unify and rally the faithful against opposing parties. From the standpoint of these writings, the Jerusalem Church, though loyal to Jesus, was regarded as viewing him wrongly, while the Jews were regarded as guilty of rejection and betrayal. The growth of the Judas-legend illustrates these conflicts. Those who, looking beneath the surface of the Gospels, discern a layer in which Judas was not a traitor but an advocate of an earthly messianic kingdom, think that they have uncovered the true, historical Judas. But they have only uncovered an earlier layer of the legendary Judas, at a stage when he represented the Jerusalem Church in its contemporary conflict with the Pauline Church.

We now come to Matthew's account of the part played by Judas Iscariot in the Last Supper:

> In the evening he sat down with the twelve disciples; and during supper he said, "I tell you this: one of you will betray me." In great distress they exclaimed one after the other, "Can you mean me, Lord?" He answered, "One who has dipped his hand into this bowl with me will betray me. The Son of Man is going the way appointed for him in the scriptures; but alas for that man by whom the Son of Man is betrayed! It would be better for that man if he had never been born." Then Judas spoke, the one who was to betray him: "Rabbi, can you mean me?" Jesus replied, "The words are yours (or: It is as you say)." (Matthew 26:20–25.)

There can be little doubt that this version is later than Mark's, since the story has plainly advanced. What is only an implication in Mark—that a conversation took place between Jesus and Judas—becomes explicit dialogue. Each of the disciples in turn poses the question to Jesus, and we are not told what Jesus replied. Only Judas's turn is highlighted, and Jesus's words of reply are given.[5] These words may appear ambiguous, but they amount (however one translates them) to an affirmative answer. Jesus knows that Judas will betray him; Mark leaves this vague and inexplicit, revealing only that Jesus knew he would be betrayed. Again we may feel a loss of artistic effect. By being more explicit, Matthew has lost something of Mark's mysterious silence. But the story has moved on: its possibilities are unfolding. Because Jesus knows in advance about Judas's treachery, Judas becomes even more a man of fate. His treachery is predestined. The words pronounced by Jesus, already in Mark, become more fraught with meaning: "The Son of Man is going the way appointed for him in the scriptures; but alas for that man by whom the Son of Man is betrayed! It would be better for that man if he had never been born." Judas is not merely fulfilling an individual decision. He is fulfilling a prophecy. Yet no credit or happiness is allotted to him for doing what is fated and necessary. His reward for his share in the salvation of mankind is accursedness and damnation. He himself is a kind of sacrifice; he is the Black Christ who, through his destructive and self-destructive action, brings delivery to his fellow human-beings. Jesus's words (or alleged words) sum up the role of the Accursed One whose contribution is required for the performance of a sacrifice that is both appalling and essential—a double sacrifice, since it requires both the death of Jesus and the damnation of Judas.

The fatedness of these events is expressed, here as in Mark, by reference to prophecies "in the scriptures", meaning the Hebrew Bible. It may be doubted, however, whether there is anything in the Hebrew Bible prophesying such events. Certainly there is nothing presaging the role of Judas. Some precedents have been cited which amount only to superficial verbal similarities, such as the twenty pieces of silver for which Joseph was sold, or the thirty pieces of silver in Zechariah 11:12–13. The betrayer of the destined sacrifice is entirely alien to the Hebrew Bible, but can be found readily enough in Greco-Roman mythology, and, in fact, in sacrificial mythology

41

throughout the world. We may note a compulsion, on the part of the Gospel writers, to ascribe to the Hebrew Bible notions that form no part of its philosophy.

The account of Matthew, as almost all scholars agree, is actually based on that of Mark, which the author of Matthew had before him as he wrote. Comparison of the Last Supper narratives certainly seems to confirm this. Matthew mostly uses Mark's words, but characteristically makes some aspects more explicit.

This is also the case in Matthew's account of the actual betrayal:

While he was still speaking, Judas, one of the Twelve, appeared; with him was a great crowd armed with swords and cudgels, sent by the chief priests and the elders of the nation. The traitor gave them this sign: "The one I kiss is your man; seize him", and stepping forward at once, he said, "Hail, Rabbi!", and kissed him. Jesus replied, "Friend, do what you are here to do (or: Friend, what are you here for?). They then came forward, seized Jesus, and held him fast." (Matthew 26:47–50.)

There are a few slight stylistic changes here from Mark, but the only substantial addition is that Jesus responds to Judas's greeting. As in Mark, no explanation is given of when Judas left the company; as far as we are aware, he is still with them until he "appears" with an armed crowd. A curious little change is that Matthew, in the sign-giving episode, substitutes an aorist for Mark's pluperfect, thus changing a previously arranged sign into one arranged on the spot. This has the effect of reducing Judas's activity as a plotter and colluder with the authorities behind the scenes, while at the same time enhancing his role as active leader in the arrest.

There is still no explanation of why a sign should be necessary in order to point out so well-known a person as Jesus. It seems that while the narrative demands a traitor, the mechanics of his treachery remain vague. The motif of betrayal with a kiss emphasizes again that the traitor is a member of Jesus's intimate circle, a point previously emphasized during the Last Supper with the words, "One who has dipped his hand into this bowl with me will betray me." This is more important to the story than any realistic details that might explain how the treachery was accomplished or even what exactly it consisted of. In a realistic narrative, the emphasis would be on Judas's treachery in revealing Jesus's whereabouts to his enemies, or leading them to Jesus's hiding-place. This would make sense of Judas's role, and we find some hints of such a scenario in later accounts. Instead, the emphasis here is on the treacherous kiss that brings death; the narrative justification, explaining how the kiss brings death, is flimsy in the extreme. If Jesus did need to be identified for some reason, Judas could presumably have simply pointed to him. But this would not have so epitomized betrayal, as does a kiss and a reverent greeting.

It has been suggested that the story was influenced by the Hebrew Bible story of Joab and Amasa, the two rival generals of King David. Joab fell into disfavour with the king, and was replaced as commander-in-chief by Amasa. But when he was charged with leading reinforcement troops to help Amasa, Joab treacherously contrived to assassinate him. "And Joab said to Amasa, 'Is it well with thee, my brother?' And Joab took Amasa by the beard with his right hand to kiss him. But Amasa took no heed to the sword that was in Joab's hand; so he smote him therewith in the groin, and shed out his bowels to the ground." (II Samuel 20:9.) Joab's motive was rivalry for the generalship, and David never forgave him for this murder (see I Kings 2:5). But Joab was loyal to David his master, and there is no hint of a sacrificial motive, so the story is not a close parallel. Nevertheless, the image of betrayal by a kiss is undoubtedly there in both stories, and it is clearly a story-motif common in the East. It is expressed also in the Hebrew Bible in the form of a proverb: "The blows of a friend are well-meant; but the kisses of an enemy are perfidious." (Proverbs 27:6.)

But there is also another possible significance in the kiss of Judas. It may mean that there was a specially intimate relationship of friendship and trust between Jesus and Judas Iscariot. This aspect has even led some commentators to suggest that Judas was in fact the "beloved disciple". Psychoanalytic commentators have suggested an unconsciously homosexual relationship between Jesus and Judas; in this reading, the betrayal was a sado-masochistic expression of this intimate bond (for further discussion of this see p. 137). However, such explanations have abandoned the mythological level. The special intimacy between Jesus and Judas is the bond between the sacrificial victim and his slayer, sometimes expressed in myth by their being twins, or at least brothers (Osiris and Set, Romulus and

Remus, Baal and Mot, Cain and Abel).[6] The slayer must be an outcast, but he must also come from within the tribe, or he loses his representative validity. He must be disclaimed by the tribe, and yet be one of them, the more closely affiliated the better. The tribe must not perform the appalling act; yet it must be performed on their behalf. And ideally it is performed by one who could act as their leader, because close to the victim-leader, and almost his *doppelganger*.

Jesus's reply to Judas's treacherous greeting is Matthew's addition to the story. The Greek is somewhat cryptic (*hetaire, eph'ho parei*). Some sources give this as an elliptical command ("Friend, do what you are here to do") and some as a question ("Friend, what are you here for?"). It may be that Matthew meant to convey both meanings: Judas takes it as a question, but Jesus (and the readers) understand it as a command. Thus Judas preserves his stance as the wicked traitor, while Jesus's quiet acceptance (expressed also in his final words to his disciples, ". . . the traitor is upon us") shows that the treachery is part of the divine plan. The delicate balance between Judas's action as a crime, and as a move in the drama of salvation, is preserved and furthered by Matthew's addition. There is also a ritual element in the exchange. A rite of sacrifice, in which participants play predetermined roles, lies behind the scene.

So far, Matthew has been following Mark with only a few but significant additions. Later, however, Matthew presents a section not found at all in Mark, giving an answer to the reader's inevitable question, "What happened to Judas?":

When Judas the traitor saw that Jesus had been condemned, he was seized with remorse, and returned the thirty silver pieces to the chief priests and elders. "I have sinned," he said: "I have brought an innocent man to his death." But they said, "What is that to us? See to that yourself." So he threw the money down in the temple and left them, and went and hanged himself. Taking up the money, the chief priests argued: "This cannot be put into the temple fund; it is blood-money." So after conferring they used it to buy the Potter's Field, as a burial-place for foreigners. This explains the name "Blood Acre", by which that field has been known ever since; and in this way fulfilment was given to the prophetic utterance of Jeremiah: "They took the thirty silver pieces, the price set on a man's head (for that was his price among the Israelites), and gave the money for the potter's field, as the Lord directed me." (Matthew 27:3–10.)

The above constitutes a proliferation of legend about the death of Judas, combined with attempts to ground the legend in prophecies in the Hebrew Bible. A very different legend about the death of Judas is found in Acts (see below); these two different continuations of the Judas-saga probably stemmed from different regions. The Gospel of Mark, omitting all mention of the punishment or death of Judas, had left a narrative need, which was filled by speculations that quickly achieved the status of fact.

Repeated emphasis is laid in the passage on the word "blood". This is a little muted in the New English Bible translation quoted, since it renders Judas's confession as, "I have brought an innocent man to his death," instead of the Authorized Version's literal, "I have betrayed the innocent blood." The thirty silver pieces are called "blood-money", and the field bought with them is called "Blood Acre". The underlying concept here is that of sacrifice. Jesus's blood has been shed in sacrifice; this is the atoning blood that brings salvation, but it is also the blood that cries for punishment of those who have shed it. We have almost a comedy of guilt-shifting: Judas attempts to shift the guilt to the priests, and they shunt it back to him. He throws the money into the Temple: an ambiguous gesture, which says both that the Temple priests must take the blame, and also that the money deserves to be consecrated as having procured salvation. We have here the ambivalence of sacrifice, as it is regarded not in Jewish, but in Greco-Roman religion; it is both holy and accursed. The priests treat the money with the same mixture of attitudes. It cannot be used in the Temple, yet it can go towards another holy purpose, the burial of the dead; but only of strangers, not the native-born, since, presumably, there is a stigma in being buried in such a place. The burial-ground is sacred, yet it is called "Blood Acre" and regarded with horror.

All the concepts here are non-Jewish,[7] but, as usual in the New Testament, they are given a Jewish veneer. From the Hebrew Bible comes a chain of citations that, on closer inspection, is a hotch-potch of misquotation and irrelevance. The field bought by Jeremiah for seventeen shekels (not thirty pieces) of silver, for purposes of agriculture not burial, was a symbol of hope and restoration, not of sacrifice and guilt (Jeremiah 32:6–15). It has been confusedly related, by the author of Matthew, to a different transaction in the book of Zechariah, in which the prophet, for a symbolic purpose, threw thirty pieces of silver, described as his "price" (or better, as in NEB, "wages") to the "potter in the house of the Lord". This has no discernible relevance to the story for which it has been adduced as a prophecy, quite apart from the fact that it belongs to the prophecy of Zechariah, not Jeremiah, the prophet cited. But the "price" or "wages" of the prophet are related, by a loose verbal association, with the "price" paid for the betrayal of Jesus, which could be said to be "his" price. The "Potter's Field" also seems to have entered Matthew's narrative by way of Zechariah, where the "potter", however, was in the Temple, not giving his name to a field. The author of Matthew, however, has apparently inserted a "field" into the Zechariah text to make his citation more plausible—or perhaps because he was quoting from memory, which would also explain his misattribution of the passage to Jeremiah.

Yet, on further examination, we find that the interpretation put on the biblical texts is not as arbitrary as it appears. In most cases, Matthew can be seen as responding to a subterranean strand in the biblical text that the Bible itself is struggling to condemn and outlaw.

This is perhaps best seen by considering the relevance of Jeremiah 19, a chapter which Kermode summarizes as follows: "... the prophet buys a flask at the potter's house and breaks it at the burial ground, as a sign that the kings have filled Jerusalem with innocent blood ..."[8] The valley of Tophet, or Hinnom, was not a burial-ground, but a dump where rubbish was burnt. Yet Kermode is not entirely wrong, for Jeremiah turns this rubbish-dump into a kind of burial-ground, by his prophecy, "Thus saith the Lord of hosts; Even so will I break this people and this city, as one breaketh a potter's vessel, that cannot be made whole again; and they shall bury them in Tophet, till there be no place to bury." (Jeremiah 19:11, AV.) There may well be another unconscious link between the "Field of Blood" and the valley of Tophet. It was in this valley (many centuries before) that the human sacrifices were performed that are condemned in the Hebrew Bible (II Kings 23:10, Jeremiah 7:31). In Matthew's mind there may have been a link between the blood of the sacrifices offered there and the blood of Jesus.

Thus Jeremiah takes a piece of pottery to a place of condemned human sacrifice, and breaks it there to symbolize the spilling of innocent blood. But whereas such blood-spilling is totally condemned by Jeremiah, the case of Jesus is regarded by Matthew more ambivalently as an appalling but necessary sacrifice. So the "valley of Hinnom" of Jeremiah 19,[9] disfigured by human sacrifice, is transmuted by Matthew into a Blood Acre bought with the blood-money of another sacrifice, equally hideous yet salvific, just as those ancient forbidden rites were thought to be by their instigators. If so, this is an example of the use of the Hebrew Bible to reverse its own intention and reinstitute the very thing that it sought to eliminate—namely the grateful acceptance of human sacrifice, mediated by an apparatus of horror and repudiation surrounding the Betrayer. Jeremiah is indeed the very prophet who inveighed more than any other against the practice of human sacrifice (see p. 13). Yet his imagery is taken over by Matthew for a very different purpose.

There is also a more overt meaning derivable from Jeremiah 19: the condemnation of the Jewish people for spilling innocent blood. To Matthew, the Potter's Field, the Field of Blood, a burial-ground of low repute paid for by blood-money, was an echo of the valley of Topheth, also a Potter's Field (in that Jeremiah broke the symbolic pottery there), also a Field of Blood (in that it is the place where innocent blood is to be avenged), and also a burial-ground (in that the people Israel is to be ignominiously buried there). Thus the message of the Potter's Field is to reinforce the impending doom of the Jews for their alleged spilling of the innocent blood of Jesus. Later Christian commentators, such as St. John Chrysostom, interpreted the miserable death of Judas as symbolic of the fate of the Jewish people.[10] Matthew anticipates this interpretation by relating his account of the death of Judas to a passage in Jeremiah prophesying the punishment of the Jews for their sins, though Jeremiah, of course, hoped to awaken his people to repentance, and did not mean his prophecy as a rejection of the Jews by God.

A difficulty remains in the text that Matthew seems to have removed the word "potter" from the passage he quotes from Zechariah. Instead of Zechariah's casting the thirty silver pieces to "the potter in the Temple", Matthew has Judas casting them down simply "in the temple". Wilhelm Gesenius was probably the first to suggest that the word *yotzer* ("potter") in Zechariah 11:13 should be emended to *otzar* ("treasury"). This makes better sense in every way, and is supported by the Targum and Peshitta;[11] it has been adopted as the correct reading by the New English Bible. It has been suggested,[12] therefore, that the author of Matthew had the reading "treasury" before him in his text of Zechariah 11:13, explaining his assertion that Judas threw down the money in the "temple" (*naos*), not to the "potter in the temple".[13] It is unlikely, however, that Matthew would use the word *naos* ("shrine") to mean "temple-treasury". The shrine was the most sacred part of the Temple, entered only by priests. The treasury was in a much less sacred part of the temple grounds, and Matthew always uses the word *hieron* for this wider area. Matthew seems to have meant that Judas flung the blood-money down in the innermost shrine of the Temple. This would have been impossible in practice, since Judas would not have been allowed to enter the shrine. But Matthew's point is really that the innermost sanctuary has been tainted by the complicity of the Jewish religious authorities in the death of Jesus. The entry of the blood-money into the heart of the Temple (even though the priests hastily remove it) foreshadows the eventual destruction of the shrine. There is thus no compelling evidence of what Matthew's reading was in Zechariah 11:13, especially as his memory of the passage is so faulty; but the appearance of the "potter" (in "potter's field") so close to the citation of the Zechariah passage, certainly suggests that he has been displaced by Matthew's desire to make a point about the shrine.

The suicide of Ahitophel is often cited as a parallel or source for the suicide of Judas. But there is only a superficial similarity. Ahitophel was the chief adviser of King David and was renowned for his wisdom. When David's son Absalom attempted to usurp the throne, Ahitophel joined the rebellion. But when he found that Absalom failed to follow his advice, he realized that the rebellion was doomed, and hanged himself (II Samuel 17:23). This was not out of remorse for his attempted betrayal of his master David, but because his plans had misfired. His treachery to King David is not treated by the Hebrew Bible narrative as an archetype of metaphysical treachery, but as a political move. King David, though often taken by Christian writers as foreshadowing the messianic Jesus, was no sacrificial figure. He was a messiah in the Jewish sense, i.e. an anointed king of flesh and blood, struggling against his human disposition to sin but seeking to establish the kingdom of God, in the face of political and other difficulties. The atmosphere of horror that surrounds the story of Judas is entirely lacking in that of Ahitophel; if any detail of the realistic Hebrew Bible story was utilized by the Gospel writer, it was in the service of a very different literary and religious aim.[14]

Thus the story of the death of Judas undoubtedly contains many echoes of the Hebrew Bible; but these echoes are used in a way that is alien to its purposes. The Hebrew Bible contains no myth of redemption through evil, except in so far as such a myth is repudiated and rejected. The meaning of the Judas legend should be sought not through parallels with the Hebrew Bible or rabbinic literature, but in the general field of comparative myth, where we frequently find the theme of salvation through the violent death of a divine sacrifice, a theme nowhere to be found in the Jewish tradition.

❖ 4 ❖

Judas Iscariot
in Luke and Acts

W e have seen by comparison of the two earliest Gospels, Mark and Matthew, that the Judas-legend was not static, but was a changing, growing phenomenon, responding to the needs of the Pauline Church in its conflict both with the Jerusalem Church and with the Jews. We now come to Luke, the third-composed Gospel, where we may expect to find new embellishments. Luke's Gospel should also be considered together with the book of Acts, since it is generally agreed that they are by the same author.

According to Church tradition, the author of Luke-Acts is none other than the Luke named as the Gentile disciple and companion of Paul in Colossians 4:14, where he is called "Luke, the beloved physician" (see also Philemon 24, II Timothy 4:11). However, Luke is not actually mentioned in the text of either Luke or Acts. The use of the pronoun "we" in the later chapters of Acts (indicating that the author shared in the travels of Paul) does suggest that the author was a companion of Paul. But this could be a feature of an earlier source incorporated into Acts by its author; and in any case, the author could perhaps have been not Luke but some other companion. Many modern scholars believe that the author of Luke-Acts was neither Luke nor any other companion of Paul. The reasons given for this conclusion are that (1) the author shows very little sign of regarding the death of Jesus as an expiatory sacrifice, as Paul does; (2) there are significant discrepancies between the biographical details given about Paul in Acts with Paul's own statements in his epistles. If this view is correct, we know nothing about the author of Luke-Acts except that he was a Gentile (as shown by his ignorance of the geography of Palestine and by his lack of semitisms). On the other hand, the ultra-sceptical opinion about the authorship of Luke-Acts is subject to objections too (not least on the grounds of its motivation, see p. 173), and the view that Luke-Acts was written after all by Paul's companion Luke the physician is still tenable.

The consensus of scholars is that the Gospel of Luke was written between 80 and 90 CE, and its sequel, Acts of the Apostles, between 90 and 100 CE. Many considerations lead to this conclusion (e.g. the detailed knowledge of the destruction of Jerusalem shown in Luke 21:20–24, and the assertion of Luke 1:1 that many gospel writings were already in existence).

Like Matthew, Luke makes great use of the Gospel of Mark, much of which he incorporates with some characteristic alterations. However, he adds many features of his own, including an account of the birth of John the Baptist, Mary's song the Magnificat (modelled on Hannah's hymn of praise, I Samuel 2:1–10), and a long section showing Jesus's activities on the way to Jerusalem. Luke's Greek is more polished than that of the earlier two Gospels, and he prefixes a prologue and dedication in contemporary literary style. His theological aim is to integrate the life of Jesus into world history, and thus to validate the historical role of the Christian Church; for he does not expect the imminent return of Jesus (as Mark and Matthew do).

As in Mark and Matthew, the first mention of Judas Iscariot in Luke comes in the list of the twelve Apostles:

> When day broke he called his disciples to him, and from among them he chose twelve, and named them Apostles: Simon, to whom he gave the name Peter, and Andrew his brother, James and John, Philip and Bartholemew, Matthew and Thomas, James, son of Alphaeus, and Simon who was called the Zealot, Judas son of James (AV: brother of James), and Judas Iscariot who turned traitor. (Luke 6:13–16.)

Here, for the first time, we have a list containing two Judases, one called Judas son of James, and the other called Judas Iscariot. This is a new development that deserves some comment, though a full treatment of the complex question of the various Judases in the New Testament narrative will be reserved for a later chapter.[1]

In Mark and Matthew, the traitor Judas is simply identified with the Apostle, and there is no hint that there may have been more than

51

one Judas among the Apostles. This position, however, was hard to maintain because there were strong traditions of an Apostle Judas who remained loyal to Jesus. There were even traditions that this loyal Judas was Jesus's own brother, though other traditions contradicted this. In any case, an escape from the perplexity was found by asserting that there were two Judases, one loyal, and one treacherous.[2] A second Judas (as will be argued in full later) was a necessary by-product of the growth of the fictitious Judas-legend. In historical reality, as we shall have good reasons to find, there was only one Apostle Judas who remained loyal to Jesus. The second Judas was in fact the return of the original Judas, who could not be wholly obliterated after all.[3]

Luke's account of Judas's deal with the priests also contains some new features:

Then Satan entered into Judas Iscariot, who was one of the Twelve; and Judas went to the chief priests and officers of the temple police to discuss ways and means of putting Jesus into their power. They were greatly pleased and undertook to pay him a sum of money. He agreed, and began to look out for an opportunity to betray him to them without collecting a crowd. (Luke 22:3–6.)

This, like Matthew's account, is based on the brief passage in Mark 14:10–11. But Luke shows evidence of growing elaborations in the oral tradition. Nothing was said about Satan in either Mark or Matthew, but now Judas is developing into a Satan-inspired character, whose betrayal thus becomes part of a cosmic conflict between good and evil. Luke also is concerned with the plausibility of the story, and adds touches to indicate how Judas's betrayal functions. Why should a betrayer be necessary at all? Why cannot the priests simply arrest Jesus, without requiring the services of a betrayer? This problem was not entirely ignored by Mark and Matthew (see above, p. 35). Luke takes their solution further: the priests were reluctant to rouse the hostility of the Jewish masses by openly arresting Jesus. It was necessary to arrange a secret arrest, "without collecting a crowd". However, the solution of one narrative difficulty creates another. The Jewish crowd, here portrayed as supporting Jesus, is elsewhere portrayed as opposing him. This is a difficulty for all the Gospel-writers, and Matthew and Luke have only added one slight dimension to it.

The greed of Judas is rather less accented in Luke than in Matthew. As in Mark (14:11), it is the priests, not Judas, who first suggest a money-payment, though in Luke this is by agreement with Judas, not by a simple unilateral promise as in Mark. Luke is clearly not building upon the text of Matthew, but making his own additions directly to the text of Mark. Since he has attributed Judas's betrayal to the intervention of Satan, he is not so much concerned to explain Judas's motivation in terms of avarice. As a person possessed by evil, Judas does not require psychological motivation. Yet we sense the beginnings of a theological problem more fully developed later: how much is Judas to blame? If possessed by an evil power, does this make him helpless and therefore not blameworthy? Yet his evil as a betrayer is essential for the efficacy of the myth. This dilemma is intrinsic to the type of myth that the Judas-story exemplifies, and will merit further discussion.

Luke's account of the Last Supper, like that of Mark, does not mention Judas by name, though his role as betrayer is strongly hinted at. After Jesus's apocalyptic and eucharistic words, he announces:

"But mark this—my betrayer is here, his hand with mine on the table. For the Son of Man is going his appointed way; but alas for that man by whom he is betrayed!" At this they began to ask among themselves which of them it could possibly be who was to do this thing." (Luke 22:21–23.)

A "jealous dispute" breaks out among the disciples about who would rank highest in Jesus's kingdom. Jesus reproves them, saying they should not be concerned with personal glory; yet he promises that they will all "sit on thrones as judges of the twelve tribes of Israel". Jesus then continues:

"Simon, Simon, take heed: Satan has been given leave to sift all of you like wheat; but for you I have prayed that your faith may not fail; and when you have come to yourself, you must lend strength to your brothers." (Luke 22:31–32.)

Thus Luke has a distinctive approach to the matter of betrayal in this scene. Where Mark and Matthew refer to the disloyalty of the other disciples in deserting Jesus at Gethsemane, and especially to Peter's denials of his master at the High Priest's house, only Luke weaves this theme into his account of the Last Supper itself. In Mark and Matthew, Jesus waits until he reaches the Mount of Olives before prophesying the disciples' defection (Mark 14:27, Matthew 26:31) and Peter's disloyalty (Mark 14:30, Matthew 26:34). Also, in Mark and Matthew, the treachery of Judas alone is mentioned at the Last Supper, in such a way as to put him into a unique category. In Luke, however, it is not too much to say that Judas is only the extreme case of a general treachery. The impression given is of a disintegration of the disciples' morale as a whole. Again Luke puts this in Satanic terms, but it is not only Judas who is the target of Satan's campaign of corruption, but the whole body of disciples, as is shown by Jesus's statement, "Satan has been given leave to sift you all like wheat" (Luke 22:31). The fact that Luke does not mention Judas's name in the Last Supper account adds to the impression that his treachery is merely the outcrop of a general malaise.

Luke was also the author of Acts, the book of the New Testament that deals with early Church history, and especially with the conflict between Paul and the Jerusalem Church. In this conflict, as indicated above (p. 23), Paul is depicted as slowly converting the Jerusalem Church to his ideas, despite initial reluctance and even hostility. Peter, in particular, is depicted as moving from a position of strong adherence to Jewish observances to a Pauline position of salvation through faith. The difficulty with this portrayal was that Paul never knew Jesus, while the leaders of the Jerusalem Church were Jesus's everyday friends and followers—men who presumably knew better than anyone what Jesus wanted. Thus the disciples had to be portrayed as never having understood him fully, and as lacking in loyalty to his purposes.

Luke's account of the Last Supper is an indispensable introduction to his later account, in Acts, of the inadequacies of the Jerusalem Church. This attitude is characteristic of Mark and Matthew too; but Luke shapes his Last Supper account more thoroughly in accordance with it. In doing so, he taints the Jerusalem Church with the sin of Judas, though he predicts that, through the success of Peter's education in Paulinism, the Jerusalem Church would eventually

54

throw off this taint. (In historical fact, the Jerusalem Church never did adopt Pauline ideas, but the official myth of Acts and later Pauline Christianity was one of reconciliation between Paul and Peter.)[4] Thus Luke makes Jesus declare to Peter, ". . . when you have come to yourself, you must lend strength to your brothers" (Luke 22:32), a prophecy not merely of the period immediately after Peter's repentance for his denial, but of Peter's alleged role in the Jerusalem Church.

We now come to Luke's account of the actual betrayal:

While he was still speaking a crowd appeared with the man called Judas, one of the Twelve, at their head. He came up to Jesus to kiss him: but Jesus said, "Judas, would you betray the Son of Man with a kiss?" (Luke 22:47–48.)

Like Mark and Matthew, Luke has provided no mechanism for Judas's appearance, since he does not tell us when Judas separated from the other disciples. There are some interesting differences, however. The "crowd" which Judas is now leading contains the "chief priests, the officers of the temple police and the elders" (v. 52) instead of being merely *sent* by "the chief priests, lawyers and elders" (Mark 14:43, Matthew 26:47). It is not said plainly that the kiss is a pre-arranged signal by which Judas identifies Jesus, but this seems to be implied by Jesus's remark (not found in Mark or Matthew). Judas now leads the crowd, whereas before he was merely "with" them. Luke has abbreviated the account he found in Mark in some ways, and expanded it in others. Having increased the derogatory material about the disciples in the Last Supper, he decreases it in the account of the arrest, for he does not portray them as running away after their brief show of resistance. Luke does add some legendary touches (especially Jesus's healing of the ear, v. 51), but not in the Judas story. His only significant alteration seems to be the realistic detail that the arresting body contained "officers of the temple police". This is derived from some source other than Mark, and does not seem to be invented, as there would be no obvious motive for such an invention. It is thus likely to be historically true, whereas the inclusion of chief priests and elders in the crowd is most implausible, since such exalted persons would not personally perform arrests. That Jesus was arrested by the temple police (acting in conjunction with

55

the Roman occupying authority, see p. 76), is historically likely, while all the others mentioned as taking part in the arrest, including Judas, are legendary additions.

Luke's Gospel contains nothing more about Judas, but the author completes his version of the story in the first chapter of his sequel, the book of Acts:

> It was during this time that Peter stood up before the assembled brotherhood, about one hundred and twenty in all, and said: "My friends, the prophecy in Scripture was bound to come true, which the Holy Spirit, through the mouth of David, uttered about Judas who acted as guide to those who arrested Jesus. For he was one of our number and had his place in this ministry." (This Judas, be it noted, after buying a plot of land with the price of his villainy, fell forward on the ground, and burst open, so that his entrails poured out. This became known to everyone in Jerusalem, and they named the property in their own language Akeldama, which means "Blood Acre".) "The text I have in mind", Peter continued, "is in the Book of Psalms: 'Let his homestead fall desolate; let there be none to inhabit it'; and again, 'Let another take over his charge.' Therefore one of those who bore us company all the while we had the Lord Jesus with us, coming and going, from John's ministry of baptism until the day when he was taken from us—one of those must now join us as a witness to his resurrection." (Acts 1:15–22.)

The only other account of the death of Judas is Matthew's, which we examined earlier (p. 44). It is remarkable how different the two accounts are. In Matthew, Judas repents, returns the blood-money to the priests (who buy "Blood Acre" with it), and then hangs himself in some unspecified place. In Acts, Judas does not repent, buys "Blood Acre" himself, and dies a horrible death, in this very field. The field is a burial-ground in Matthew, but not in Acts. In Matthew, the name "Blood Acre" derives from the blood-money used for purchasing it, while in Acts it derives from Judas's bloody death. Matthew's designation of the field as previously a "potter's field" (and all the connections made thereby with Hebrew Bible passages about potters or pottery) is missing in Luke, whose linkages with the Hebrew Bible are quite different. About the only thing in common between the two accounts is the presence of a field in the story with the name "Blood Acre", though only Acts gives an Aramaic equivalent for this. The discrepancies between the two stories are so great as to tax the powers of even the most determined harmonizers.[5] This is clearly a developing story that took off in two directions.

Yet the two stories of the death of Judas, irreconcilable as they are on the logical level, form a kind of psychological unity, for together they explore the range of mythical possibilities in answer to the question, "What happens to the Betrayer?" The worshippers whose hopes of salvation depend on the sacrifice of Jesus nevertheless wish to absolve themselves from all participation in bringing about his death. They need, therefore, to load the figure of Judas with all possible guilt.

In practice, there are thus three possible ways of handling the topic of Judas's story subsequent to his betrayal of Jesus (or four, if one includes ignoring the matter, as do Mark and John):

1) Judas is overcome by his own guilt and commits suicide;
2) Judas, unrepentant, meets with punishment and death;
3) Judas is banished and wanders, like Cain, through the world, a marked man, bearing the guilt of his betrayal.

The New Testament stories in Matthew and Acts explore only the first two possibilities. The third is explored in later Christianity in relation to the Jewish nation, whose exile and wanderings were regarded as a punishment for their part in the crucifixion of Jesus. The Jews, as the Judas-nation, contribute, through Christian interpretation of Jewish experience, to the development of the Judas myth. The Christian folk-legend of the Wandering Jew also expresses the notion that the wanderings of the Jews are a punishment for their crime of deicide, though this legend also envisages the possibility that, at the end of time, the Jew may expiate his sin through his sufferings and gain forgiveness.

The first possibility too, found in Matthew, holds out the hope of forgiveness for Judas. His suicide has the appearance of a self-inflicted punishment, rather than an act of mere despair. He refuses to benefit by his treachery, and seeks to return the money he received. It is as if he has come to his senses after a bout of madness, and now cannot understand why he acted as he did. Matthew, unlike Luke, does not explicitly mention the Satanic possession to explain Judas's conduct, but his denouement of the Judas story suggests such an explanation.

The idea of Judas's ultimate redemption is paralleled in sacrificial myths of other cultures. In Greek and Roman mythology, for example, we often hear of the eventual purification and atonement of the perpetrator of the unspeakable act.[6] The eventual redemption of the Jews, or Judas-people, was so important in Christian mythology that their conversion came to be regarded as the indispensable preliminary to the Second Coming of Christ.[7] The fact is that the Betrayer or Executioner of the necessary sacrifice is so important to salvation that his ultimate redemption is a kind of recognition of his services. Together with the loathing and horror inspired by his deed, there is a submerged feeling that he is in some way a holy person. Indeed he is himself a kind of victim, since he must sacrifice his happiness and innocence to bring about the necessary murder.

The death of Judas in Acts is a far more complex story than in Matthew, and it is interesting to probe it for this sort of ambivalence. In this story, Judas is not just a criminal; he shows subtle indications of being himself a sacrificial figure. His death in a "field of blood", by the pouring out of his entrails, recalls the deaths of certain figures in pagan myth and sacrificial ritual, who fertilize the fields with their blood. The very death of Judas in a field (rather than in the unspecified location of Matthew's account) deepens the mythological aspect by arousing associations with the agricultural rites of sacrifice that underlie all mystery religion. The "field of blood" in which he dies echoes, or parodies, the "place of a skull" in which Jesus died. When one considers the prominence of blood in the sacrificial imagery surrounding the death of Jesus, from the blood of the Communion to "the blood of the lamb", the graphic phrase "field of blood" cannot be without resonance.[8] It is a phrase that could as easily describe a place of sacrifice as one of guilt and punishment. The death of Judas, in part at least, is that of a Black Christ, who undergoes his own Passion in order to spare mankind the deadly sin which he commits on their behalf.

While the mythological content of the Acts version is richer than Matthew's, the latter is not without its own evocative touches. In Matthew, Judas hangs himself, and the image of the Hanged Man too recalls many mythological figures of sacrifice, from Attis to Jesus himself. In Acts, Judas dies by divine intervention (a common theme in sacrificial myth); in Matthew, Judas dies by his own hand, also a motif often paralleled in mythology, for example, by the self-inflicted sacrificial death of Odin. As long as we mistakenly view the death of Judas as an historical event, we can see only contradictions in the evidence: Judas cannot have hanged himself if he died by a bursting of the entrails; he cannot have died in a field, and also somewhere else; the field cannot have been named "field of blood" both for the reason given in Matthew and for that given in Acts. But as soon as we abandon the historical approach and consider the story as a myth, the contradictions vanish, and turn into variations on a theme. As Lévi-Strauss has shown, the variant versions of a myth form a totality; what had to be omitted from one is supplied by another. Judas died both by hanging and by bursting, both by divine intervention and by his own hand, and so on, because all these variations add something to his function as Betrayer of the sacrificial victim, bearer of guilt, and Black Christ.

The writer of Acts, like the writer of Matthew, is concerned to ground his version of Judas's death in the Hebrew Bible, though he uses different texts. He says for example (in v. 16) that Scripture, "through the mouth of David", prophesied the punishment of Judas; and in v. 20, he gives the quotations from the Psalms that he has in mind. These (Psalms 69:25 and 109:8) are hardly convincing "prophecies", as they are merely generalized curses against King David's enemies. Nothing points to Judas in particular, or indicates that the Psalmist meant them as prophecies, rather than as judgements on events of his own day.

Yet we saw that Matthew's account derived from certain aspects of the Hebrew Bible, albeit viewed from a primitive point of view alien to the Bible itself. A similar point may be made about Acts. The graphic picture of Judas's blood and entrails spilling on to the raw earth of an open field evokes the story of Cain and Abel; Abel's blood was also spilled in a "field" (Genesis 4:8). God said to Cain, "... thy brother's blood crieth unto me from the ground. And now art thou cursed from the earth, which hath opened her mouth to receive thy brother's blood from thy hand" (Genesis 4:10–11). The Hebrew Bible's doctrine that the spilling of blood dries up the land is a late development in human history; behind it lies the opposite idea that precisely the spilling of blood in human sacrifice renders the land fertile. The image of the earth "opening her mouth" to receive blood is very ancient; originally this was a hungry acceptance by the earth goddess of her due.

The story of Cain and Abel, as we find it in the Hebrew Bible, is one of simple murder; but more than one scholar has argued that it is a transfigured account of human sacrifice, in which the earth was not accursed, but blessed, by Abel's blood.[9] Several times the New Testament delves back to the ancient remnants of human sacrifice that lie like archaeological strata under the Hebrew Bible's civilized and sophisticated stories. For the New Testament's story of salvation through the death of Jesus (and secondarily through Judas) is a "return of the unconscious", in which prehistoric ideas are revived.

Judas, on the surface of the story, is not a saviour, but the direct opposite, a killer and sacrificer. But, as we see in the study of sacrificial myths, the identities of victim and sacrificer frequently blend with each other. Often the sacrificer is the brother of the victim (Cain and Abel, Romulus and Remus, Osiris and Set); sometimes he is the twin brother, which brings the identification even closer. Here only note that the death of Judas has many sacrificial features, especially in the more complex version of Acts, and that, for whatever reason, it functions as a horrible parody of the death of Jesus.

5

Judas Iscariot in John

The latest and in some respects most elaborate account of Judas appears in the Gospel of John. Here Judas receives some touches that fill out his character in almost novelistic style; he is no longer a bare Opposer, with only the most rudimentary motives. In particular, John extends the theme of Judas's greed by making him into the corrupt treasurer of the band of disciples. The picture of Judas carrying his money-bag thus entered Christian iconology with tragic results to the Jews as a whole. At the same time, the mythological theme of the fated crime achieves more conscious expression, so that Judas appears even more as a person manipulated by cosmic forces, rather than as one acting in accordance with his own inclinations. How can Judas be both more motivated and more predetermined?

The Gospel of John is remarkably different from the other three Gospels. Not only does its sequence of events differ widely from that of the three "Synoptic" Gospels (so called because of their similarity), but the portrayal of Jesus himself is such that John's Jesus is a different person. Jesus's ministry lasts two years, instead of one, he spends six months in Jerusalem instead of one week, and the location and timing of the events often varies. Jesus, in John, is given to long speeches absent in the Synoptics, but his parables are entirely missing. Most notably, Jesus in John claims divine status, while in the Synoptics he does not. John is the most antisemitic of the Gospels, portraying Jesus as in conflict not with Pharisees or Sadducees, but simply with "the Jews".

Most scholars agree that John was composed around 100 CE, since its theological standpoint is late. The place of composition may have been Antioch. The author of the Gospel is unknown. The Church tradition that the author was Jesus's disciple John son of

61

Zebedee cannot be true, since there is evidence that the author has used both Mark and Luke. Details of the career of John son of Zebedee known from the other sources are omitted from this Gospel, and its author shows no interest in John's birthplace, Galilee. It is doubtful whether the author was a Jew, despite his accurate geographical references, which may have come from some Church source. The Church tradition of authorship is based partly on chapter 21 of the Gospel, which claims that the author was Jesus's "beloved disciple", but this chapter is a late addition.

Though late, the Gospel of John is of some historical value, because its author used some sources, whether written or oral, that were either unavailable to the Synoptics or ignored by them. However, the author has used his sources with great imaginative freedom, producing a pattern of events and characterization of his own.

John does not list Jesus's disciples, so that he does not contribute in this way, as the other Gospels do, to the discernment of how one Judas was multiplied into two. But John does retain a vivid trace of a period when there was only one Judas in the story. This is the episode referring to "Judas, not Iscariot" (14:22), who urges Jesus to "show himself to the world", i.e. to take a place on the political stage. As we argued earlier (p. 32), the close similarity between this episode and that of Jesus's "brothers" (7:5) giving him the same advice points to the conclusion that the original Judas was Jesus's brother, especially as we know from Matthew (13:55) that Jesus did have a brother called Judas. Thus we find in John's Gospel a separate and individual way of working out the transition from one Judas to two. The careful definition, "Judas, not Iscariot" shows that the author is concerned that some confusion may exist between the two Judases.[1] His solution is not (as in the Synoptic Gospels) to have one totally innocuous (indeed featureless) Judas, along with another who is the evil betrayer. John retains a less innocuous non-Iscariot Judas, one who gives Jesus bad advice and does not understand his mission of death on the Cross, thinking that Jesus aims at worldly success. This figure actually represents a transition between the original Judas and his more evil *doppelganger*. Evidently, John works independently of the other three Gospels, and makes his own use of the material at his disposal. Some of it may even be earlier and more authentic than the sources used by the Synoptic Gospels, though the use of source-material in this Fourth Gospel shows the latest standpoint of all.

John's chief addition to the story is to turn Judas Iscariot into the treasurer of Jesus's movement. Being thus soiled by contact with money, Judas can more credibly turn to evil. Even before his thoughts begin to dwell on betrayal, he has stolen from the common purse. This expansion of Judas's money-corruption was a most fateful development for the history of antisemitism. The association of the Jews with money in later times, and indeed the compulsion of Christian society to drive the Jews into money-lending as their sole permitted occupation, owes much to this emblematic portrayal of Judas.

The theme first appears in connection with the story of Martha and Mary:

> Then Mary brought a pound of very costly perfume, pure oil of nard, and anointed the feet of Jesus and wiped them with her hair, till the house was filled with the fragrance. At this, Judas Iscariot, a disciple of his—the one who was to betray him—said, "Why was this perfume not sold for thirty pounds (three hundred denarii) and given to the poor?" He said this, not out of any care for the poor, but because he was a thief; he used to pilfer the money put into the common purse, which was in his charge. (John 12:3–6.)

This story is a conflation of two other stories found elsewhere in the Gospels. The first (Mark 14:3–9; Matthew 26:6–11; Luke 7:37) also takes place in Bethany. An unnamed woman pours precious ointment on Jesus's head, and is reproved—not by Judas Iscariot, but by "some of those present" (Mark) or by the "disciples" (Matthew)—for wasting ointment that could have been sold to benefit the poor. In Luke this story is given an anti-Pharisee bent; the grumbling of the Pharisees, however, is directed not against the waste of money, but against Jesus's failure to distance himself from the woman, whom Luke turns into a prostitute. (Luke does not identify this prostitute as Mary Magdalene, or even as Mary of Bethany.)[2] The second story (Luke 10:38–42) concerns the two sisters Martha and Mary; but it is situated only in "a certain village", not Bethany, nor does it refer to precious ointment. Mary sits at Jesus's feet drinking in his words, while Martha does the serving, but Martha's complaint is rejected by Jesus. Again, Judas Iscariot is not mentioned.

Thus the episode of the ointment is an excellent example of the free imaginative development of stories in the Gospels, quite unhampered by any consideration of historical fact. Luke uses it to drive one more nail into the Pharisees, though the story did not concern Pharisees originally; then John transforms it into an episode in the Judas saga, while weaving it together with another quite unrelated story, that of Martha and Mary. John's picture of Judas as the corrupt controller of the money-bag is, of course, constructed out of hints already present in the narrative. Judas's greed is suggested by the fact that he sells Jesus for thirty pieces of silver, though even this motif, as we have seen, has gone through several phases. That Judas is a thief is John's own contribution, a first adumbration of the increasingly unpleasant character which builds up in the subsequent history of the Judas personality. That the betrayer of Jesus must have been a wicked person from the first seems a natural deduction. The drama is also increased by the opposition between the purity and innocence of Jesus and the stained and corrupt character of his betrayer.

Yet as Judas is progressively blackened, certain narrative questions intrude. How did such a person become an Apostle in the first place? And if Judas's motive was mere vulgar greed, does this not trivialize the confrontation between good and evil? We therefore turn to the complementary, if somewhat inconsistent, trend of John's narrative, which represents Judas's betrayal as a cosmic event, rather than the result of individual criminality. Here again, John builds on elements already present in the story, but he develops them in a deeper and more extreme way.

John insists more than any other Evangelist on Jesus's foreknowledge. In John's account, Jesus is fully aware that he will be betrayed and by whom. Moreover, this is an active rather than a passive foreknowledge, in that Jesus actively promotes his own betrayal and designates Judas as its agent. This makes Judas a fated figure. His betrayal may arise from his defects of character, but it is also his destiny.

We become aware of this quite early in John's story. The first hint of the betrayal is in Chapter 6. It is interesting that this prevision of betrayal arises out of Jesus's declaration of the theme of the Eucharist, "Whoso eateth my flesh, and drinketh my blood, hath eternal life; and I will raise him up at the last day. For my flesh is meat indeed, and my blood is drink indeed. He that eateth my flesh, and drinketh my blood, dwelleth in me, and I in him." (John 6:54–56.) This declaration might be expected to offend the Jews, not only because of the cannibalistic imagery and the strict prohibition in Jewish law against consuming any kind of blood, but also because such religious language was typical of the communion-meals of paganism. But what is stressed, rather, is that it offends many of Jesus's own disciples: "Many therefore of his disciples, when they had heard this, said, This is an hard saying; who can hear it? When Jesus knew in himself that his disciples murmured at it, he said unto them, Doth this offend you?" (6:60–61.) Then follows: "But there are some of you that believe not. For Jesus knew from the beginning who they were that believed not, and who should betray him." (6:64.) The rupture between Jesus and his disciples reaches such a point that "from that time many of his disciples went back, and walked no more with him." (6:66.) The Twelve, however, stay with him, and Simon Peter declares their loyalty; to which Jesus replies, "Have not I chosen you twelve, and one of you is a devil?" Upon this the comment follows, "He spake of Judas Iscariot the son of Simon; for he it was that should betray him, being one of the twelve."

We thus have a crescendo of betrayal in this passage. "Many" of Jesus's disciples desert him, even the Twelve become suspect in their loyalty, and one of them is finally announced as the arch-betrayer. All of this occurs in the context of eucharistic assertion of the magical efficacy of the mystical ingestion of Jesus's body and blood, which will produce both immortality and union with Jesus himself. It seems that betrayal is being equated with a denial of the efficacy of this sacrament.

The theme of the Eucharist is found in the other Gospels only in the Last Supper. In John, however, it is entirely absent from the Last Supper, appearing only in the Galilee setting, and in association with desertion by Jesus's disciples. John's Gospel is evidently not concerned with an actual incident in the life of Jesus (to whom the Eucharist was unknown[3]) but with controversies in the early Church about the Eucharist. The test of loyalty to the Pauline Church was acceptance of this sacrament. The mystical Pauline interpretation of the death of Jesus was in conflict with the view of his early followers that Jesus was a Jewish messiah who would return to resume a mission of political salvation. Only for a mystery-religion scenario was the figure of a Betrayer required. Judas Iscariot thus appears not only as the apex of a pyramid of betrayal consisting in denial of the efficacy of the Eucharist, but also as the arch-betrayer needed for the story which gave the Eucharist its sacrificial significance.

Here we come upon an interesting difference between John's story and that of the other three Gospels. John contains no episode of a meeting between Judas and the Jewish priests to arrange the betrayal of Jesus for money. Despite the fact that John alone portrays Judas as a miser and embezzler of the disciples' funds, there is no hint in his Gospel of a money-motive for Judas's act of betrayal. It seems that John is so keen to emphasize the fated nature of Judas's act that he is reluctant to assign any earthly motive to it. At the same time, he emphasizes far more than the other writers the general corruption of Judas's character. The result is that even Judas's evil traits contribute in a way to the theme of fate and foreknowledge: for Jesus knows Judas's character only too well. We feel, though it is never said quite explicitly, that Jesus has purposely chosen Judas to be one of the twelve disciples, knowing his evil character, so that he can eventually perform this evil function. This comes close to being made explicit when Jesus says, "Have not I chosen you twelve, and one of you is a devil?" (6:70.)

This is actually the first reference to Judas Iscariot in John's Gospel, and it presents us at once with a diabolical being, imbued with Satanic influence, hardly human, and yet a fully fledged member of a group hand-picked by Jesus himself. Yet when we next come across Judas in chapter 12, in the incident of Mary and Martha, he appears wicked and despicable rather than demonic. He has shrunk from supernatural to merely human status. Thus Jesus's previous description of him as a "devil" appears to be a prophecy, foreshadowing what will happen when Judas becomes Satan's agent. We see Judas in chapter 12, mean and dishonest, as the kind of man whose soul invites diabolic possession. This actually occurs for the first time in chapter 13, though here again, the narrative equivocates. First, in verse 2, we are told that even before the Last Supper, the devil had "put it into the heart of Judas Iscariot, Simon's son, to betray him". Then, in verse 27, we are told that it was just after Jesus handed Judas the sop, during the course of the Last Supper, that "Satan entered into him".

How are we to understand this three-fold introduction of Judas's diabolism? Perhaps we may see in it not a contradiction, but John's portrayal of the gradual unfolding of a diabolic mission. First, Judas prepares himself by a general program of mean-spirited evil; then the thought of a great act of betrayal enters his mind, suggested by Satan himself, who has selected him as a suitable instrument; finally, the thought of this betrayal so pervades him that he loses all individuality and becomes the incarnation of Satan. For to John, more than to the other Gospel-writers, the death and resurrection of Jesus form part of a cosmic drama in which Jesus is locked in combat with Satan, the "prince of this world" (John 12:31, 14:30, 16:11).

Here we may pause to appreciate the special artistry of John. He has added dramatic depth to the story by his picture of the gradual damnation of Judas. He has integrated the themes of Judas's personal wickedness and the fatedness of his role by showing him as evil's chosen instrument. But he has also revealed a cosmic background in which the real struggle is not between Jesus and Judas themselves but between opposing supernatural forces. While Luke had briefly introduced the theme of Satanic possession (Luke 22:3), his was a perfunctory treatment compared with John's dramatic preparation and development. It is in John that Judas achieves almost supernatural status as the embodiment of evil, and this, together with John's continual indictment of the "Jews" as Jesus's cruel and uncomprehending antagonists, has burned the image of the Jews into the Western mind as hateful and sinister figures, not merely bound to gross materiality, but imbued with a kind of negative spirituality deriving from the Devil.

Next comes John's great set piece, his account of the Last Supper. Here he gives Judas Iscariot a larger role than the other Evangelists, in keeping with his enlarged conception of Judas's destined and necessary role. Indeed, John presents, in chapter 13, a picture of the Last Supper in which Judas's betrayal is the central motif. This contrasts with the Synoptic accounts of the Last Supper, which pursue other important themes, namely Jesus's institution of the Eucharist and also the account of what is known as the "avowal of abstinence", Jesus's assertion that he will not drink wine with his disciples until the coming of the Kingdom of God. It is a startling fact that John here omits altogether the theme of the Eucharist. This is not because the Eucharist is unimportant to John—on the contrary, in chapter 6, he portrays Jesus as flaunting the most provocative and apparently cannibalistic aspects of the Eucharist before disapproving Jews, even alienating some of his own disciples. Why then does John omit it from the Last Supper? The answer is partly to make the theme of Judas's betrayal more central. At the same time, the omission of the Eucharist shows that its presence in the Last Supper was not fully established in John's time—a further confirmation of the view that Jesus's institution of the Eucharist is unhistorical, and that it was actually founded by Paul.

By several touches, not found in the other Gospels, John draws attention to the presence of a traitor at the Last Supper:

> It was before the Passover festival. Jesus knew that his hour had come and he must leave this world and go to the Father. He had always loved his own who were in the world, and now he was to show the full extent of his love.
>
> The devil had already put it into the mind of Judas son of Simon Iscariot to betray him. During supper, Jesus, well aware that the Father had entrusted everything to him, and that he had come from God and was going back to God, rose from table, laid aside his garments, and taking a towel, tied it round him. Then he poured water into a basin, and began to wash his disciples' feet and to wipe them with a towel.
>
> When it was Simon Peter's turn, Peter said to him, "You, Lord, washing my feet?" Jesus replied, "You do not understand now what I am doing, but one day you will." Peter said, "I will never let you wash my feet." "If I do not wash you," Jesus replied, "you are not in fellowship with me." "Then, Lord," said Simon Peter, "not my feet only; wash my hands and head as well!"
>
> Jesus said, "A man who has bathed needs no further washing; he is altogether clean; and you are clean, though not every one of you." He added the words "not every one of you" because he knew who was going to betray him. (John 13:1–11.)

Jesus draws the moral that they should all wash each others' feet in common allegiance to him. But then he continues:

"I am not speaking of all of you; I know whom I have chosen. But there is a text of Scripture to be fulfilled: 'He who eats bread with me has lifted his heel against me.' I tell you this now, before the event, so that when it happens you may believe that I am what I am." (John 13:18–19.)

The incident here described, in which Jesus washes his disciples' feet, is found in no other Gospel. It seems to have been invented by John on the basis of Jesus's saying, recorded by Luke, "I am among you as he that serveth" (Luke 22:27). But the purpose is not just to point a moral about service. Jesus seems to be carrying out a ritual of purification, by which his disciples are cleansed of their sins in preparation for the great time of testing. Acceptance of this purification is required for inclusion in the "fellowship". After the ceremony, Jesus declares his disciples to be "clean", with one exception. Presumably, Judas has been included in the ceremony; but Jesus hints that the ceremony has not been efficacious for all. Knowing everything, Jesus knows already who will betray him, and that the suggestions of the Devil are already working in Judas's mind. The incident throws light on the statement, near the beginning of the passage, that Jesus "loved his own who were in the world". The expression is redolent with Gnostic associations. These chosen souls have been selected for rescue from the evil "prince of this world". They walk in this world, but belong to another. Judas, however, is not merely "in the world" but belongs irremediably to it, together with all those who reject Jesus's divinity.

When Jesus says, "I know whom I have chosen", there is a measure of dramatic irony. Ostensibly, he means only that he knows whom he has chosen for fellowship and love; but there is an implication that he has chosen Judas too, although for a mission of evil. John goes further than any other writer in depicting Jesus as actually designating Judas as his betrayer. He does this by purposely choosing him as a disciple, knowing him to be a "devil". Other signs of Jesus's complicity with Judas soon appear.

A further touch of destiny is added by the biblical quotation now adduced by Jesus to prove that the betrayal is part of God's plan. The quotation is abbreviated from Psalms 41:9: "Yea, mine own familiar friend, in whom I trusted, which did eat of my bread, hath lifted up his heel against me." It is interesting that John omits the first part of this verse, since it is inappropriate to his portrayal of Jesus's total foreknowledge. In the Psalm, David is referring to his own life, not to someone far in the future, and the "familiar friend" was no doubt Ahitophel, his trusted counsellor, who joined the rebellion of Absalom (II Samuel 15:12). But John wishes to show that the betrayal by Judas was fated and foretold, so he twists and truncates David's autobiographical remark into a prophecy. The effect is to enhance the mythic quality of Judas's betrayal. This is not just an individual act of treachery, but a cosmic event foretold in prophecy. There is also the important dimension of fulfilment and continuity. Christianity has always sought to ground itself in the Jewish tradition, though in fact the Christian myth contains elements common in pagan myth, but alien to Judaism. Similarly, the role of Judas, as betrayer of the divine sacrifice, has many parallels in pagan myth but has no real analogue in Jewish religion, despite attempts to find supporting texts for it in the Jewish scriptures.

John, however, is the only Gospel-writer who finds an actual Old Testament quotation purportedly prophesying the role of Judas. The other Gospels have the saying, "The Son of Man goeth as it is written of him," followed by a curse on "that man by whom the Son of Man is betrayed" (Matthew 26:24, Mark 14:21, Luke 22:22), but no proof-text is offered to support the assertion that these things are "as it is written". John's proof-text concerns the fact that the betrayal is by one who eats at the same table as Jesus. This aspect is indeed included in the other Gospels, though not with any attempt to prove a Scriptural "fulfilment" ("He that dippeth his hand with me in the dish, the same shall betray me", Matthew 26:23, Mark. 14:20). It is an aspect of particular horror, since in the East there was a special obligation of loyalty to those with whom one had shared bread. But it also has a deeper mythic meaning, for, as we have seen, a close connection must exist between the sacrificial figure and his Betrayer, who must also represent the community for whose benefit the evil deed is done. The sharing of the meal provides an element of closeness that might otherwise be supplied by twinship or brotherhood.

It is rather surprising that John's Gospel does not contain the sonorous and impressive saying included in all three Synoptic Gospels:

The Son of man indeed goeth, as it is written of him: but woe to

70

that man by whom the Son of man is betrayed! Good were it for
that man if he had never been born.

This saying sums up the whole ethos of human sacrifice, with its
emotions of sorrow, guilt, tragedy, inevitability and thankfulness.
The deed of blood is accepted as utterly necessary, but the guilt is
transferred to a dark and doomed figure whose lot is regarded with
horror. The source for this saying is Mark, from whom both
Matthew and Luke have taken it. It seems likely that the saying, or
something like it, belonged originally to some mystery-cult in the
region where Mark's Gospel was composed (probably Rome).[4] The
saying is put into the mouth of Jesus, but it reads rather like a speech
of the chorus in a Greek tragedy. Indeed, Athenian tragedy sprang
from a background of sacrificial ritual, just as the Elizabethan drama
sprang from the medieval Passion plays.

   Though John does not use this classic formulation, he develops his
story, even more than the previous Gospels, in the spirit of an act of
doomed and destined betrayal. Now comes a passage that seems
designed to show Jesus's foreknowledge of his betrayal and
awareness of the identity of his betrayer:

After saying this, Jesus exclaimed in deep agitation of spirit, "In
truth, in very truth I tell you, one of you is going to betray me."
The disciples looked at one another in bewilderment: whom
could he be speaking of? One of them, the disciple he loved, was
reclining close beside Jesus. So Simon Peter nodded to him and
said, "Ask who it is he means." That disciple, as he reclined,
leaned back close beside Jesus and asked, "Lord, who is it?"
Jesus replied, "It is the man to whom I give this piece of bread
when I have dipped it in the dish." Then, after dipping it in the
dish, he took it out and gave it to Judas son of Simon Iscariot.
As soon as Judas had received it Satan entered him. Jesus said to
him, "Do quickly what you have to do." No one at the table
understood what he meant by this. Some supposed that, as
Judas was in charge of the common purse, Jesus was telling him
to buy what was needed for the festival, or to make some gift to
the poor. As soon as Judas had received the bread he went out.
It was night. (John 13:21–30.)

71

This complex passage raises many questions. Who was the "disciple he loved", and why is his name not mentioned? When we are told that no one understood what Jesus meant by his gesture and speech to Judas, surely this must exclude the beloved disciple, who could not have failed to understand? And what about Peter? Surely, after urging the disciple to ask, he must have wanted to know the result?

Traditional commentators took the view that the anonymous disciple is intended to be none other than John, son of Zebedee, the purported author of this Gospel. This is attested by a passage very near the end of the Gospel, where Jesus appears after his resurrection to Peter and the other disciples:

> Peter looked round, and saw the disciple whom Jesus loved following—the one who at supper had leaned back close to him to ask the question, "Lord, who is it that will betray you?" When he caught sight of him, Peter asked, "Lord, what will happen to him?" Jesus said, "If it should be my will that he wait until I come, what is it to you?" It is this same disciple who attests what has here been written. It is in fact he who wrote it, and we know that his testimony is true. (John 21:20–24.)

Here we are told that it was the "disciple he loved" who wrote this Gospel. That this disciple was in fact John, son of Zebedee, is not said anywhere within the Gospel itself, but was a tradition handed down in the Church, and incorporated into the title of the Gospel itself. This ascription and the accompanying tradition gave a peculiar authority to the Gospel of John, which was accepted as an eye-witness account of the life of Jesus, written by his favourite disciple. As mentioned earlier, however, modern scholars do not accept this attribution, and indeed regard the Gospel as being of unknown authorship. Further, it is thought to be the latest-composed of the four, and certainly not the work of an eyewitness. Moreover the last chapter, which claims "the beloved disciple" as the author, is now generally agreed to be a later addition which converts the Gospel into one of those pseudepigraphic works that have played so great a role in the history of religion. Whether the beloved disciple was actually John son of Zebedee is itself by no means certain, and in any case the real John son of Zebedee was one of the leaders of the

Jerusalem Church, and was a fully observant Jew all his life. Nothing could be more alien to such a person than the Hellenistic, inflated spirituality of the "Gospel of John".

Even without the fiction of privileged authorship, the Last Supper narrative in the Fourth Gospel has an air of personal authenticity that is absent in the Synoptic Gospels. The author claims that he knows exactly what went on between Jesus and Judas at the Last Supper. The other Gospels only hint that Judas was designated to perform his evil mission, but John makes this explicit from personal knowledge. The complicity of Jesus is perfectly expressed in the detail that as soon as Jesus gave the sop to Judas, the latter was entered and possessed by Satan. In the other Gospels, this "possession" took place before the Last Supper, and without any prompting from Jesus. The complicity is further emphasized by the instruction then given by Jesus: "Do quickly what you have to do."

This amazing co-operation between Jesus and Satan, however, is part of the logic of the story, and can be paralleled in other myths of human sacrifice. Even though the Slayer or Betrayer is portrayed as evil, his victim is willing and co-operative. In this way, the two incompatible aims of human sacrifice are fulfilled: to ensure that it happens (for otherwise there will be no salvation), and to disclaim responsibility. To kill the victim is evil, and must therefore be the work of Satan; but the good consequences that flow from the death of the victim are so desirable that, in some way, the services of Satan must be enlisted. This paradox was developed in the thought of the Church in later times to produce the theory that Satan was "duped" into bringing about the salvation of mankind, which without his evil ministrations would never have occurred.[5]

The statement "No one at the table understood what he meant by this" seems to contradict, in a strange way, the privileged knowledge given to the beloved disciple. Perhaps we are meant to take it in this way: even though Jesus said to his beloved disciple that the traitor would be the one to whom he gave the bread, this information magically vanished from the mind of the beloved disciple, and was only recalled by him later in the light of the event of betrayal. This kind of magical intermission of memory is not unknown in folktales. This would also explain Peter's failure to follow up his own enquiry.

A further magical element appears at the end of the Gospel in the added passage that recalls the Last Supper, where mysterious reference is made to the alleged author's immunity to death. Peter asks what will happen to the beloved disciple who asked about betrayal at the Last Supper, and Jesus replies, "If it should be my will that he wait until I come, what is it to you?" This answer seems to mean that the beloved disciple will be preserved until the Second Coming.[6] This legend underwent a curious transmutation in later history. Instead of a faithful disciple living on in tranquillity until the return of Jesus, the concept arose of the Wandering Jew, who would live on in suffering repentance and expiation of his sins until released by Jesus's return. This derivation is supported by the nomenclature: the name given at first to the Wandering Jew was John; only later was it changed in northern areas to Ahasuerus, and in Spain it remained Juan. One reason for this transformation of the legend was the knowledge that the beloved disciple had actually died (see note 6). Perhaps also his intimate knowledge about Judas gave him, in the popular mind, a certain air of complicity that fitted him for the role of a penitent. After all, Judas himself was a "beloved disciple" ("mine own familiar friend", in the words of the Psalm Jesus quotes in this Gospel). The more beloved Judas was, the greater horror in his betrayal. There is thus, as in a dream, a coalescence between Judas and the beloved disciple. The Wandering Jew is a kind of repentant Judas, as well as being a derivative of the beloved disciple.

An interesting incidental feature in John's account of the Last Supper is the naming of Judas as "Judas son of Simon Iscariot" (13:26). This is the reading of the NEB translation, where the more familiar AV reading has "Judas Iscariot, son of Simon". Both readings have manuscript support, but, as the NEB reading indicates, the weight lies on the side of "Iscariot" in the genitive, making it agree with "Simon", not with "Judas". It should also be noted that the words "son of" do not appear in the Greek, and that the translation "brother of" is equally in accordance with Greek usage. In any case, it would seem from this text that "Iscariot" was a name, or nickname, borne not just by Judas himself, but by at least one other member of his family. The only parallel expression is in John 6:71, where there is a similar disagreement among the manuscripts. In no other Gospel are we given the name of Judas's father (or brother); nowhere else is the name "Iscariot" applied to anyone except Judas himself. We shall see some significance in this text when we come to discuss the question of the meaning of the name "Iscariot".

Our conclusion regarding John's Last Supper account is that it centralizes the theme of Judas's betrayal and especially of Jesus's foreknowledge and even participation in it. The account ends with the brief and expressive sentence, "It was night." As many commentators have noted, this sentence possesses a considerable symbolic force. Judas, going out into the night, has become totally identified with the powers of darkness. From now on, Jesus will move towards inexorable death. Yet he himself has fully acquiesced in this. In the course of his ensuing disquisition to his disciples, he says, "I shall not talk much longer with you, for the Prince of this world approaches" (14:30). The phase of tragedy has begun, in which only death and darkness can be envisaged, and the hope of resurrection is too remote to be mentioned. There is a mythic resonance about this, for in a ritual of death and rebirth it is essential that each phase should be experienced fully and without adulteration. The wailing of the women for Adonis is unrelieved by any hope of resurrection, so that when this eventually happens, joy too can be unadulterated and have the quality of unexpectedness. The Gospel of John displays this separation of emotions, as in the passion plays of all mystery cults; but the dualism that pervades this Gospel makes the separation even sharper. Jesus, by his reference to the "Prince of this world", shows that his death is the triumph of Satan. He must come under Satan's complete thrall in order to experience the total submission and defeat that must precede his resurrection and eventual victory.

The next we hear of Judas Iscariot is in the scene of the arrest of Jesus:

After these words, Jesus went out with his disciples, and crossed the Kedron ravine. There was a garden there, and he and his disciples went into it. The place was known to Judas, his betrayer, because Jesus had often met there with his disciples. So Judas took a detachment of soldiers, and police provided by the chief priests and Pharisees, equipped with lanterns, torches, and weapons, and made his way to the garden. Jesus, knowing all that was coming upon him, went out to them and asked, "Who is it you want?" "Jesus of Nazareth," they answered. Jesus said,

75

"I am he." And there stood Judas the traitor with them. (John 18:1–5.)

This is the last we hear of Judas in John's Gospel. About the further life of Judas, John, like Mark, is silent. Matthew portrays a repentant, and Acts an unrepentant Judas; John has neither. Mark's silence is part of his general reticence; John's, we may feel, has an artistic purpose. Judas has become swallowed up in the power of darkness, and has lost all individuality. He performs his role of treachery, as he is doomed to do, and disappears from life.

There are some interesting new features in John's account of the betrayal and arrest of Jesus, and also some interesting omissions. John says nothing about the kiss with which Judas, according to the Synoptics, identified Jesus. On the other hand, John provides a more plausible account of why a traitor was required to find Jesus. The "garden" is a less public place than the vale of Gethsemane, in the Mount of Olives, where the Synoptics place the arrest, and would presumably need special knowledge to find—knowledge which Judas, as an intimate of Jesus, could supply to the arresting authorities. Another important point is that John involves the Romans in Jesus's arrest, as the Synoptics do not. The Greek word for a "detachment of soldiers" (v. 3) and for "troops" (v. 12) (*speira*) can only refer to a Roman military unit. Judas guides these troops together with Jewish police (*huperetas*) to the garden, and stands by while the arrest takes place. The involvement of the Romans in Jesus's arrest is a touch of real history which has survived in John's Gospel, though apparently suppressed by the Synoptics. Here is one of the details supplied by John that go back to earlier sources.[7] It was inevitable that John, using independent sources, should occasionally preserve details suppressed by the Synoptics. Not that John is any less selective, but he makes his own choice of what to preserve and what to invent.

The Gospels are, on the whole, pro-Roman, and seek to minimize the role of the Romans in Jesus's arrest, trial and execution (see p. 99). But here something of the historical reality, the arrest of a subversive Jew by Roman occupying troops with the collaboration of Jewish quisling police, is allowed to appear. In this version of events, Judas (who in John makes no arrangement with the Jewish priests) functions as a collaborator, betraying a leader of the Jewish resistance to the Roman occupation; though in fact this is in contradiction to John's picture of Jesus as totally non-political. John is even more concerned than the Synoptics to deny any involvement of Jesus in politics, but careless editing has apparently let through a significant detail—that Jesus was arrested by Roman troops. On the other hand, John involves the Pharisees in Jesus's arrest, a detail which appears in none of the other Gospels. The notion that the Pharisees had "police" to send is absurd. Only the High Priest—who was a Sadducee, not a Pharisee—deployed police in his capacity of Gauleiter for the Romans. But this malicious little addition, attempting to implicate the Pharisees in Jesus's arrest, may safely be dismissed as unhistorical. The accounts of the Synoptics and of John, while equally biased, overlap sufficiently for the historical facts to be discerned in their interstices; the lacunae of one account are often supplied by another.

John's picture of Jesus being arrested by Roman troops ties in well with the following episode, unique to John, in which Jesus does not undergo any Sanhedrin trial. Instead he is interrogated by Annas, the High Priest's father-in-law, who then sends him "bound" to Caiaphas, the High Priest, who hands him over directly to the Roman Governor, Pilate. This is a most revealing sequence of events. The alleged Sanhedrin trial, described in all three of the Synoptic Gospels, is full of improbabilities, and many scholars have regarded it as unhistorical. If John is correct, Jesus was never tried by the Sanhedrin on a religious charge. Rather he was arrested by Roman and quisling Jewish troops on a political charge of subversion against the Roman occupation of Judaea. This makes the role of Judas, in John's account, very different from that described in the other Gospels. Judas is here hand in glove with the Romans and their Jewish acolytes, not with the Jewish religious establishment.

But this cannot be regarded as an insight of John himself into the character of Judas. It is the outcome of John's individual mixture of truth and fiction. If Jesus was arrested as a political subversive, then his betrayer would have to be a political collaborator with the Romans, a role for which nothing in the foregoing story prepares us. John inadvertently turns Judas into a political figure, simply because John, at this point, retains an authentic indication, derived from early sources, that Jesus was a political figure. John himself does not see the implications of the fact that Jesus was arrested by Roman and high-priestly troops. Nor does he see the implications of Jesus's interrogation in the High Priest's house, rather than before the Sanhedrin. The High Priest, to John, as to the other Gospel-writers, is a religious rather than a political authority. The position of the High Priest as a Roman-appointed Gauleiter is nowhere explained in the New Testament, though it is possible to see from certain New Testament passages (the trials of Peter and Paul) that he had no deciding authority in religious matters. Nevertheless, John reveals, however unintentionally, some valuable historical facts: that Jesus was arrested as a rebel against Rome, and that he was never tried on a religious charge.

❖ 6 ❖

The Beginnings of Folklore

A study of the New Testament materials reveals that Judas Iscariot develops from a featureless Opposer to a well-rounded figure of evil, pre-elected for a role to which his evil traits are admirably suited. In the Christian literature that followed the composition of the Gospels, the character of Judas continued to develop, entering the realm of popular folklore and myth. Here we find stories about the childhood of Judas, prefiguring his later treachery; he begins to be charged with sexual enormity; and we also find Judas endowed with a wife, who shares in, or even instigates, his wrong-doing. This is the natural continuation of the process begun in the Gospels, answering the need to know more about a fascinating figure of evil.

But at this point we should pause and ask whether or not our survey so far confirms the view that the treachery of Judas is intended to represent and symbolize that of the Jews as a whole.

The chief device which links the two is the representation of Judas as defecting to the enemies of Jesus who are themselves the leaders of the Jews. Only the Gospel of John portrays Judas as an agent of Roman, not Jewish, authorities, and even here the matter is obscure. The name "Romans" does not appear even in John to describe persons actually present at the scene of the arrest; their presence can only be deduced from the word *speira* (a Greek word regularly used to translate the Latin *manipulus*, a unit of the Roman army), which is retained from an earlier source (see p. 76). Indeed, throughout the Gospels, the Romans are almost invisible. When they are mentioned, their oppressive occupation of Judaea is ignored, and instead they are given a mild and benevolent aspect. Those depicted as the enemies of Jesus are the leading Jewish groups—the Pharisees, the High Priest and his entourage, the elders, scribes, and lawyers—all conceived as representatives of the most authoritative Judaism. Jesus thus appears as being pitted against the very essence of Jewry. In John, even the distinction between the leaders and the mass of Jews is dropped, and Jesus's enemies become simply "the Jews". Thus the meaning of Judas's betrayal is simple: he has gone over to the Jews. His name then, which continually echoes *Ioudaioi*, acquires the meaning "Jew". Judas now encapsulates the aura of treachery and hostility emanating from the Jews that has been shown surrounding Jesus throughout. Judas's treachery is now not only seen as the culmination of a lifetime of meanness, but as the fulfilment of the potentialities of his name. His innate Jewishness, in other words, now bursts the bonds imposed by his discipleship. He shows his real character, and thereby exposes the character of his entire nation.

A parallel is created at every point in the myth between the career of Judas and that of the Jewish people. Just as Judas, a chosen disciple, abandoned Jesus, so the Jews, God's chosen people, abandoned Him by rejecting his Son. In each case there is treachery, for betrayal means to turn against one's own. John emphasizes this when he says of the Jews, "He came unto his own, and his own received him not." (John 1:11.) Moreover, the alleged crime of the Jews, as of Judas, was to hand over Jesus to destruction, rather than destroying him themselves, an act of treachery rather than one of direct violence. Just as Judas is given a past history of evil thoughts and deeds (his embezzlement of funds) in order to explain his defection, so the Jews, despite their divine election, are given a past history of rebellion against God (Matthew 23, Acts 7). Just as Judas is a fated instrument of both Satan and God (he is possessed by Satan, but unwittingly performs an act of salvation), the Jews as a whole are "blind" to the message of Jesus because this is the fate which has been prophesied for them (Matthew 13:14, Mark 4:12, John 13:37–41, Romans 11:7–11); salvation also comes to the Gentiles through the "blindness" of Israel ("through their fall salvation is come to the Gentiles", Romans 11:11). Just as Judas, despite being selected for the task by Jesus himself, is doomed to a terrible punishment, so the Jews, despite their fated role, must suffer punishment throughout the generations. This is why Matthew depicts the Jews as calling a dire punishment upon themselves with the words, "His blood be on us and on our children" (Matthew 27:25). The destruction of the Temple was interpreted by Christians as the punishment of the Jews for their rejection of Jesus, a belief which may be found in the New Testament itself (Luke 19:44, I Thessalonians 2:16).

As I have argued elsewhere,[1] none of this is based on historical fact. The Jews did not reject Jesus. The Pharisees, the religious leaders of the people, were not in conflict with him and played no part in his arrest or trial. The High Priest, who was indeed Jesus's enemy, was a henchman and appointee of the Romans, not a figure of authority to the vast majority of the Jews, who regarded him as a heretic and a quisling. When Jesus died on a Roman cross, he was mourned as yet another failed Messiah, who had died in the attempt to restore the Jewish monarchy and independence. The need to detach Pauline Christianity from the Jewish rebellion against Rome led the evangelists to transfer the conflict between Jesus and Rome to an alleged struggle between Jesus and the Jewish religion. This produced the image of the Jews as a Judas-nation, and to the invention of Judas himself as the arch-traitor who encapsulates Jewish treachery. Thus the more the Jews were blackened, the more easily could Pauline Christians disclaim anti-Roman intentions, dispelling quite natural suspicion of a group who worshipped a Jew who had died by crucifixion, the Roman punishment for subversion.

This identification of Judas with the Jewish people as a whole would seem to have been unconscious, as far the New Testament itself is concerned. It is only in later Christian literature, notably the writings of Jerome (c. 340–420), that this identification is made explicit. But the parallel is so striking, and its artistic effect so compelling, that it cannot be missed by anyone reading the New Testament with the eye of a literary critic. When the legend of Judas Iscariot was created, there must have seemed a certain inevitability about it that precluded any sense of conscious forgery. Myths are created in a creative ferment that is very far removed from the critical stance needed to explicate them. When the death of Jesus began to be seen not as the unfortunate failure of another messianic claimant, but as a divine vicissitude pregnant with meaning for the future of the cosmos, the narrative developments followed with the force of mythic necessity. The death of a god demands an antagonist of equal, or near-equal, status. This figure could only be Satan. Thus Jews became the dedicated acolytes of Satan (John has Jesus say to the Jews, "Ye are of your father the Devil", John 8:44). This

81

identification had already been made in the Hellenistic world by the Gnostics, who regarded the Jews as people of the Demiurge, the evil Creator of the material world. But the urgent narrative pressure of the developing Passion play of Jesus, during his emergence as a new mystery-god, demanded a single *dramatis persona*, who would act as a focus of hate. So the character of Judas emerged, rapidly acquiring fullness of characterization, dramatizing and crystallizing the role of the villainous nation which supported him somewhat like a Greek chorus (except that the latter is usually on the side of the victim). That Judas was elected for this role was probably not a conscious decision. Still if the traitor had been Simon or James, there would not have been the same resonance. It must have seemed a divine inspiration when the treacherous disciple emerged from the mythopoeic melting-pot as no other than Judas, the eponymous representative of the Jews.

Again, the developments in the character of Judas in post-Gospel Christian literature, while often motivated by sheer narrative curiosity ("What was Judas like as a child?" or "Did Judas have a wife?"), never escape the need to maintain an analogy between Judas and the Jewish people as a whole. The literature with which we are concerned in this chapter consists mainly of what are called "the New Testament Apocrypha". These writings were written in imitation of the New Testament itself, being Gospels, books of Acts, and Apocalypses, often purportedly written by prominent New Testament characters (Peter, Andrew, James, Thomas, Paul, Nicodemus, even Pilate). The actual dates of composition range from the third to the fifth century CE. During the period in which these works were written, the Christian Church changed from a minority cult to the official religion of the Roman Empire.[2] Much polemical literature was being written by Christian theologians and historians against the Jews and Judaism, and the main lines of Christian antisemitism were being laid down by figures such as Chrysostom, Eusebius, Tertullian, Irenaeus, Origen, Jerome and Augustine.

However, the earliest evidence of continuing interest in Judas may be found not in the Apocrypha but in a fragment from the writings of Papias, in which the death of Judas is narrated with a lurid fascination. Papias, who died about 140 CE, was Bishop of Hierapolis in Phrygia (Asia Minor). His work, a collection of traditions called *Exposition of the Lord's Sayings*, did not survive, but extracts from it were quoted by later writers.

As a great example of impiety, Judas walked about in this world. He was so swollen in his body, that where a wagon could go through easily, he could not go through; nay, he could not even insert the mass of his head. His eyelids were so swollen, it is said, that he could not see the light at all, nor could his eyes be seen even with an optical instrument; so deep did they lie from the surface.

His genitals were repellent and huge beyond all shamelessness. From his whole body flowed blood mixed with worms, which exuded particularly during his natural needs.

After many trials and sufferings, they say, he died in his own place, which, because of the stench, has remained deserted and uninhabitable to the present day. Until today, no one can pass by that place without holding his nose. So great was the exudation from his body that spread over the ground.[3]

This account is based on the premise that Judas did not die when he hanged himself. Since the story of Judas's suicide in Matthew 27:5 contradicts the account of his "bursting" in Aceldama, as described in Acts 1:18, a harmonizing version arose in which Judas did indeed attempt to hang himself, but was cut down in time to save his life. This enabled him to survive long enough to suffer the gruesome death allotted to him in Acts.

Papias's subsequent account shows a desire to ascribe terrible sufferings to Judas in punishment of his treachery. The idea that his body swelled up grotesquely does not appear in our text of Acts. Yet it may have once been there. For the word used by Papias for "swollen"—*presthes*—is rather similar to the word used in Acts—*prenes*—meaning "headlong", a word which scholars have found difficult in that context. It has been suggested, therefore, that the text of Acts 1:18 should be corrected, in the light of Papias, from *prenes* to *presthes*, in which case Acts too would be picturing a swollen Judas. This amended reading makes more sense of his death by "bursting", as well as being more plausible linguistically.[4]

The picture of a grossly swollen Judas, exuding noxious liquids and worms, clearly owes something to well-known descriptions of the deaths of certain tyrants—particularly that of Herod I, a near contemporary who, as it happens, also shared with Judas the thankless role of archetypal Jew in the medieval passion plays.

Herod, because of his alleged Massacre of the Innocents, by which he attempted to murder Jesus in his infancy (a mythical event based on Pharaoh's massacre of the Israelite infants in Exodus 1:16), was also an Opponent to the divine Saviour, though not as significant as Judas, since his attempt came to nothing. However, his terrible death was an historical fact (see Josephus, *Antiquities*, xvii, 168), involving swelling, exudation of liquids and worms, rotting of the genitals, and a noisome stench. Furthermore, Herod Agrippa I, the grandson of Herod I, also died by a sudden illness in which he was "eaten of worms",[5] after executing James son of Zebedee. It seems then that Judas, in Papias's account of his death, has inherited the real or fancied symptoms of a variety of alleged persecutors of Jesus or the Church.[6]

The inclusion of genital symptoms is especially interesting here. This may simply be a transfer from the death of Herod I, whose "privy member was putrefied and produced worms". But Papias also introduces a monstrous swelling of Judas's member, which makes a grotesque picture of pathological lasciviousness. Judas in his final illness thus becomes a kind of gross priapic figure. One cannot help seeing here a forerunner of the priapic Jew, who in medieval and Nazi propaganda, threatened the pure virgins of Christendom or the Aryan race with his enormous and repulsive appetites. Equally prophetic is the ghastly stench affecting Judas both in life and death, which may be seen as a forerunner of the *foetor Judaicus* (Jewish stench). It was believed by many generations of medieval Christians that this adhered to Jews, who only become free of it if they became converted to Christianity (see p. 112). The fantasies that clustered round the figure of Judas were always liable to be transferred to the Jews as a whole.

A further touch in Papias's portrait that casts a shadow forward is his remark that Judas, an example of impiety, "walked around (*periepatesen*) the world". This picture of a peripatetic Judas naturally reminds us of the Wandering Jew, who as we have already seen (p. 12) has a good deal in common with Judas. The Wandering Jew, in medieval legend, was a penitent and a convert to Christianity, who nevertheless wandered in torment until his eventual release at the Second Coming. But there were other versions of the legend, current especially in Germany, in which he was unpenitent and malevolent. These images would seem to be derived from, or at least cognate with, Papias's Judas.

84

Another fragment of Papias, however, preserved by Irenaeus (writing at about 180 CE[7]), gives us a rather different slant on Judas (*Haer.* v. 32):

The elders who saw John the disciple of the Lord remembered that they had heard from him how the Lord taught in regard to those times, and said: "The days will come in which vines shall grow, having each ten thousand branches, and in each branch ten thousand twigs, and in each true twig ten thousand shoots, and in every one of the shoots ten thousand clusters, and on every one of the clusters ten thousand grapes, and every grape when pressed will give five-and-twenty metretes of wine. And when any one of the saints shall lay hold of a cluster, another shall cry out, 'I am a better cluster, take me; bless the Lord through me.'" In like manner, he said that a grain of wheat would produce ten thousand ears, and that every ear would have ten thousand grains, and every grain would yield ten pounds of clear, pure, fine flour; and that apples, and seeds, and grass would produce in similar proportions; and that all animals, feeding then only on the productions of the earth, would become peaceable and harmonious, and be in perfect subjection to man. Testimony is borne to these things in writing by Papias, an ancient man, who was a hearer of John and a friend of Polycarp, in the fourth of his books; for five books were composed by him. And he added, saying, "Now these things are credible to believers." And Judas the traitor, says he, not believing, and asking, How shall such growths be accomplished by the Lord? the Lord said, "They shall see who shall come to them."

In this passage, Judas is shown primarily as an unbeliever. This conforms to the tradition that Judas, even before his final treachery, showed evil traits. In the Gospel of John he is a thief; but here his sin is to doubt the word of Jesus, who foretells the earth's amazing productivity in the coming messianic age.

Particularly interesting is the fact that this passage does not sound very Christian. What does mainstream Christianity have to do with a messianic age of abounding fertility? According to Paul, the Second

Coming would bring about a transfiguration of all believers ("in the twinkling of an eye") that would set them far above such mundane considerations as unprecedented harvests of grapes or grain (I Corinthians 15:52). Though there has always been a millenarian strain in Christianity, it has been a minority trend. Irenaeus himself, however, as can be seen from the whole of book 5 of his work, was decidedly a millenarian, which may have led him to include the passage cited above. On the other hand, the millenarian hope formed a mainstream belief in the Jerusalem Church, which retained the Jewish doctrine of a messianic kingdom, an era of world peace and boundless prosperity, in accordance with the prophecies of the Hebrew Bible. Thus Irenaeus is probably handing on a tradition derived from the Jerusalem Church.

Further evidence lies in the fact that parallels to this story about Jesus can be found in Jewish writings. Descriptions of the messianic kingdom's amazing agricultural productivity are commonly found in the intertestamental literature (e.g. 2 Baruch 29:3–30:1). Even more striking is the following rabbinic parallel to the story of Jesus and the doubter:

Once Rabban Gamaliel sat and expounded: "In the future world, women will give birth every day, as it is said, 'She will conceive and give birth simultaneously'" (Jeremiah 31:8). A certain student jeered at him, quoting, "There is no new thing under the sun" (Ecclesiastes 1:9). He said to him, "Come and I will show you something like it in this world." Then he went out and showed him a hen. Again, Rabban Gamaliel sat and expounded: "In the future world, trees will bring forth fruit every day of the year, as it is said, 'That it may bring forth branches and bear fruit' (Ezekiel 17:8). Just as branches are there every day, so fruit will be there every day." The same disciple jeered again, saying, "Does not Scripture say, 'There is no new thing under the sun'?" He said to him, "Come and I will show you something like it in this world." So he went out and showed him a caper-bush. Again Rabban Gamaliel sat and expounded: "In the future world, the land of Israel will produce fine loaves and garments of fine wool, as it is said, 'There shall be bread and raiment in the land'" (Psalms 72:16). The same disciple jeered again, saying, "'There is no new thing under the

86

This represents the scene of the Anointing, in which Judas (according to John) was indignant at the waste of precious ointment. This miniature in a psalter from the Upper Rhine shows Judas (sitting next to the beardless John, the "disciple whom Jesus loved") with a bedraggled beard and ugly, Semitic features and expression, contrasting with the benign Nordic features of all the others. This dates from about 1260. (*Psalter, Besançon.*)

The same scene by a 15th century artist, Nicholas Froment. Judas, of ugly but not pronouncedly Semitic appearance, points his finger angrily at the kneeling Mary. All the figures here seem to have been painted from models. (*Painting, 1461, Wing of an altarpiece, Florence.*)

This 13th century Spanish portrayal of a Disputation between Christians and Jews differentiates the Jews from the Christians not merely by dress, but facially. The exaggeratedly hooked noses of some of the Jews shows the beginnings of facial stereotyping, while the Christians all have the same straight-nosed look of lamb-like innocence. (*Escorial, Madrid, Library of St. Lawrence.*)

Here we have the scene of Judas's acceptance of blood-money from the Jewish priests. Thi dates from 1250–60, and is a sculpture on the rood screen of the cathedral at Naumburg. Th close kinship of Judas to his fellow-Jews is stressed by the fact that like them, he wears th anachronistic pointed hat (*pileus*). The solidarity of Judas and the priests is emphasised als by the remarkable compactness of the whole group, huddling together conspiratorially. Th faces, however, are not markedly Semitic. (*Naumburg Cathedral, West rood screen.*)

In Giotto's famous painting of Judas receiving the blood-money from the priests (c. 1305), we see a special conception. Judas is young and handsome, constrasting with the grave, long-bearded father-figures of the priests. Yet behind Judas we discern the shadowy figure of the devil. Giotto is concerned with the point of transformation of Judas from apostle to traitor. Judas remains a figure of light and youth, still hovering on the verge of succumbing to corruption. Giotto therefore abandons the traditional conception of Judas as already corrupted long before his act of treachery. It is a powerful and artistic portrayal, which has some roots in earlier art and some consequences in later, but it is far from typical of the medieval view of Judas. (*Wall-painting, Padua.*)

Did Judas actually participate in the first Communion by drinking the wine and eating the bread distributed by Jesus? Commentators have disagreed about this. A manuscript illumination of 820–30 solves the problem in the way advocated by St. Augustine. As Judas eats the eucharistic sop, a black bird, symbolizing evil, enters his mouth together with the bread, thus illustrating the words of Paul, "... he that eateth and drinketh unworthily, eateth and drinketh damnation to himself" (1 Cor. 11: 29). (*St-Germain-des-Prés, Stuttgart Psalter, Stuttgart.*)

Judas becomes the subject of a psychological study in the powerful portrayal of the Last Supper by Rubens. Judas is isolated from the other disciples, not by the simple device of physical isolation at the wrong side of the table (as in medieval depiction), but by the composition itself, which shows Jesus looking upwards while all the disciples, except Judas, gaze adoringly at him. Judas is thus isolated by his inability to share in this adoration. His look is profoundly introspective and unhappy. He is the cynic who hates and fears his own cynicism, and wishes he could share the illusion of his companions. This is a tragic, Shakespearean conception, and it is not too much to say that Judas, rather than Jesus, is the centre and subject of the painting. Yet the composition owes much to medieval motifs. Even the little dog lying at Judas's feet (but not included in the previous oil sketches) occupies a position earlier reserved for a recumbent dragon-figure, symbolizing Satan. Rubens has given us a humanist version of a story previously treated as myth. (*Pinacotecca di Brera, Milan.*)

In a painting by Phillippe de Champaigne, Judas is sitting at the Last Supper in isolated position. In contrast to Rubens's conception, Judas is not looking away in despair and self-loathing, but staring full at Jesus with a self-confident, sceptical or challenging expression. Jesus has his eyes turned up to heaven, and perhaps Judas is questioning his other-worldly stance. This too is a humanistic, rather than a mythic, treatment; yet there is continuity with the medieval conception of Judas, in that he is wearing a gown of a boldly yellow colour. Perhaps unconsciously, the artist thus preserves Judas's role as representative of the Jewish people. (*Louvre, Paris.*)

A miniature in the Stuttgart Psalter (820–830), shows the Kiss of Judas, alongside the Death of Judas (almost in cartoon-strip style). Two soldiers are arresting Jesus just as Judas is kissing him. Judas's death is by hanging on a tree, as in the version of Matthew 27: 5. A black bird, symbolizing the Devil, hovers near him to seize his soul. (*St-Germain-des-Prés, Stuttgart Psalter, Stuttgart.*)

A painting of the Last Supper from the workshop of Lucas Cranach (1565) incorporates propaganda for the Reformation, by portraying all the Apostles, except Judas, as contemporary Reformation leaders. Judas sits in isolation, holding his money-bag surreptitiously behind his back. His features contrast strongly with the grave dignity of the "Apostles", and the idealized Jesus; Judas has debased features of a Semitic cast. He wears the traditional yellow garments. (*Altarpiece of the Reformers, Schlosskirche, Dessau.*)

Giotto's well-known painting of the kiss of Judas is a dramatic composition in which the unity of Judas with the arresting forces is emphasized. All lines in the composition lead to the sorrowful, reproachful face of Jesus. Judas embraces him, enveloping him in the yellow cloak of betrayal, while the staves of the surrounding Jews are raised in a kind of arch above the embracing pair. At the extreme edge of the crowd, cut off from effective participation, is Peter, striking out with his sword at Malchus's ear. (*Wall painting, c. 1305, Padua.*)

In a powerful, almost frenzied, woodcut by Dürer, Jesus is shown in unusual fashion as undergoing agony at the time of his arrest, rather than as accepting it with calm sorrow. While the arresting soldiers are laying ropes on him, Judas continues to kiss him, gazing avidly at his distress. This portrayal seems to anticipate modern psychoanalytic interpretations of Judas's betrayal as an expression of erotic sadism. (*Woodcut, 1510, Staatliche Museum, Berlin.*)

An ivory relief of 420–30 is especially interesting because it shows the symbolic parallelism between the death of Jesus and the death of Judas. Judas and Jesus are shown side by side, Judas hanging from the tree and Jesus from the Cross. Here are portrayed the two Saviours, the Black Christ and the White Christ, one accepting the sacrifice of obloquy, death and damnation, the other that of death only. (*North Italy, casket, British Museum, London.*)

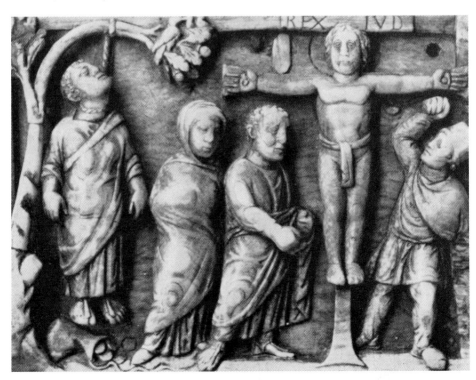

sun'." He said to him, "Come and I will show you something like them in this world." He went out and showed him mushrooms and truffles, and, corresponding to garments of fine wool, he showed him the bark of a young palm-shoot. (b. Shabbat 30b. See also a similar prognostication of the world to come in b. Ketuboth, 111b, though without the jeering disciple).

Here we find not only the description of future productivity, but also the sceptical disciple[8] and the teacher's rebuke, though this takes the form of a reasoned refutation, not a threat of exile from the world to come.[9] This would seem to be a stock story in rabbinic Judaism. It is not quite clear whether the teacher here is Gamaliel I or Gamaliel II. If the former, he was the contemporary of Jesus who is mentioned favourably in Acts 5.

In the Jerusalem Church, the same story was naturally told about the teacher, Jesus. Perhaps at first, the sceptical disciple was left anonymous, as in the rabbinic story; but when the tale was taken up by those Pauline Christians who retained the millenarian doctrine, such as Papias and Irenaeus, the disciple was given a name—and what more suitable name than Judas? As the sinful disciple *par excellence*, Judas would be the natural repository for stories of disciple-failure, even when these were originally attributed to others or were left anonymous. Scepticism as a form of spiritual failure is preserved most famously in the story of Doubting Thomas (John 20:25), and it may even be that other "doubting" stories were current about Thomas, whose real name was Judas. The Gospel of Thomas gives his full name as Didymos Judas Thomas. But Thomas, like its Greek equivalent Didymos, was merely a sobriquet meaning "twin", and the transition from Didymos Judas Thomas to Judas Iscariot would be an easy one.

Here, then, we have an example of a story about Judas Iscariot that has a genuine Jewish origin, though it was not originally attached to him. This accounts for its relative mildness. Judas is merely a sceptic here, not a thief or traitor, though its function is to show that Judas, even in the early days of his discipleship, had a rebellious streak that would eventually turn treacherous.

Another document from the period of the early Church may throw important light on the historical Judas, rather than on his legend. This is the fragment that survives from the Gospel of Peter. The document, buried in a monk's grave at Akhmim (anciently Panopolis) in Upper Egypt, was discovered in 1886. It was written on parchment that dates from the eighth century at the earliest, but the Gospel of Peter itself is attested by Serapion (Bishop of Antioch, 190–203) as having existed at the end of the second century, and there can be little doubt that the fragement we have comes from the attested Gospel. Serapion, however, and after him Eusebius, rejected the Gospel of Peter as uncanonical. Eusebius (*H.E.*, ii., 25, 6) includes it among the forged heretical gospels, of which he says in general, "The character of the style itself is very different from that of the apostles; and the sentiments, and the purport of those things that are advanced in them, deviating as far as possible from sound orthodoxy, plainly proves that they are the fictions of heretical men." However, this judgement need not prevent a modern researcher from regarding a statement in one of these works as providing more valuable historical information than the canonical gospels.

The statement in question occurs at the end of the fragment, after the death and resurrection of Jesus have been described.

> Now it was the last day of the unleavened bread, and many were going forth, returning to their homes, as the feast was ended. But we, the twelve disciples of the Lord, wept and were grieved: and each one, being grieved for that which was come to pass, departed to his home. But I Simon Peter and Andrew my brother took our nets and went to the sea; and there was with us Levi the son of Alphaeus, whom the Lord ...

Here the fragment breaks off. The extraordinary phrase in this passage is "we, the twelve disciples of the Lord", for at this point, as the canonical Gospels and Acts are at pains to emphasize, there should be only eleven disciples. It seems from this phrase, however, that the Gospel of Peter knows nothing of the defection of Judas. We thus have an interesting corroboration of the evidence previously discussed, from Paul's writings (p. 24), that there was a period after Jesus's death when the story of Judas's defection did not exist.

Even in its fragmentary state, the Gospel of Peter clearly displays a pro-Roman, anti-Jewish bias, so it cannot be regarded as a document of the Jerusalem Church. Certain details suggest a Gnostic influence, especially Jesus's silence on the Cross "as if he had no pain". It may be, however, that this Gospel was originally a Jewish-Christian document later adapted by Gnostics. There is evidence from Theodoret (*c.* 455) that there was a Nazarene Gospel of Peter. The Gnostic editor may have neglected to correct the number of disciples given in his source at this point. We do not know what account the Gospel gives of the Last Supper or the arrest of Jesus, since the fragment starts at Pilate's washing of hands. But a Gospel with such far-developed antisemitism is unlikely to have omitted Judas's alleged treachery altogether. The "twelve disciples", therefore, stand out like a sore thumb; they cannot be there as part of the design of the editor, and must be counted as a revealing mistake, stemming from an earlier stratum of the Gospel. We thus have confirmation here that the canonical Gospels, which are so careful to number the disciples as eleven at this point, had a text before them which said twelve: otherwise, they would surely have simply said "the disciples" without specifying their number.[10]

Commentators who have been unwilling to accept that there was a time after the death of Jesus when the defection of Judas was unknown have found the above-discussed phrase in the Gospel of Peter particularly disconcerting. One such commentator, Werner Vogler, has suggested that Judas may have remained a member of the group of disciples even after his betrayal—a most unlikely thesis.[11] Other explanations offered are hardly more plausible.[12] The existence of this striking phrase, especially when taken in conjunction with I Corinthians 15:5, must be regarded as historically significant.

In the later apocryphal Gospels and Acts, the Judas legend begins to be embroidered in the manner of a folk-tale. The Arabic Gospel of the Saviour's Infancy[13] describes how young Jesus cured people possessed by demons and performed other wonders. This Gospel also provides some fantastic details of Judas's childhood, prefiguring his role as an adult:

Another woman was living in the same place, whose son was tormented by Satan. He, Judas by name, as often as Satan seized him, used to bite all who came near him; and if he found no one near him, he used to bite his own hands and other limbs. The mother of this wretched creature, then, hearing the fame of the Lady Mary and her son Jesus, rose up and brought her son Judas with her to the Lady Mary. In the meantime, James and

89

Joses[14] had taken the child the Lord Jesus with them to play with the other children; and they had gone out of the house and sat down, and the Lord Jesus with them. And the demoniac Judas came up, and sat down at Jesus's right hand: then, being attacked by Satan in the same manner as usual, he wished to bite the Lord Jesus, but was not able; nevertheless he struck Jesus on the right side, whereupon He began to weep. And immediately Satan went forth out of that boy, fleeing like a mad dog. And this boy who struck Jesus, and out of whom Satan went forth in the shape of a dog, was Judas Iscariot, who betrayed him to the Jews; and that same side on which Judas struck Him, the Jews transfixed with a lance. (John 19:34.)

Here we find an extension of the canonical attempt to find grounds for Judas's treachery in his earlier character. When Satan possessed Judas, just before or during the Last Supper, it was not his first experience of Satanic possession. As a child he had been a demoniac, and had been the subject of a miracle cure by the child Jesus. Moreover, Judas's behaviour towards the child Jesus had fore-shadowed his adult treachery. He tried to bite him, but only succeeded in striking his right side. Notably, Judas's conduct is regarded as emblematic of that of the Jews. The blow to Jesus's side was later echoed by the Jews, transfixing Jesus with a lance. The fact that it was not the Jews but a Roman soldier who, according to John, struck Jesus with a lance does not inhibit the author from ascribing this deed to them. For throughout the history of Pauline Christianity, the Jews have been blamed for everything. The Romans are merely pawns, manipulated by the Jews. Every action performed by the Romans—the arrest of Jesus, his scourging, his crucifixion—is attributed to the Jews, whose physical non-participation only makes their machinations more despicable and eerie. The story of Pilate washing his hands of guilt sums up the Pauline determination to whitewash the Romans. In so doing, Christians detached themselves from the Jewish protest against Roman imperialism, declared the Christian desire for rapprochement with Rome, and conveyed an important message of the Gospels: "Christians are not Jews."

This little cameo of Jesus and Judas in childhood, despite its aim of merely adding to the popular folklore about "Judas the traitor", brings out unmistakably the function of Judas in Christian antisemitism. As Hans-Joseph Klauck points out, "Satan, Judas and the Jews form, in this remarkable piece of narrative, a trio which co-operates fatefully against Jesus."[15]

A recently discovered text of great interest in relation to the developing Judas-legend is the Coptic Gospel of Bartholemew.[16] The text has been assigned to the fifth century, and consists of a number of fragments, which can be assigned to the Gospel of Bartholemew, known from fuller versions in Greek, Latin and Old Slavonic stemming from the third century. Bartholemew appears in the New Testament only as a name in the list of Jesus's disciples, usually paired with Philip. As in the case of other disciples, attempts were made to fill out his character[17] by featuring him in an apocryphal Gospel in which Jesus gives him a special revelation.

A number of points may be noted in the fragmentary Coptic version of this Gospel. In the miracle of the loaves, Judas is excluded from distributing the bread, as being unworthy to approach Jesus. Further, in this version it was Judas's wife who persuaded him to betray Jesus and to accept blood-money for it. As a result, Joseph of Arimathea's seven-month-old child rejects her as a wet-nurse. This appears to be the earliest mention of Judas's wife, although stories about her proliferate later in which she is made to bear a large burden of guilt. Misogyny thus combines with antisemitism in the development of the saga. In Bartholemew's account, Judas's wife not only brings about his treachery, but encourages him to steal money meant for the poor out of the common purse of the Apostles. This Gospel further presents Judas's suicide as having been prompted by Satan, who persuaded him that Jesus would have pity and release him with the other souls during the Harrowing of Hell. In the event, however, Jesus left three souls behind there: Judas, Cain and Herod. Andrew later visited Hell and spoke to Judas, but was unable to save him, since Judas had prayed to Satan before hanging himself.

The Gospel of Nicodemus also contains a late interpolation concerning Judas's wife. The story has survived to modern times in the form of a popular myth.

And he went home to make a rope out of rushes to hang himself, and he found his wife, who was sitting and roasting a cock in a pan at the hearth for a meal. He said to her, "Up, wife, get me some rushes for a rope; I want to hang myself, as I deserve." His wife replied, "Why are you saying such things?" He said, "Know in truth, that I have wickedly handed over my master Jesus to the elders, whereby Pilate is executing him. Jesus, however, will rise again on the third day, and then woe to us." His wife said to him, "Do not speak or think so. This cock, which I am roasting over the fire, can just as well crow, as Jesus can rise again, as you say." And as soon as she uttered these words, the cock fluttered its wings and crowed three times. This convinced Judas even more, so he made the rope from rushes and hanged himself, and so breathed out his soul.

In this obvious folk-tale, Judas's wife appears as a sceptic rather than an instigator of his wickedness. But the introduction of this character raised narrative possibilities which later story-tellers found irresistible. The part played by Eve in Adam's sin, possibly even the complicity of Zeresh in the murderous plot of Haman in the Book of Esther, suggested that also in the case of the ultimate crime, the betrayal of Jesus, a woman might ultimately be to blame.

An interesting and singular line of thought about Judas was developed by a group within the Gnostic movement, who noted that without him there would have been no salvation. Therefore a positive image of Judas emerged, as having a good aim which could only be accomplished by the betrayal of Jesus. Unfortunately, the writings of this group have not survived. Nevertheless, we have an account of them by Irenaeus:

> Others again declare that Cain derived his being from the Power above, and acknowledge that Esau, Korah, the Sodomites, and all such persons, are related to themselves. On this account, they add, they have been assailed by the Creator, yet no one of them has suffered injury. For Sophia was in the habit of carrying off that which belonged to her from them to herself. They declare that Judas the traitor was thoroughly acquainted with these things, and that he alone, knowing the truth as no others did, accomplished the mystery of the betrayal; by him all things, both earthly and heavenly, were thus thrown into confusion. They bring forward a fictitious history along these lines, which they call the Gospel of Judas. (Irenaeus *Haer.* 1, 31, 1.)

The Cainites, as they were called, carried to a logical conclusion the Gnostic inversion of the story of the Hebrew Bible. All Gnostics subscribed to this inversion to some degree. Thus they all believed that the God of the Hebrew Bible was not omnipotent and good, as represented, but an evil and limited deity who had indeed created the world, but in his own evil and limited image. The true High God was far above this world, and the aim of Gnostics was to escape to Him, which meant evading the power of the Creator God, or Demiurge. They are aided in this attempt by a high feminine power, called Sophia, who is linked to the High God. The Gnostics also maintained that it was the evil Creator who dictated the Bible to the Jewish prophets, who were his dupes. The whole Jewish people were thus the chief agents and acolytes of the Demiurge, falsely believing him to be the ultimate God. The Gnostics did think that the Bible contained a good deal of historical truth ; but since it was inspired by the Demiurge, its system of values was wrong. Consequently, its heroes were really villains, and its villains heroes. This interpretation, however, was not advanced consistently. For example, while all Gnostics agreed that Adam performed a fine deed, not a sin, when he defied the command of the Demiurge and ate the fruit of the forbidden tree, and moreover that the inhabitants of Sodom were good Gnostics whose destruction was plotted by the evil Demiurge, most did not go so far as to approve of Abel's murder. This final step was taken by the Cainites, who also made a hero of Judas Iscariot.

Further light is thrown on the doctrine of the Cainites by Epiphanius, who reports their belief that the betrayal of Jesus was meritorious, since it delivered mankind from the power of the Demiurge (Epiphanius, *Haer.* xxvi, 2). Irenaeus, on the other hand, seems to think that the Cainite doctrine sprang not so much from a desire to further the process of salvation as from a general inversion of moral values. The Cainites, he says, like another Gnostic sect, the Carpocratians, believed that liberation of the soul could be achieved by performing sins, the more horrific the better. "An angel, they maintain, attends them in every one of their sinful and abominable actions, and urges them to venture on audacity and incur pollution. Whatever may be the nature of the action, they declare that they do it in the name of the angel, saying, 'O thou angel, I use thy work; O thou power, I accomplish thy operation!' And they maintain that this

93

is 'perfect knowledge', without shrinking to rush into such actions as it is not lawful even to name."

Throughout the history of religion, certain groups have tried to achieve spiritual freedom and "perfect knowledge" through emancipation from morality. Where the aim of religion, as in the case of the Gnostics, is to attain a god-like status, the trammels of morality are seen as part of the lowly human status which the initiated desire to shed. Thus the performance of acts normally regarded with horror, such as incest or murder, becomes the index of spiritual progress. In the modern world, nihilistic terrorists have a similar philosophy, which is more or less embodied in the writings of the Marquis de Sade. Viewing normal morality as fundamentally corrupt, or as stemming from class oppression, they have regarded acts of terror and disruption as redemptive gestures, making all things new and cleansing the world. This sort of nihilism is attributed to the Cainites by Irenaeus when he says they praised Judas since "by him all things, both earthly and heavenly, were ... thrown into confusion".

If Judas is defended on the ground that he committed the ultimate sin, thus proving himself a good Gnostic, this will hardly rehabilitate him in the eyes of non-Gnostics. Such a defence merely confirms his status as the arch-sinner. On the other hand, the claim that Judas, who realized that salvation could only come through Jesus's death, somehow found the moral courage to bring about this necessary sacrifice, might seem a more acceptable defence. At least it would amount to an honest acknowledgment, which the majority of Christians are unwilling to make, that there is great hypocrisy in claiming to benefit from the death of Jesus, while regarding the person who brought this about with loathing and abhorrence. Christians *want* Jesus to die on the Cross; otherwise they cannot be saved. To avoid this frightful thought, they have delegated Judas (and the Jews) to murder Jesus on their behalf. By washing their hands like Pilate, and mourning and bewailing the death of Jesus every Easter, they hope to avoid complicity in his death. The more they cover Judas and the Jews with obloquy and hatred, the more they can distance themselves from responsibility.

The Cainites, on the other hand, refused to share in this hypocrisy. By expressing admiration for Judas, they acknowledged their complicity in the deed and gloried in it. This may be considered a moral advance in a way, though historically it is a kind of throwback. For civilizations which felt no guilt for human sacrifice have been rare. One example in the ancient world were the Phoenicians, whose honoured priests performed their human sacrifices. The Aztecs are another example of guilt-free human sacrifice. When humanity "advances" by being ashamed of such a sacrifice, it deputes an accursed figure like Judas to perform the deed. To revert from this stage of society to unashamed ritual murder, as the Cainites proposed, may be more honest. But it is a step in the wrong direction. The real advance would be to abolish human sacrifice, as Judaism did, not even retaining it in the form of myth, as did Christianity.

Some modern thinkers have adopted a neo-Gnostic attitude towards the crime of Judas and the Jews. The French Catholics Léon Bloy (1892), an antisemite, and Charles Péguy, a philosemite and anti-Dreyfusard, both stressed the Jews' and Judas's God-given mission of betrayal. Even Jews have occasionally been attracted to the idea of Judas's divine mission of betrayal, since such an interpretation might seem to rescue Judas from obloquy and the Jews themselves from antisemitism. A curious example of a Jewish espousal of the Gnostic standpoint is the story by Bernard Lazare, called "La gloire de Judas". Here Judas is held up to admiration as the disciple who deliberately accepted eternal shame in order that the prophecies might be fulfilled, and the tyrannous reign of the Jewish God might be ended. Jesus, returning to earth, appears to him and calls him, "My beloved disciple", but tells him that he must continue to bear the burden of his sacrifice. This story was written in Bernard Lazare's youth, before the Dreyfus affair (see p. 119) woke him from his Gnostic dreams, and enlisted him firmly in the camp of Judaism.

However, it should be mentioned that the Cainites, like other Gnostics, did not believe that Jesus really suffered on the Cross. The so-called Docetic doctrine, to which the Gnostics subscribed (from the Greek *dokeo*, meaning "to appear"), was that Jesus only *seemed* to suffer. Either his place was taken by a simulacrum, or he did not feel the pains of crucifixion. In either case, it was not fitting for a person of his divine status to undergo such a humiliating torture. Consequently, Judas's betrayal cannot be regarded as a heinous crime, as in orthodox Christian thought, since he was not betraying Jesus to an agonizing death, but merely to an early and painless translation to heaven. This means in effect that the Gnostics, including the Cainites, did not believe in human sacrifice. Whereas the agony of Jesus, for the ordinary Christian, was essential to salvation and atonement, for the Gnostic it was really inessential. For the Gnostics believed in *gnosis*, or enlightenment, rather than atonement. Jesus, for them, was simply the culminating Gnostic teacher, whose mission was to show us the key to transcendence. The Gnostics were not concerned about the problem of sin. Such a concern, for them, was the mark of an inferior soul. Jesus's death meant simply his return to the Pleroma, and his triumph over the vain machinations of the Demiurge. Thus, it was relatively easy for Gnostics to see Judas's betrayal as a meritorious act.

Gnosticism existed as a doctrine before Christianity, and only took on a Christian colouring in the first and second centuries CE. But it notably lacked the sacrificial element which Christianity (in its Pauline form) shared with mystery-religion.[18] What then was the attitude of Christian Gnosticism to the Jews? It might be thought that the Jews could perhaps receive the hero-worship given by the Cainites to Judas. But the Jews, to all Gnostics including the Cainites, remained the people of the Demiurge—or, in Christian terminology, of Satan. Though Judas could perhaps be credited with good motives, the Jews, as acolytes of the evil Demiurge, were viewed as simply assisting him in his war against the High God without realizing that Jesus's death would bring him final victory. The Gnostic literature is full of ludicrous attempts by the Demiurge to defeat the Enlightened by bringing about their destruction, failing to understand that this only makes them more powerful.

One group of people had an even stronger motive for rescuing Judas from obloquy—the Jews. Among them folklore tradition arose from the sixth or seventh century onwards known as *Toledoth Jeshu* (the history of Jesus). This history consisted of a version of events in which the Jews were exonerated from Christian charges of deicide, while Jesus himself was displayed as a sinful sorcerer and idolater who deserved his death. This folklore saga, circulating among the common people, and never officially recognized by learned Jewish authorities, is known in various versions. In some, Judas is a praiseworthy champion of Judaism who combats Jesus's sorceries, and eventually brings him to punishment.

The name of Judas in this saga is Rabbi Judah ish Bartota, which means "man of Bartota". That this name is intended to be a version of Judas Iscariot is shown by incidents which echo events in the New

Testament story. How then did "Judas Iscariot" become "Judah ish Bartota"? The explanation is fairly simple. The authors of the saga must have surmised that the first syllable in "Iscariot" represents the Hebrew *ish*, a view that many modern scholars have endorsed (though wrongly, as argued on p. 129). Searching round the rabbinic literature for a name compounded with *ish* and sounding vaguely like "Iscariot", they came across the name "Eleazar ben Judah ish Bartota" (Mishnah, Abot 3:7, Orlah, 1:4, Tebul Yom, 3:4). Bartota is a place in Upper Galilee, the birthplace of Rabbi Eleazar and of his father Rabbi Judah. The latter was thus elected to be the equivalent, in Jewish folklore, of Judas Iscariot. Since Rabbi Eleazar was born around 50 CE, his father could have been alive in the time of Jesus. "Judah ish Bartota" was close enough to "Judas Iscariot", though no Talmudic text identifies the two—indeed, no Talmudic text mentions Judas Iscariot or his alleged role.

The Talmud, however, does mention Jesus, though very briefly. It dismisses him as a sorcerer and "seducer to idolatry", who was tried by the Sanhedrin and executed by stoning (b. Sanhedrin 43a). This story is evidently late, and was intended to counter Christian missionary activity. There is no authentic memory of Jesus in the rabbinic writings, since Jesus was regarded as just another failed messiah-figure and was immediately forgotten, except by those who believed in his resurrection. Judas of Galilee, whom we know from Josephus and the New Testament as a formidable messianic claimant, receives no mention at all in the Talmud, and even Bar Kochba, the most successful of the messiah-figures, receives very little. Jesus too would probably have gone unmentioned but for the need to counter Christian propaganda. The Talmudic story thus essentially says: "If Jesus really claimed to be God and performed miracles as you Christians say, then he must have been an idolater and a sorcerer, and the Sanhedrin would have been right to execute him." The New Testament does not say that Jesus was executed by stoning or by the Sanhedrin, although, given its anti-Jewish bias and its concern not to offend the Romans, it would doubtless have preferred to say so, rather than admit that he was crucified by the imperial authorities. The New Testament is thus very good evidence for a non-Jewish execution,[19] and the Talmud's account, dating from no earlier than 250 CE, is plainly unhistorical.

But the Jewish popular saga of Jesus naturally bases itself on the

Talmud, which it proceeds to embroider in the manner of all folklore. It accounts for Jesus's miracles not by denying them, but by saying that Jesus had illicitly acquired the secret Name of God, which enabled him to fly and perform other wonders. Judah ish Bartota was chosen by the Sanhedrin to encounter Jesus in a contest of magic, including a flying contest that seems to derive from the similar contest between Peter and Simon Magus in Acts of Peter 32 (unless both derive from some earlier Oriental tale). Later, we find Judah acting as a secret agent for the Sanhedrin. He joins Jesus's band of Apostles in disguise, learns their secrets, and identifies Jesus for arrest by a kiss, just as in the Gospels, except of course that in this version Judah is an intrepid undercover agent instead of a base traitor. (This part is evidently based on the Gospels themselves and actually provides a more plausible rationale for the kiss than is found in the Gospels.) Jesus is then tried and executed by decree of the Sanhedrin, as in the Talmud.

The story ends with an exploit of Judah in which he foils Christian attempts to establish belief in Jesus's resurrection. He hangs Jesus's body on a huge cabbage-stalk in his own garden, and triumphantly produces the body when the empty tomb is proclaimed as proof of the resurrection. The cabbage-stalk motif is a curious combination of Jewish law and general folklore. By Jewish law, the body of an executed criminal had to be hung up on a wooden post or tree for a short period before burial. Jesus, however, while alive, had magically administered an oath to all trees not to act against him, so no tree or wooden post would hold his corpse. The giant cabbage in Judah's garden, however, not being a tree, was not bound by this oath. The folk-theme of the "oath by all trees", by the way, reminds us of a similar element in the Norse myth of Balder, which had mystery-religion antecedents.

The Jewish view of Jesus as a powerful sorcerer, and of Judas as his heroic opponent, provides a positive image of Judas Iscariot to counter the highly negative one current in Christian circles. The Jewish saga of Jesus employs material from the Talmud, the New Testament and pagan folklore to build up an alternative narrative. But it is plainly a pathetic attempt of a beleaguered people to sustain their morale in the face of denigration. It had no counter-influence, of course, on the further development of the antisemitic Judas Iscariot legend in Christendom.[20] The Jewish version circulated by

98

word of mouth and in manuscript among Jews, and served to strengthen popular morale. When Christian scholars first became aware of it in the seventeenth century, they put it forward as a horrifying proof of Jewish malevolence.

But this Jewish version of the Judas myth is based on the Christian account of Jesus, who is shown as an opponent of Judaism and the Jewish religious leadership. From the Middle Ages onwards, Jewish scholars began to doubt this account, and to see Jesus instead as a loyal Jew whose messianic claim had been misinterpreted by the Gentile Church as a claim to personal divinity. It therefore began to be seen that the Talmudic opposition to Jesus was unnecessary, since the historical Jesus was not as represented by the Church. Indeed, since the eighteenth century, about 300 books have been written by Jews urging the Jewishness of Jesus.[21] To argue that Jesus never intended to found a new religion, but only to implement Jewish prophecies of a human messiah, has been called "the Jewish view of Jesus", though many non-Jews have also advocated it.

But the treatment of Judas Iscariot in the *Toledoth Yeshu*, while understandable, is even further from historical truth than the Gospels. For in this Jewish saga, the Romans vanished altogether. The Gospels do their best to minimize the Roman role, but cannot quite obliterate it. In Christian preaching and missionary activity, the Romans faded out, and the simplified charge became that it was the Jews who crucified Jesus. A move in this direction can even be observed in the Gospels; for John's deliberately ambiguous use of pronouns can easily leave the impression that the crucifixion was carried out by Jews. When Jews came to construct their own version of events, they were reacting to the missionary account, not to the Gospels themselves, which they did not study closely until the Middle Ages. Their response then was, in effect: "Yes, we did execute Jesus—not crucify, since this was punishment unknown in Judaism—but only after a fair trial and because he was found guilty of capital offences, as you Christians testify when you say that he set himself up as God, in defiance of the First Commandment."[22] From this perspective, Judas Iscariot falls into place as a doughty defender of Jewish monotheism against Jesus's new idolatry. When medieval Jewish scholars first came to study the Gospels and discovered that, except in John, Jesus could not be seen to indulge in self-deification, the whole basis of their previous position was shattered. By this time,

99

however, the age of saga-making was over for Jews, and their new reaction was expressed in argument and scholarship. In promoting a new image of Jesus as a loyal adherent of Judaism who was misinterpreted after his death as a Hellenistic god, the status of Judas in this new scenario was overlooked. One of the aims of the present book is to fill this lacuna. The mythic status given to Judas as the betrayer of the god-sacrifice gives his role an imaginative quality that takes it out of sober history. Once this mythic aura has been analysed and removed, it will be possible to ask who Judas actually was.

7

Judas and the
Growth of Antisemitism

The ongoing elaboration of the Judas legend in the early Church was undertaken for its own sake, without the conscious intention of linking the terrible sin and fate of Judas with that of the Jews as a whole. But the life and growth of a story have their own momentum. Some scholars have seen the growth of the Judas saga entirely in these terms: they would argue that it has no meaning external to itself. It unfolded like a flower, following its own narrative potential. But this is a superficial, narrowly aesthetic view. Every story has some message to convey. The great myths that have shaped civilizations are stories with a capacity to shape and orient men's thoughts, deeds and communal life. The Judas saga is not a great myth, but it forms part of one, that of the descent, violent death and resurrection of Jesus Christ. A myth of such universality and power has the capacity to create a whole cycle of subordinate legends and sagas, and the Judas saga is one of these. The subordinate units echo endlessly the great theme of the controlling myth. The Judas saga, with its theme of fated treachery, thus echoes the central *mythos* of the apparent defeat and annihilation of the divine Saviour by the Evil Power, whose minions and instruments were the Jews.

The thinkers and theorists of Christianity, during the years in which the Judas saga was being formed, did, however, consciously realize that Judas was a symbol for the Jews. This is a favourite theme of Saint Jerome (340–420), the greatest scholar of the Church, who translated the whole Bible into Latin.[1] It is also a frequent topic in the diatribes of Saint John Chrysostom (345–407) against the Jews[2] (see Appendix A). This eloquent saint, whose sobriquet means "golden-mouthed", is rivalled only by Hitler in the virulence of his attacks on the Jews, whom he accused of a whole catalogue of crimes, including cannibalism.[3]

101

Despite the venomous writings of these learned and impressive leaders, antisemitic feeling was slow to develop among the general Christian population. During the so-called Dark Ages (from about 600 CE to about 1100 CE), frequent synods condemned the over-friendliness of the Christian masses towards the Jews. Regulations were passed at successive synods prohibiting Christians from eating with Jews, or taking part in their festivals. It was even necessary to issue an edict to ban Christian farmers from having their fields blessed by rabbis. During this period of cultural breakdown in Europe, following the barbarian conquests of the various regions of the former Roman Empire, the masses were imperfectly Christianized.[4] When the period known as the Middle Ages began (about 1100 CE), a new flowering of culture was accompanied by a more organized and sophisticated campaign against the Jews, whose numbers had increased considerably in Europe following the decline of their great centre in Babylonia. Another important factor in Europe was the growth of a closer relationship between Church and State, which made co-operation between them against the Jews more feasible. The Church made great efforts to reach the masses through popular religious art and literature of various kinds. These were most successful in fostering faith and piety to an extent seldom seen in the world history; they were also most successful in fostering antisemitism, which was seen as an essential form of Christian piety.

The Judas-legend expanded in the Middle Ages, in free and imaginative detail. It would be a mistake to think that such late embroiderings of the story can be discounted as "inauthentic". Lévi-Strauss has urged that all variations of a myth need to be accepted, and that the sum of these variations comprises the myth. Sometimes what may seem a late and inauthentic variation contributes some essential, though temporarily mislaid, element. The medieval saga of Judas is a freewheeling fantasy based on the Gospels; but it also contributes to their understanding. The range of this saga may be gauged from the following outline, culled from various sources, including the great repository of folklore, the *Legenda aurea*.[5] The tale is a curious mixture in which Judas is amalgamated with other mythic figures, including Cain, Moses and Oedipus:

Judas was the son of Jewish parents, who lived in Jerusalem. The name of his father was Reuben, and the name of his mother was Cyborea. One night, Cyborea dreamt that she would become pregnant, and that the child was fated to destroy the whole Jewish people. In great agony of mind, she told Reuben her dream. He told her not to pay any attention to such things, since they came from an evil spirit. After the stated time, however, her son was born. The memory of the dream returned, and out of fear that it might turn out to be true, the child Judas was put into a small chest on the sea. Wind and wave brought him to the island of Skariot, from which his name was derived.

The Queen of the island, who had no children and was looking out for a young prince to follow her on the throne, discovered the child, who was very pretty. She let it be known in the land that she was pregnant, and let Judas be looked after by a wet-nurse until she could acknowledge him as her own child. Thus Judas was brought up in a royal manner, as heir to the kingdom.

But after a time, the Queen conceived a son of her own from the King. The two children grew up together, but not a long time passed before the evil that lay in the nature of Judas came to expression. Frequently he struck or mistreated in other ways his so-called brother. He did this despite the continual exhortations of the Queen not to mistreat the true prince, until in the end, in an outburst of anger, she made known to him his irregular origin. In fury over hearing this, Judas seized the first opportunity to kill his brother. Then out of fear of the consequences, he embarked on a ship and sailed to Jerusalem.

There his courtly manners and evil tendencies secured him a place in the entourage of Pilate. One day Pilate looked into the garden of his neighbour and was seized by an irresistible longing for a fruit which he saw there. Judas promised to obtain it for him. The garden, however, and the fruit, without his knowing it, were the possessions of his own father, Reuben. Before he could pluck the fruit, Reuben appeared. There followed an argument, which developed into a fight, and finally Reuben was slain. Since there was no evidence of murder, it was given out that Reuben had died suddenly, and Judas, with the agreement of Pilate, married the widowed Cyborea, and took possession of her house and property.

The newly married wife was unhappy from the first and often sighed. When her husband one day asked about the cause of her grief, she told him enough of her story for Judas to be in a position to know his double crime of patricide and incest. Both of them were filled with repentance, and, on the advice of Cyborea, Judas decided to go to Jesus, to seek pardon and forgiveness. He was soon a favourite disciple, and was chosen to look after the money-box. But his evil nature asserted itself again, and he betrayed his Master to the Jews for thirty pieces of silver. Then he repented again, gave the money back, and hanged himself.[6]

This medieval Judas-romance is extraordinary in its unconscious symbolism, by which Judas, in every particular, echoes in his life the role of the Jews in the Christian myth and psychology. Like the Jews, Judas is chosen for a great role, but he is not really the true heir, and his evil nature will not allow him to accept the true heir when he arrives. Judas's life on the island is a mirror-image of his later life, and also an allegory of the history of the Jews, who, in Christian theory, played the role for a time of God's chosen people, but turned in rage to destroy the true Son of God when he came. The picture of Judas as a royal prince owes nothing to the New Testament, and has been created by the medieval imagination. Of course, it has utilized biblical material, chiefly the story of the infancy of Moses and his discovery by Pharaoh's daughter. But this has been made to serve a purpose alien to the narrative of the Hebrew Bible, which does not portray Moses as desiring an Egyptian princedom. The narrative is closer in spirit to the Greek myth of Oedipus, as the sequel shows, in which Judas kills his father and marries his mother. But there is also the great difference that Oedipus is brought up by humble parents in ignorance of his noble birth, while Judas is raised by noble parents in ignorance of his humble birth. Thus when Judas commits the Oedipal double sin, this is a domestic, rather than a communal, tragedy. There is no communal plague, only an individual repentance.

This is an interesting opportunity to compare a Jewish, a Christian and a Greek treatment of the same mythological theme, the transfer of an infant from his true parents to foster-parents. The Greek story, as Freud pointed out in *Moses and Monotheism*, expresses the child's disappointment with his own parents, and the fantasy of belonging to parents who are not vulnerable to disillusion. The child's longings are fulfilled by the discovery of his noble origin, but the fulfilment of one childhood fantasy leads to the tragic fulfilment of the main fantasy which in adulthood needs to be repressed. The Jewish version, on the other hand, expresses the older child's acceptance of his real parents, despite their lack of the childhood glamour for which "nobility" is a metaphor. Moses returns to his real parents, who are not a King and Queen, but ordinary Israelites, and finds an adult mission in following their footsteps. What, then, does the Christian variation mean? It means that he who loses the childhood dream is a lost soul. There is no adult mission, but only the glamour of childhood, which Judas temporarily recovers by adherence to Jesus—the perpetual child, and son of the noblest Father of all, beyond all possibility of disillusion. But Judas has gone too far from innocence to retain the vision.

At the same time, it is noteworthy that in this romance, Judas is after all treated as a hero-figure. The story of the baby floating in a casket and found by a princess is a well-known hero-motif, found not only in the instance of Moses, but in the tales of other legendary heroes such as Sargon. Judas, then, is here a negative hero, chosen by fate for a great and tragic mission, a kind of kamikaze pilot who brings salvation through the death of his own soul. The prophecy to his mother in her dream predicted that he would bring destruction to the Jews; but the unspoken prophecy is that he would bring salvation to the Christians. Here the link between the fate of Judas and that of the Jews becomes explicit. Whereas in the Arabian Gospel of the Infancy of Jesus, Judas's childhood was entirely without distinction (since he was the demoniac child of an ordinary woman), the saga of Judas's childhood, as it developed, needed something more impressive to explain why Judas was chosen by fate for such a tremendous role. If he was not of noble birth, he was at least believed to be for a time, and even brought up to believe it himself, just like his brethren the Jews. And like them too, his rage at being told the truth—that his nobility was merely temporary—drove him to murder the true prince.

The evil nature with which Judas is cursed from birth also finds a more elaborate form than in the other infancy narrative. Judas is not just a biting demoniac; he has an attractive side to his personality. The Queen found him "pretty" as a baby; and even after his murder of the prince, his "courtly manners" secured advancement in the court of Pilate. He is also capable of repentance—a feature derived from Matthew. In short, he has become a character suitable for novelistic or dramatic treatment. One can imagine Shakespeare writing a play about this complicated character, with his fundamentally vicious nature, and his doomed impulses towards goodness and nobility. Yet this aspect too does not arise from aesthetic considerations alone, but has mythic significance. It is particularly interesting that the medieval saga emphasizes the brother-relationship between Judas and the "true prince" who symbolizes Christ. Judas is a kind of prince too, because the myth requires him to share in the royal aura of his victim. While the Gospels suppress the brother-relationship between Jesus and Judas (see p. 146), the unconscious mythic drive restores it in the medieval saga. Like Cain and Abel, Set and Osiris, or Romulus and Remus, the two protagonists of the Christian ritual murder must be brothers.

In the medieval Judas-saga, Cyborea is a tragic Jocasta-figure, losing her husband Reuben only to find herself married to her own son, her husband's murderer. Judas, who had earlier in life been a conscious murderer of the prince, here stumbles unwittingly into parricide and incest. The effect is to display Judas as a natural sinner. He cannot escape sin, which has been his fate from childhood, and therefore he is a fit person to commit the greatest sin of all. In his Oedipal role, Judas is symbolic of mankind in general as well as of the Jews. He represents in particular the lure of sex; the chief obstacle to spirituality in Gnostic thought, and the source of all evil in medieval Christian thought. He represents the fallen state of inescapable evil—incurred sometimes willingly, sometimes unknowingly—which is inseparable from being human, and which the death of Christ expiates. Yet he remains, of all mankind, unexpiated, since he is chosen to be the instrument of expiation for others. In this as well he represents the Jews. He is thus the symbol of unregenerate humanity, unredeemed by the sacrifice of the Cross, and like the Jews in medieval and later Nazi propaganda, he is imagined as rampant in his sexual desires and unimpeded by moral restraints. In short he represents the secret desires of Christians themselves, and this only adds to the hatred they feel towards him.

In some medieval sources, however, Judas's wife has a less pitiable role than Cyborea, who is as much the victim of Judas as anyone else. In the other versions, she is not his mother but a wife who is his partner in crime, and indeed often instigates his evil deeds. She is often a scold, who nags Judas into dishonesty by complaining about their poverty. Elsewhere, his sins are multiplied. In one source, the thirteenth-century "Ballad of Judas", he commits incest not with his mother, but with his sister. Through gambling, he loses thirty pieces of silver belonging to Jesus, with which he was supposed to buy the materials of the Eucharist for the Last Supper. In order to replace the lost money, Judas in desperation agrees to betray Jesus to the Jews for this sum. Thus the bread and wine used in the first Eucharist were bought with Judas's blood-money. This is an interesting variation on the pervasive Christian theme of salvation through sin; if the salvation of the Cross was brought about through the sin of Judas's betrayal, it is only natural if the continual daily salvation brought by the sacrament of the Church had its origin in the same betrayal.

But it was undoubtedly the Passion Plays that contributed most both to the development of the Judas-image and to its potency as an instrument of antisemitic indoctrination. The Passion Plays began in the thirteenth century and became so popular in the fourteenth that they have been compared in popularity to the football matches of our own days. The villains of these plays were always the Jews, and the performances were violent, ribald and often obscene. All work in a town or village would stop, and the spectacles were often followed by a pogrom in which the local Jews were indiscriminately killed and maimed in a religious fervour, though the political authorities usually prevented all-out massacres. The tortures of Christ were enacted with extreme realism and abundance of artificial blood, and the Jews were always depicted as relishing these tortures, spitting on the agonized Christ, and thinking up fresh indignities. Earlier, the tortures were shown as performed by Roman soldiers, in accordance with the Gospels, while the Jews only rejoiced and advised; later, the Jews were represented as performing the tortures themselves, since the Gospels were too restrained for the antisemitic expectations of the audience. In the French play attributed to Jehan Michel, for example, the Jews compete to pull out handfuls from

Jesus's beard, pulling away flesh at the same time; then they draw lots for the parts of his body that each will abuse. Here is an extract:

1st Jew: See the blood streaming, and how his whole face is covered with it!
2nd Jew: Here, you false, blood-stained man! I don't pity your pain. You are only a vile trifler, the lowest of the low.
3rd Jew: Let us play at pulling out his beard. It's too long anyway.
4th Jew: I've torn him so hard that the flesh has come away too.
5th Jew: I'd like to have my turn at tearing him.
6th Jew: Look at this clump I'm pulling away like lard!

Thus the Christian populace indulged in an orgy of dramatic sadism, performed by imaginary Jews, for whose imaginary cruelty the real Jews were punished with real cruelty.[7]

Integral to these revolting spectacles is the scene in which Judas haggles with the Jewish elders for his blood-money. Here the kinship of Judas to his fellow-Jews is emphasized by their common avarice, and their desire for the death of Jesus. The myth of Jewish avarice, a vital ingredient in antisemitism, was thereby fostered in the minds of the Christian populace. Judas was given grotesque "Jewish" characteristics, which identified him with the contemporary German or French Jews whose outlandish looks were a result of their exclusion from all honourable professions and the laws regulating their dress. The image of the Jews as moneylenders had been established by Christian pressure, but this did not prevent Christians from despising and vilifying Jews as usurers. The Jews depicted in the Passion Plays were all moneylenders, although in the time of Jesus, Jews were mostly agriculturists. Thus children, seeing a Jew, would immediately identify him with the stage Jews whom they had been taught to loathe, and to whom the connotations of "Judas" (traitor, murderer, miser) were effortlessly transferred. The indoctrination of children by the vivid and emotionally stirring Passion Plays thereby brought about an ingrained and intense antisemitism (especially in Germany,[8] where the Passion Plays were particularly brutal).[9]

An additional feature of Judas in the Passion Plays was his red hair. This was not part of the general Jewish stereotype, but an identifying mark of Judas himself, which he shared with Herod (who was also a staple character in the Passion Plays). It may be that redness, as the colour of blood, was reserved for those taking the leading murderous parts—Judas for his acceptance of blood-money and his association with the Field of Blood, and Herod because of his massacre of the Innocents.

In addition to the Passion Plays, which were concerned with the betrayal, trial and crucifixion of Jesus, there were many other forms of medieval drama in which Jews figured.[10] The Easter Plays, for example, beginning in the eleventh century, featured debates between two actors, one representing the Church and the other the Synagogue, the aim being to prove that Judaism had been rendered obsolete by the advent of Christianity. At first the Synagogue (as in Church art of the early period) was given a fairly dignified role. But as time went on, the tone of these Easter plays deteriorated, and the character representing Judaism in these debates became an anti-semitic caricature.

There were also the Morality Plays, of which the most famous is "Everyman". These could reach a level of high seriousness in drama-tizing the Seven Deadly Sins and their punishment. Yet many of these plays were marred by antisemitism, since the character of Satan was given the same identifying features as Judas in the Passion Plays— red hair and beard, long nose and chin, and Jewish garments. Thus the old triple identity of Jew-Judas-Satan was reinforced.

From the fourteenth century onwards, European drama began to detach itself from its religious origins, and a secular form of drama arose dealing with contemporary life. However, it inherited from the religious drama the requirement that the role of villain should be assigned to Jews. Jews were portrayed as plotting against Christians, or poisoning wells. A frequent theme was ritual murder. Jews were graphically portrayed on stage as abducting Christian children, crucifying them, and extracting their blood for Passover rituals; these plays were based on allegedly historical incidents, such as the death of William of Norwich.

In such plays, there was no specific role for a character named Judas, but his name is not infrequently mentioned in them as a general epithet for "Jewish traitor". Indeed, the theme of Jewish perfidy runs throughout these performances, and it is not too much to say that obsessive attacks on the Jews and Judaism are the main theme of medieval Christian drama. The Passion Plays remain, however, the purveyors of antisemitic rage at its most intense, and as the chief popular instrument of antisemitic indoctrination. In recent times there has been much controversy about a Passion Play that still survives, being performed every ten years at Oberammergau in Bavaria. In response to criticism, some of its more obviously antisemitic aspects have been changed; yet it remains a distressing spectacle to Jewish viewers. The organizers argue that it must surely be permissible to give dramatic expression to the central Christian story. However, the study of the historical role of the Passion Plays, especially in this area, in fostering the loathing and paranoia that eventually produced the Holocaust, can lead to only one decent solution: to abandon cosmetic attempts, and abolish the Oberammergau Passion Play altogether.[11]

The Passion Plays, however, are best understood not as mere orgies of antisemitism, but as reinforcements of Christian belief in the efficacy of the death of Christ for salvation. The continual repetition of the agonies of Jesus on the Cross was a dramatic renewal of the process by which every Christian attained the salvation of his soul. The renewal of Jew-hatred was part of this religious process. There is much truth in the ironic saying of Erasmus, "If it is the part of a good Christian to detest the Jews, than we are all good Christians" (*Si christianum, est odisse judaeos, hic abunde omnes christiani sumus*). Only if Christ truly suffered was there salvation for Christians. Every pang of pain, every contortion of agony, witnessed on the stage and enacted in the theatre of the believer's soul, contributed towards release from the hell-fire which terrified the medieval Christian. The good Christian must feel sorrow for the agonies of Christ and never allow into consciousness his thankful and happy awareness that only these agonies stood between him and damnation. The best defence against such awareness was to hate and blame the Jews. The more he hated them, the more innocent he was of desiring the crucifixion of Christ.

In this double exercise of mourning and hate, the Christian was re-enacting an ancient ritual. The same ambivalence characterizes primitive societies, where the community demands a human sacrifice, but rejects with horror the means by which it is procured. Mankind has always felt the need not merely to perform the sacrifice, but to renew it periodically in symbolic ways. We know of ancient ritual performances, such as the week-long re-enactment of the vicissitudes of Attis in Rome (taking place at the season later known as Easter).[12] It is probable that the origins of drama itself can be traced to such performances. Certainly the Athenian drama still retains strong features of a religious origin—including sacrificial elements—and was performed as part of a sacred festival. The origin of tragedy should be sought in just the kind of ambivalent mourning that we find in the mystery-religions.

The message of the Passion Plays was reinforced by the powerful visual stimulus of medieval Christian art. The depiction of Judas Iscariot was an important ingredient in the general antisemitic depiction of the Jews. Of this, Joseph Reider has written, "We find art playing a very important role in disseminating distorted conceptions and false notions of the Jews, often depicting them in unnatural colours and derogatory poses, sometimes even as frightful monsters without any redeeming virtues. The artists thus helped to fan the bias and hatred of the populace, who knew them for the most part from these misrepresentations and caricatures and not from close personal contact. In an age of rampant ecclesiasticism and furious sacerdotalism, when reason was garrotted and superstition held full sway, it was not unnatural that art should contribute its share in formulating and promulgating the well-known myth of His Satanic Majesty, the medieval Jew."[13]

From early times, the Church and the Synagogue were frequently portrayed by female figures, one wearing a crown and holding a chalice and cross, the other blinded and mourning, with a fallen crown, carrying in one hand the tables of the Law, and in the other a broken banner. Examples are the stained glass windows at St. Denis on the Seine and at Bourges Cathedral. Thus the defeat of Judaism and the triumph of the Church were symbolically conveyed, but without the degree of malice and contempt that characterized later forms of portrayal of Judaism and the Jews. Chief among these later manifestations was the portrayal of Judaism as a sow, from which representative Jews are depicted as suckling. This idea, like nearly all the most offensive and brutal antisemitic notions, sprang from Germany, where it is found first in the thirteenth century, sculptured on the Cathedral of Magdeburg. From the German churches, the sculptured sow travelled to those of France and Holland, and is found also in countless antisemitic drawings and caricatures, especially after the invention of printing. The most famous sow was that of

Wittenberg, of which Luther gave an enthusiastic description in the course of his antisemitic writings; he was especially captivated by the scatological aspect of this church sculpture.

Even more potent for antisemitic indoctrination by art was the stereotypic depiction of individual Jews. The constituents of this stereotype (not necessarily all used simultaneously) have been listed by Zafran[14] as follows: 1. the pointed hat; 2. the yellow badge; 3. badge adorned with representation of a pig or a scorpion; 4. Hebrew script; 5. an evil face; 6. face depicted in profile. The facial stereotype has been the subject of disagreement among iconographers. According to Shachar,[15] a specifically Jewish facial stereotype is not found until the seventeenth century, while Zafran finds it from the thirteenth century on. My own impression is that the stereotype (consisting mainly of hooked nose and bulging eyes) exists in the earlier material, but is not used consistently until the seventeenth century. In the woodcuts depicting alleged ritual murders, for example, a group of Jews will contain one, or at most two with stereotypical Jewish features, while the rest have nondescript faces, amounting to mere facial diagrams. It seems that the effort of comprehensive characterization seemed unnecessary, as long as one at least of the group had the facial stereotype, while the rest were labelled as Jews by some more easily drawn feature such as a pointed hat. On the other hand, the portrayal of deformed or degraded facial structures may be regarded as an objective aspect, whether or not we define such deformations as ingredients in a specifically "Jewish" stereotype.

A study of the artistic evidence shows once again that Judas Iscariot was treated as symbolic of the Jewish people as a whole. When we see pictures of Judas bearing the unmistakable characteristics of the medieval Jewish stereotype (while the other apostles, and Jesus himself, are portrayed as Christians), there can be no doubt that Judas and the Jews belong together.

One alleged characteristic of the Jew, in medieval Christian folklore, might seem impossible to portray in art: the *foetor iudaicus*, or "Jewish stench". Yet surprisingly enough it does appear in art, as Zafran has pointed out. We saw above (p. 84) that one of the earliest post-biblical developments of the Judas saga was to ascribe to him an insupportable stench. From the thirteenth century onward, we find references to the alleged Jewish stench, which could only be removed by baptism. In a fifteenth-century engraving of the Last Supper by the Dutch Master IAM of Zwolle, Judas (identified by his moneybag) is portrayed as having the Jewish stench, as is shown graphically and unmistakably by the fact that the disciple sitting next to him is holding his nose. This engraving inspired other similar portrayals of a stinking Judas in Church art. Since by this time belief in the *foetor iudaicus* was almost universal, the portrayal of Judas as suffering from it in consequence of his contemplated betrayal was a most effective way of instilling the equation of Judas and the Jews. Without the use of words, but by visual indoctrination alone (far more effective), the message was conveyed, "The stinking Jews are the Judas-nation."

In the earliest artistic portrayals of Judas (as in the earliest portrayals of Jewish characters generally) the aim of debasement and degradation has not yet appeared. Judas is a wicked, but not yet a subhuman, character. These are the portrayals of Judas in Brescia, the Theodosian sarcophagi, in St. Apollinare, Ravenna, and in the Codex Rossanensis. Judas is differentiated from the other apostles in various ways: if they are bearded, he is shown as beardless, and if they are wearing haloes, he has none, or a dark one; he carries a purse. But his features are not degraded or bestial or exaggeratedly Semitic. He is often portrayed as having a low forehead, but this does not mark him out particularly as a Jew. Even when he is shown with a dishevelled beard, this does not indicate specific Jewishness at this stage, rather than mere personal disreputableness. Indeed in the early art of the Mediterranean, neither the caricatured Judas nor the caricatured Jew appears: he is not found in the biblical cycles presented on the mosaics of the churches Santa Maria Maggiore in Rome, Capella Palatina in Palermo, the Cathedral in Moreale in Sicily or St. Mark's in Venice. Nor is it found in the biblical cycles of Lorenzo Ghiberti on the bronze doors of the Baptistery at Florence, of Benozzo Gozzoli in the Campo Santo at Pisa, of Raphael on the ceilings of the Loggie of the Vatican or of Michelangelo on the ceiling of the Sistine Chapel. Nevertheless, even in these relatively civilized portrayals, some device is found to express the link between Judas and the Jews, such as the yellow cloak.

The dehumanizing of both Judas and the Jews begins to be found in the art of Central Europe and Germany in the thirteenth century, particularly in pictorial representations of the blood-libel accusations. It was this kind of accusation that lowered the status of the Jews to a subhuman level, and prepared the way for the Nazi attitude to the Jews as vermin. The popular art of Germany and Central Europe has a heavy responsibility for this development. Church art too contributed its quota of degraded-looking Jews both in pictorial representations in churches and in popular illustrated Bibles, notably the *Biblia Pauperum* and the Moralized Bible.

In addition to the features of the Jewish stereotype, Judas was given special characteristics of his own. Chief among these were his red hair and his yellow gown. Both of these were also characteristic of the Judas of the Passion Plays. The red hair (which is sometimes found in the portrayals of other Jews, particularly Herod) is probably not specifically Jewish, but derives from an ancient (pre-Christian) prejudice, and should probably be explained as deriving from fear of blood; it is ascribed to all those mythologically regarded as guilty of bloodshed or blood-betrayal. Since it was also the colour of Satan's hair in the Passion Plays and in art, the triple identification, Judas/Jews/Devil, was reinforced by this coloration. The yellow gown, on the other hand, is cognate to the yellow badge which Jews were compelled to wear, and which was a regular feature of their portrayal in art. Thus Judas's yellow gown marks him out as a super-Jew, whose main item of costume is nothing but an enlarged yellow badge. The colour yellow, in medieval symbolism, stood for treachery and ignominy.[16] So again, without words, the mere coloration instilled the message of the essential identity of Judas and the Jews.

It should be added that the money-bag which Judas invariably carried acted as a powerful link with the popular Christian conception of the Jews. Though this detail of Judas's appearance was derived from the New Testament, it had acquired a specifically Jewish connotation because of the Christian policy of channelling the Jews into the profession of money-lending, by their exclusion from all other trades and professions. Jews are frequently depicted in the popular art as carrying money-bags in pursuance of their profession as usurers. This is a case of transmission of a characteristic from Judas to the Jews, rather than from the Jews to Judas (as when Judas is given a pointed hat). But the link was just as effectively made, and there can be no doubt that whenever Christians saw Judas portrayed with his money-bag, they thought of him as a typical Jew in this respect. It is a constant feature of paranoid pathology not only to see certain loathed characteristics in the target of hostility, but to make efforts, when circumstances favour such victimization, to create those characteristics in an objective form, so that the paranoia can be justified "objectively". The Nazis, for example, having fantasized Jews (who were objectively of very clean habits) as unclean ("dirty Jews"), deliberately turned them into objectively dirty Jews by depriving them of all means of hygiene in the death-camps. Similarly, medieval Christendom turned the Jews into usurers so that they would conform to the image of Judas with his money-bag. Once this social operation had been successfully completed, the money-bag could function as a symbol of Jewishness.

The antisemitic art of modern times is to be found especially in the field of caricature. The grotesque Jews of Nazi antisemitic caricature derive directly from the religious art of the middle ages, including the frequently portrayed figure of Judas Iscariot. Some powerful artists, however, have not been satisfied with a simplistic portrayal of Judas as archetypal villain, and have sought to probe and understand his motivations. An outstanding example is Rubens's painting of the Last Supper (Ermitage, St. Petersburg), whose Judas is isolated from the Apostles by a cynical but unhappy freedom from illusion. This is a subtle conception that detaches Judas from religious myth and makes him the subject of a psychological study. In Dürer's strange woodcut of the kiss of Judas, there seems to be an anticipation of modern psychoanalytic interpretations of the betrayal as an expression of erotic sadism. Such portrayals constitute important steps towards demythologization and away from antisemitism, as in certain modern literary developments (such as *The Last Temptation of Christ* by Kazantzakis)—yet they still remain too much under the spell of the Gospel story to question it fundamentally.

The medieval drama too had a profound influence on later European secular drama. Some famous Renaissance plays still show signs of this derivation. Marlowe's *Jew of Malta*, whose villain, Barabas, poisons wells and plots to destroy Christians, derives from the late-medieval antisemitic secular plays. Marlowe, however, uses this medieval material for his own purposes. Barabas is a typical Renaissance villain, and his Jewishness simply adds an extra dimension of horror. Like Tamburlaine, the protagonist of another Marlowe play, Barabas glories in unbridled individualism and freedom from inhibition, and one even feels that Marlowe, the freethinker, has some secret sympathy for him. But Shakespeare's *Merchant of Venice* shows great affinity to the medieval drama and expresses a more serious kind of antisemitism. Antonio takes a symbolic Christ-role, and the Jewish usurer, Shylock, plots his death. The scene in which Portia acts as judge and saves the Christian from the Jew echoes the medieval "processes" in which this role is played by the Virgin Mary, who descends from heaven for this very purpose. The relationship between Shylock and his comic servant Lancelot Gobbo is modelled on that of Satan and Vice in the Morality Plays. Shylock, however, does not display the special characteristics of Judas himself, and in fact is modelled on another New Testament stereotype, namely the Pharisee. From the moment when he first sees Antonio and exclaims, "How like a fawning publican he seems!" (recalling Luke 18:10–14, where the publican, or tax-collector is compared favourably with the Pharisee), Shylock displays all the classical Pharisee traits—cruelty, self-righteousness (he never legally commits a crime), and insistence on the letter of the law. Shakespeare never knew a practising Jew in person (though he may have met some Jewish converts to Christianity), for all Jews had been excluded from England since their brutal expulsion in 1290. But the New Testament provided amply for the construction of a Jew, and his portrait of Shylock, despite its vaunted "humanity", bears the traces of this origin. Shylock represents Judaism, with its alleged emphasis on the cruel letter of the law, while Portia represents the Christian law of love and mercy. Thus the play, as well as being a secularized version of the Passion Plays, derives partly from the Easter Plays, with their dramatized debates between Christianity and Judaism.[17]

As for the progeny of the medieval Judas in later European literature, I suggest that the figure of the double-dyed plotting villain that appears so frequently in Western drama and fiction is derived from this source. In the Arthurian saga, he is Mordred; in the Roland saga, he is Gamelin. In Shakespeare, he is Iago. This motiveless, treacherous villain, who plots evil for its own sake, is endemic to Western literature, and is found nowhere else. The medieval drama is a mediate influence, but the New Testament itself has been the direct source of these pathological villains. Certainly there is no model for them in the Hebrew Bible, which contains no motiveless villains. Cain, for example, has a comprehensible motive of jealousy, and proves capable of remorse. Laban, the antagonist of Jacob, is mean and crafty, but hardly evil; Jacob is crafty too, and the contest of intellects provides an enjoyable spectacle. Ahitophel, who has sometimes been regarded as a model for the New Testament Judas, is no villain (see p. 48). He is a politician with good reasons for taking a certain line, and commits suicide after his fellow-conspirators fail to take his advice. His role is more like that of Cassius in Shakespeare's *Julius Caesar* than that of Iago.

However, the Judas-surrogates of Western literature cannot properly be regarded as part of the history of the Judas-figure itself. Even if a character such as Iago has undertones relating him to Judas, and so (at another remove) to the Jews, this link is too indirect to add significantly to the growth of antisemitism. However, it does reveal the predisposition of the Christian mind to derive satisfaction from hating villainous characters. While not part of the antisemitic pattern, it does reflect the mind-set created by the basic myth of Christian civilization.

A certain important exception should be mentioned, however. The greatest poem of the Middle Ages, Dante's *Divine Comedy* (written about 1310), shows a conscious effort to avoid connecting the perfidy of Judas with the dishonour of the Jewish people as a whole. In the *Inferno*, Dante describes the position in hell of all the great malefactors of the past. The possibilities for antisemitic treatment were great, but Dante does his best to sidestep them. Judas is placed at the very centre of hell, next to Satan himself, one of whose three mouths continually gnaws him. The other two mouths gnaw Brutus and Cassius, whom Dante regards as the sinners who destroyed the possibility of a universal Christian state when they murdered Julius Caesar. Thus Judas is regarded as one of the three greatest sinners in history. But nothing is said about his sin being typically "Jewish". The depiction of the Jews in hell is moderate by medieval standards. The High Priest Caiaphas, his father-in-law Annas, and the elders of the Sanhedrin (earlier called "Pharisees"), who allegedly condemned Jesus, lie crucified on the ground, trodden on by all who pass (Canto 23). It is hinted, as commentators have pointed out, that the exile of the Jews is a similar crucifixion ("Thus racked for ever on the shameful cross/In the everlasting exile", ll. 124–125), but this is not really spelled out. Dante himself was personally friendly with many Jews, notably the poet Immanuel of Rome. (Such friendships, however, did not always preclude antisemitism in one's writing, as with Origen and Jerome.[18]) Moreover, the Italian temper was usually less antisemitic than that of Germans, French, Spaniards and English, perhaps because the close proximity of the Papacy bred scepticism, a great solvent of antisemitic fantasies, or perhaps because of the cosmopolitan spirit fostered by Italian trade with the Levant and Muslim countries. Whatever the reason, it is pleasant to be able to record that Dante's treatment of Judas and the Jews is civilized compared with the antisemitic virulence of the Passion Plays and other products of the Christian imagination, many of them written at about the same time.

In the post-medieval period, as we have seen, the image of Judas transmigrates into other forms in European literature. This is because this literature becomes secular, and the Passion story is no longer mainly used as a subject for plays, poems or stories. But the Jew remains as an important character in secular literature, and the depiction of him owes much to the medieval figure of Judas. One characteristic of the medieval Judas, for example, was red hair, and this feature can be traced in the villain-Jew of European literature down to our own days. Perhaps the most famous example is Dickens' Fagin. A seventeenth-century verse description of the typical stage-Jew, as depicted in the plethora of plays of which *The Jew of Malta* and *The Merchant of Venice* are only the most prominent examples, is as follows:

> His beard was red; his face was made
> Not much unlike a witch's;
> His habit was a Jewish gown,
> That would defend all weather;
> His chin turned up, his nose hung down,
> And both ends met together.[19]

Dickens, to be sure, did not really know that in giving Fagin red hair he was perpetuating a centuries-old anti-Jewish icon; but in fact a continuous tradition lay behind this unconscious choice. Indeed, the tradition of a red-haired Betrayer goes back to prehistoric times. Set, the brother, betrayer and murderer of Osiris, had red hair—no doubt the device is intended to symbolize the spilling of blood. Red hair was also a characteristic of the Devil in the medieval drama, so that "Judas" and "Devil" tended to become almost synonymous. The Man with Red Hair who plots and betrays is such a well-established archetype in human culture that he can be relied on to arouse villainous associations in the minds of most readers. When the red-haired man is also a Jew, the circle of associations is complete.

Such literary epigones of the medieval Judas as Fagin can always be discounted by someone prepared to dismiss the resemblance and to insist that Judas Iscariot, as a specific character in imaginative literature, did not survive the Middle Ages. Where he did unmistakably survive was in antisemitic propaganda, the interminable books and pamphlets which proclaimed the "menace of the Jews". These productions began in the eighteenth century as a furious reaction to the beginnings of Jewish emancipation, reached their apex in the Nazi propaganda and have continued with hardly diminished energy up to the present day. In all such writings, the equation of "Jew" and "Judas" is a commonplace. The growth of modern nationalism has been a great spur to this identification, since almost every national group of Christian background whose aspirations have been disappointed is ready to blame it on those "traitors" the Jews, and for evidence cite the arch-traitor, Judas. The leading instance of this reflex was the German conviction of Jewish betrayal after the First World War. Despite the fact that German Jews had fought loyally in the war, gaining medals for valour out of proportion to their numbers in the population, the need for a scapegoat led inevitably to the archetypal "traitors". This solution was accepted with enthusiasm by the majority who voted Hitler into power. The Judas archetype has thus been an important factor in modern European politics, and should not be dismissed as merely an aspect of literary or religious history.

The Dreyfus case of 1894–1906 offers a classic instance of the use of the Judas–Jew–traitor equation in modern times. Alfred Dreyfus, a Jewish officer in the French army, accused of handing over information and documents to the Germans, was found guilty and sentenced to Devil's Island. A certain Colonel Picquart, however, discovered evidence clearing Dreyfus and proving that the real culprit was an officer named Esterhazy. But the authorities were unwilling to accept the evidence, and Picquart was ordered to drop the matter. When he refused, he was transferred to a remote part of Tunisia.

Shortly after this, a letter was brought forward by Colonel Henry, a high official of the information branch, further implicating Dreyfus in treason. It was soon discovered, however, that this letter was a forgery. Picquart, before setting off for Tunisia, had managed to interest some important persons in the case, who began to agitate for a further enquiry into the question of Esterhazy's guilt. Esterhazy was courtmartialled but acquitted, and after a virulent press campaign against the Dreyfusards, Colonel Picquart was accused of divulging official secrets and thrown into prison. Many non-Jewish liberals, including George Clemenceau (later the Premier who carried France to victory in World War I), Jean Jaurès, the Socialist leader, and Emile Zola, the famous novelist, took part in a campaign to clear Dreyfus. Jewish intellectuals too, including Léon Blum (later Premier) and the writer Bernard Lazare, contributed to the campaign. A press onslaught of extraordinary bitterness was launched against them, and the country was divided on the issue. On 13th January, 1898, Zola's article "J'accuse" was published in the newspaper *L'Aurore*. It was a shattering indictment of the corruption and injustice of the Government and the Army. Zola was put on trial for defamation, and he was thereby able to give maximum publicity to the details of the affair. In the same year, there were anti-Jewish riots throughout France, instigated by the anti-Dreyfusards. Eventually Dreyfus was completely cleared, and reinstated. Colonel Henry, the forger of the incriminating letter, was arrested and committed suicide in prison.[20]

The reactionary anti-Dreyfusards ran their campaign almost entirely on antisemitic lines. Dreyfus was bound to be guilty, because he was a Jew, and Jews, in the tradition of Judas, were natural traitors.

One of the leading anti-Dreyfusards was Léon Daudet, a celebrated novelist and contributor to *Action Française*, the antisemitic paper founded by Charles Maurras. Daudet called his memoirs of the Dreyfus era *Au Temps de Judas*. Another leading anti-Dreyfusard was Maurice Barrès, an essayist and novelist who became a politician supporting the royalism and antisemitism of Charles Maurras.[21] Barrès titled his account of the ceremony in which Dreyfus was stripped of his rank "La Parade de Judas". During one of Dreyfus's trials, Barrès wrote, "That Dreyfus is capable of treason, I conclude from his race ... Through these long hearings, I have watched the face of Dreyfus, sweating treason." The most virulent antisemite of the period was Edouard Drumont, author of the influential book *La France juive devant l'opinion* which claimed to unmask a vast Jewish conspiracy. He wrote:[22]

The affair of Captain Dreyfus ... is simply another episode in Jewish history. Judas sold the God of mercy and love. Deutz gave up the heroic woman who had entrusted herself to his honour.[23] ... Captain Dreyfus has sold to Germany our mobilization plans and the names of our intelligence agents. This is all just a fatal running to type, the curse of the race. And it is ourselves and not the Jews who are really guilty; for they could quite rightly say to us: why have you broken with the tradition of your ancestors? Why do you entrust your secrets to those who have always betrayed you?

The Dreyfus affair brought many such views to the surface, for the Judas/Jew equivalence had long been an antisemitic commonplace in France. For example, Léon Bloy wrote, "Judas is their type, their prototype, their archetype, or, if one prefers, the definitive paradigm of the ignoble and sempeternal conjugations of avarice."[24] Even when the name "Judas" is not explicitly mentioned, the Jewish association with treachery is an unmistakable allusion to the Judas myth. For example, the Italian Jesuit periodical *La Civiltà Cattolica* declared: "The Jew was created by God to serve as a spy, wherever treason is being prepared."[25] It is interesting to note here the survival of the notion that Judas had a divine mission of betrayal. But of course this notion of destiny never lessens the hatred felt either for Judas or for the Jews.

Frequently, however, the association between Jews and Judas is made explicit in the antisemitic literature. For example, René, Marquis de La Tour de Pin, a religious antisemite who advocated the expulsion of all Jews from France in the interests of a Christian state, wrote in 1898, "... (we) must never lose sight of the fact that France is the kingdom of Christ, and that if the deicide nation comes near it, it can only be to give it the kiss of Judas."[26]

The Jewish statesman Léon Blum took part in the Dreyfus campaign in his youth, and later wrote a book about it called *Souvenirs sur l'Affaire*, in which he wrote:

121

To appreciate "the Affair" correctly, one must remember that Dreyfus was a Jew, that once a Jew always a Jew, that the Jewish race is impervious to certain moral concepts, that it is marked by certain hereditary taints. And one of these ethnic traits, indefinitely inheritable, was it not precisely the innate predisposition to treason? Had not whole centuries shunned the Jewish race as the descendants of Judas? . . . the antisemites thus did not hesitate to . . . presume Dreyfus guilty, simply because he was a Jew. The race of the criminal provided them with an overriding explanation for the crime.[27]

The Dreyfus affair vividly underlines the identification in the Christian mind between "Jews" and "Judas". Though often unspoken, it rises to the surface and becomes explicit in times of stress. The non-Jewish traitor Esterhazy almost went scot-free because it seemed so right and inevitable that the traitor should be a Jew. Even those who knew with certainty that Dreyfus was innocent continued in many cases to proclaim his guilt because the facts seemed irrelevant; the Jews were guilty, even if Dreyfus individually was not. The Jews, like Dreyfus, are accused of treachery whenever the need for a traitor arises. The Jews are the natural victims of such a charge, despite their assiduous and often pathetic efforts to prove their loyalty, because they are the archetypal traitors in the Christian myth.

The survival of this ancient link in modern antisemitism simply extends the tradition of previous centuries. Pope Gelasius I (492–496) observed, "In the Bible the whole is often named after the part; as Judas was called a devil and the devil's workman, he gives his name to the whole race." In the catechisms used to educate children in the basic principles of Christianity, the Jews were linked with Judas Iscariot as the betrayers and murderers of Jesus. The catechism of Abbé Fleury (1640–1723) was very widely used. Part of it runs:

Did Jesus have enemies?—Yes, the carnal Jews.—To what point did the hatred of Jesus's enemies go?—To the point of causing his death.—Who was it who promised to hand him over?—Judas Iscariot.—Why was this city (Jerusalem) treated in this way?—For having caused the death of Jesus.—What became of the Jews?—They were reduced to servitude and scattered throughout the world.

Another catechism, that of Adrien Gambart, contains the following:

Is it a great sin to take communion unworthily?—It is the greatest of all sins, because one makes oneself guilty of the body and blood of Jesus Christ, as Judas and the Jews were; and one becomes the object of His judgement and condemnation.

By such means, young children were indoctrinated in the belief that the treachery of Judas was typical of Jews. This collocation was instilled so deeply that it became part of the Christian psyche.

In literature, too, the connection between Judas and the Jews was often mentioned, usually in a casual way that shows it to be taken for granted. For example, in Christopher Marlowe's play *The Jew of Malta*, one of the characters, Ithamore, jokingly referring to the Jew Barabas, says, "That hat he wears, Judas left under the elder when he hanged himself."[28] Sometimes, however, the Elizabethan drama hinted at the connection in a more indirect way. As Celeste Wright has pointed out, the fact that the usual end of the Jewish usurer in Elizabethan drama is by hanging is not fortuitous. "In view of the close connection between Avarice and Usury, the idea [of hanging] may reasonably be traced back to the story of Judas."[29]

An interesting example of conscious contemplation of the relationship between Judas and the Jews is the poem "Self Condemnation" by the seventeenth century Metaphysical poet, George Herbert (1593–1633):

> Thou who condemnest Jewish hate
> For choosing Barabbas a murderer
> Before the Lord of glory,
> Look back upon thine own estate,
> Call home thine eyes, that busy wanderer,
> That choice may be thy story.
>
> He that doth love, and love amiss
> This world's delights before true Christian joy,

Hath made a Jewish choice:
The world an ancient murderer is;
Thousands of souls it hath and doth destroy
With her enchanting voice.

He that hath made a sorry wedding
Between his soul and gold, and hath preferred
False gain before the true,
Hath done what he condemns in reading;
For he hath sold for money his dear Lord,
And is a Judas Jew ...

Here Herbert condemns those who put the joys of this world before their religious allegiance. Such people align themselves both with the Jews (who betrayed Christ by preferring Barabbas) and with Judas (who sold Christ for money). The poem does not intend primarily to condemn the Jews, but comprises a moral lesson on the subject of worldliness. However, the use of the Jews together with Judas as a negative example shows how deep-grained this collocation is, and how even so sweet-natured a person as Herbert has no scruple about reinforcing a view of the Jews that had become an axiom.

Another gentle, whimsical soul, from the following century, was Laurence Sterne (1713–68), whose much-loved book *The Life and Opinions of Tristram Shandy* contains the following passage:

"Your son!—your dear son,—from whose sweet and open temper you have so much to expect,—Your BILLY, Sir—would you, for the world, have called him JUDAS? ... Would you, Sir, if a Jew of a godfather had proposed the name for your child, and offered you his purse along with it, would you have consented to such a desecration of him? ... you would have trampled upon the offer;—you would have thrown the temptation at the tempter's head with abhorrence ... the sordid and treacherous idea, so inseparable from the name, would have accompanied him through life like his shadow, and, in the end, made a miser and a rascal of him, in spite, Sir, of your example."

Here it is taken for granted that a Jewish godfather would be proud of his connection with the traitor Judas Iscariot and would therefore propose this name for his godson. This proposal is called "sordid and treacherous", being accompanied by a money bribe. The

Jewish godfather is thus comprehensively identified with Judas himself.

In the nineteenth century, the identification of Judas with the Jews took a strongly political turn, as we have seen in the upheaval of the Dreyfus case. But it would be wrong to think that only right-wing politicians made this identification. There was an antisemitism of the Left too, and it was only with difficulty that Jean Jaurès persuaded the Socialists to support Dreyfus. Left-wing antisemitism (of which Marx himself was a conspicuous example) regarded the Jews as essentially bourgeois and capitalist (though in fact the majority of Jews were poverty-stricken). Some of the Left-wing expressions of antisemitism made use of the same equation of Jews and Judas that is found on the Right. For example, the French socialist E. Cannot wrote:

"Jews! To the heights of your Sinai . . . I humbly lift myself. I stand erect and cry out to you, on behalf of all my humble equals, of all those whom your spoliation has brought to grief, who died in misery through you and whose trembling shades accuse you. Jews! for Cain and Iscariot, leave us, *leave us*! Ah, cross the Red Sea again, and go down there to the desert, to the promised land which is waiting for you, the only country fit for you; you wicked, rude and dishonest people, go there!"[30] The early Socialist Charles Fourier even wrote: "The Jew is, so to speak, a traitor by definition."[31] Modern left-wing antisemitism, with its equation of Zionism and Western imperialism, is only a variation on this theme.

The old religious antisemitism may have given way in many respects to secular versions, but it persisted in its authentic medieval form in the Roman Catholic Church where the Jews were still seen in the image of Judas. For example, a certain Father Constant published a book in 1897 called *Les Juifs devant l'Église et l'histoire* in which he wrote: "Ever since the great betrayal at Mount Calvary, the spirit of the Iscariot had infested the Jewish race. In the heart of every Jew, there flows a traitor's blood. They showed their gratitude to the princes of Spain by summoning the Arabs of Africa." Here the Jews are blamed for the Muslim invasion of Spain, which they allegedly plotted in "the spirit of Iscariot". Father Constant further claimed: "The Church always takes up its standpoint on the firmly established fact that the Jew as such, and just because he is a Jew, is predisposed to treason." In a reference to the Catholic liturgy, he wrote: "It was not without reason that in the most solemn moment of its liturgy, at the foot of the bleeding cross of its Lord, in the hour when the Church offers to Heaven this blood for all humanity, when none is excluded from its prayers, in that hour which of all hours is that of compassion, it was for that reason that the Church thought fit to pray for the forgiveness of the Jews only by adding the epithet which justice commanded, namely 'perfidious'. Let us also pray for the perfidious Jews."

Father Constant's book was published in Paris with the full approval of the Catholic Church of the time. The prayer to which he refers is *"Oremus et pro perfidis Judaeis"*, in the Collect for Good Friday, the oldest form of public prayer in the Church. The word *perfidis* was recently dropped by the Catholic Church in response to criticism. It forms only a small part of the Church pattern of Jews as traitors, tainted with the sin of Judas.

A well-known American antisemite, W. D. Herstrom, who regularly promulgates paranoid attacks on a Jewish world-conspiracy, appealed to the religious background of antisemitism in these words: "If you say that you are not anti-semitic, it is tantamount to saying you are not a Christian or that your profession of Christianity is not genuine. Such a person is a Judas Iscariot, playing both sides to retain prestige and popularity."[32]

An interesting and instructive piece of sociological research was carried out by Charles Y. Glock and Rodney Stark, who asked in a widely-distributed questionnaire, "When you think of Judas, do you think of him as a Jew, a Christian, or neither?" The answers revealed that 44 per cent of the Protestants and 47 per cent of the Roman Catholics thought Judas was a Jew, while only 13 and 19 per cent of these groups thought the apostles were Jews.[33]

It is hardly surprising that after the Russian Revolution, which to many in England seemed a typical instance of Jewish treachery, the London *Times*' correspondent on Russian affairs, a certain Robert Wilton, reported that the Bolsheviks had unveiled a statue to Judas Iscariot in Moscow.[34]

8

Who Was Judas Iscariot?

We have pursued the Judas saga from its bare beginnings as a sketchy scenario of betrayal to elaborate narratives covering every phase of Judas's life from birth to death. We have seen that the name "Judas" became a byword signifying "traitor" in European languages, and, more significantly, that "Judas" never lost its semantic association with "Jew". Whenever a person has been stigmatized as a "Judas", even in a context where no Jews are involved, the implication has been clear: "This person is as bad as a Jew; he has betrayed his trust in the same way the Jews betrayed Christ." Thus the word "Judas" as a term meaning "traitor" carries at all times an antisemitic charge, even when applied to non-Jews. Inevitably, however, the full antisemitic potential of the word is only realized when the person or persons accused of treachery are Jews. Since the Jews figure in the fantasy-life of Christians and even post-Christians as the archetypal traitors, the Jews are often chosen for this role in times of crisis and defeat.

This situation has not been affected by the declining belief in Christianity. When a religion declines, its dogmas may decay rapidly, but its fantasies take much longer to disappear. The name "Judas" will retain its antisemitic charge as long as post-Christian movements continue to echo the Christian cosmic myth of good and evil. Indeed, the antisemitism of post-Christian movements is even more implacable, for these movements lack the Christian conception that the Jews, with all their evil, are somehow necessary for the continuance of Christian life. The post-Christian movements of Nazism and Communism inherited the belief in the evil of the Jews, together with the millenarian conviction that the Jews were no longer necessary for salvation and could therefore be obliterated. For Christians, the millennium lay far in the future; but for the post-

127

Christian movements it had already arrived—and that spelt death for the Jews.

But what historical reality, if any, lies behind the Judas myth? Who was the real Judas Iscariot, and what role did he play in the story of Jesus of Nazareth? This question must lead us back to the Gospels, in which the process of freewheeling fantasy has not yet destroyed all the traces of earlier more factual records.

When we come to reconstruct the historical Judas (as in the case, indeed, of Jesus), we have to read between the lines in the documents that are available to us, catching hints from passages that seem to have survived from earlier accounts. This enquiry is not merely academic and theoretical. It helps us understand how myths arise, and it helps to dispel prejudices still remaining from myth-derived indoctrination. Even if we are left finally with a question-mark, and a theory that reaches only to the probable, we nevertheless strengthen the rational approach that aims primarily at the probable, and eschews the bigoted certainty of minds imbued with myth and fantasy.

The starting-point of most theories about the historical Judas has been the name Iscariot. What is the derivation of this name? Is it Hebrew, or does it come from some other language? Is it a nickname, or a surname, or a place-name? Is it given to Judas alone, or did he inherit the name from his family?

The common explanation regards Iscariot as a Greek transliteration of two Hebrew words: *ish*, meaning "man", and *qeriyoth*, being the place-name Kerioth, found three times in the Hebrew Bible.[1] "Iscariot" would therefore mean "man of Kerioth". In Jeremiah and Amos, the word comes in a list of places in Moab; but in Joshua it is included among places in Judah. In the Septuagint of Joshua, however, the Hebrew *qeriyoth* is not translated as a place-name, but as meaning "cities" (Greek, *hai poleis*), i.e. cities connected with Hazor, or Hezron, a broad area, as recent excavations have shown. Thus it is doubtful, even in the one biblical passage where *qeriyot* occurs as situated in Judah, whether this is in fact a place-name—and no one has suggested that Judas came from Moab.[2]

Nevertheless, in the absence of any other theory, it has been widely accepted that Judas came from a place in Judah called Kerioth. Two considerations have helped to strengthen this view. First is the evidence, found only in John, that Judas's father (or possibly brother) Simon was also called Iscariot (John 6:71 and 13:26). This seems to rule out the possibility that Iscariot is a nickname, since two people are not likely to have the same one. But it does seem quite plausible that two people of the same family should be familiarly referred to as coming from the same town. The Gospel of John provides another piece of evidence: in certain manuscripts of this Gospel we find, instead of "Iscariot", the Greek expression *apo Karuotou*, meaning "from Karyotos".[3] This shows that in one textual tradition, at least, "Iscariot" was regarded as meaning that Judas came from a certain place; though it remains doubtful whether this is a genuine geographical tradition, or an early attempt to find an etymology for a name whose meaning had already become mysterious.

Attempts were made to locate the town of Kerioth more precisely. The German scholar Frants Buhl, in his *Geographie des Alten Palästina*, identified the ancient Kerioth with the modern Arab township Qaryaten, relying on the fact that place-names are often extraordinarily long-lived, so that it is not far-fetched to suppose that a name has survived for two thousand years with only slight changes. This identification was widely accepted. Unfortunately, Qaryaten is not in quite the right area, being far removed from the ancient site of Hazor, with which Kerioth is associated in the Bible. It also seems significant that the place-name Kerioth is nowhere mentioned in the post-biblical literature. This suggests either that there never was such a place, or that it had ceased to exist in the time of Jesus.

A further question is whether "Iscariot" is indeed a compound name combining *ish* ("man") and *qeriyoth* (Kerioth). If Iscariot means "man of Kerioth", why does the New Testament leave the first word, *ish*, untranslated? Why not translate it into Greek as "man" (*aner*)? Certainly the expression "man of . . ." is idiomatic in Hebrew of this period.[4] But the expression "man of . . ." is never regarded as part of the name, and is always translated explicitly when the name is transferred into another language.[5]

On the whole, despite its wide acceptance, the "man of Kerioth" theory is very flimsy. Yet far-reaching conclusions have been drawn from this premise, and are now so firmly entrenched that they have almost acquired the status of unchallenged fact. Thus we repeatedly encounter the assertion that Judas Iscariot, unlike the other disciples, was a Judean, not a Galilean. This made him the odd man out among the disciples; he never quite fitted into this company, who shared a Galilean outlook with Jesus himself. Judas, the argument continues, was of somewhat higher social standing than the others, because his southern extraction made him familiar with the manners of the metropolis, Jerusalem. This again alienated him from the rustic disciples and from Jesus himself. He was thus the one most likely to defect. His upper-class background made him ambitious for high status in the "kingdom of God". But when he found that Jesus had no desire for political power, he became disillusioned and betrayed him.

All this depends on the assumption that Judas was born in a Judaean town called Kerioth, a notion that in turn depends entirely upon the suspect etymology described above. There is not a shred of evidence, apart from this, to show that Judas was a Judaean. The name "Judas" certainly does not show this, for it was a common name in Galilee. The famous Judas of Galilee, the founder of the Zealot movement, is an obvious example. Another is Jesus's brother Judas (Matthew 13:55). The greater likelihood is thus that Judas Iscariot, like the other disciples, was a Galilean.

Many scholars dissatisfied with the "man of Kerioth" theory have attempted other explanations of the name. Some suggest that Iscariot is a form of "Issacharite", meaning a member of the tribe of Issachar. Etymologically, this is quite an attractive idea; but the theory is unlikely to be correct, since the tribe of Issachar had ceased to exist many centuries earlier. The Assyrian conquest of the Northern Kingdom had brought about the exile and dispersal of the Lost Ten Tribes, of which Issachar was one.

Others hold that the name Iscariot is not derived from a place-name, but was rather a nickname borne by Judas because of his role as the disciples' treasurer. On this theory, "Iscariot" is derived from the Latin word *scortea*, which means a leather bag. Judas is indeed said to have "had the bag" (John 12:6; 13:29). The Greek word used here is *glossokomon*, which is nothing like Iscariot. But this theory is hardly persuasive, since our earlier investigations have indicated that the concept of Judas as treasurer of the band is not early or authentic, but a product of the developing legend of Judas as avaricious.[6]

One view worth discussing is that Iscariot derives from the place-name Sychar, which occurs in John 4:5, described there as "a city of

Samaria". The suggestion is that Iscariot means "man of Sychar", i.e. that the first element in the name is *ish*, as in the "man of Kerioth" theory, but the second element is whatever Hebrew name underlies the Greek transliteration "Sychar". By this theory, Judas is even more the odd man out than if he were a Judaean; here he becomes a Samaritan, a sect regarded as heretical by the main body of the Jews. It seems impossible, however, that this could be so. The attitude of Jesus towards the Samaritans, as described in the Gospels, was reserved. He ordered his disciples not to enter their cities (Matthew 10:5). On his journey to Jerusalem, the Samaritans prevented him from passing through their territory, showing their usual hostility to pilgrims (Luke 9:52). Though Jesus rebuked his disciples for wishing to destroy the offenders with fire from heaven, the incident does not suggest friendly relations between the Jesus group and the Samaritans. Though he spoke kindly to the Samaritan woman, he told her that the Samaritans, unlike the Jews, "worship ye know not what" (John 4:22). Like the rabbis, he commended the Samaritans when they performed good deeds (Luke 10:30–36) and used such incidents as an example, but he insisted that "salvation is of the Jews" (John 4:22). These attitudes are hardly compatible with the acceptance of a Samaritan as one of his Apostles.

In addition, the name Sychar presents problems. No other source, Jewish or non-Jewish, mentions this place-name. The probability is, as many scholars have suggested, that Sychar is a corruption of the well-known Samaritan city, Shechem. The first to make this identification was Jerome. This is all the more probable because of John's remark that it "was near to the parcel of ground that Jacob gave to his son Joseph".[7] Nevertheless, some modern scholars have preferred to identify Sychar as the modern Askar, which is some distance from Shechem. The only evidence for this view is the similarity of names, which may be coincidental, and the evidence from John favouring Shechem is hereby ignored. If Shechem is meant, then the attractiveness of the suggested derivation of Iscariot is lessened, while if Askar is relevant, this derivation becomes linguistically stronger.

However this may be, the basic difficulty with the "man of Sychar" theory is the same as that with "man of Kerioth"—it is hard to see why the expression for "man" was not translated into Greek, instead of being amalgamated with the place-name to make a compound in a way that has no Jewish precedent.

Another theory about the meaning and origin of "Iscariot" that is free from these difficulties has been apparently neglected for ideological reasons. This is the view that Iscariot is derived from the Latin *sicarius*, meaning "dagger-man". This word was explicitly applied to members of the Zealot movement, who were active opponents of the Roman occupation of Judaea and engaged in acts of armed resistance. What makes this theory particularly strong is not only its linguistic plausibility, but the remarkable fact that another of Jesus's disciples was known as "Simon the Zealot". This shows that Jesus recruited at least one disciple from the Zealot movement, and it is not at all impossible that he recruited another, whose nickname may also have signified previous membership in the movement. A transliteration of *sicarius* into Aramaic is already known from the rabbinic literature, where a certain prominent rebel during the Jewish war against Rome (66–70 CE) is known as "Abba Sikra" or Abba the Zealot (see b. Gittin 46a). This combination of given name and nickname corresponds exactly to the combination Judas Iscariot. True, the rabbinically-recorded name lacks the introductory "i" found in Iscariot, but it is not unusual for a transliterated name to be found in various forms, since different areas of Palestine would find their own solutions to the problem of pronouncing a foreign word. Indeed, in some New Testament manuscripts the name Iscariot is found without the "i" in the form Skariotes, Skarioth or Scariota.[8]

To think of Judas having a war-like career as a Zealot before entering Jesus's band of apostles requires a shift of thinking that has proved too difficult for most scholars. It was hard enough to accept that even one of the disciples had this background; a second was too much. But as we shall see, there is good reason to suppose that at least two more of Jesus's disciples had the same background. A shift of thinking may therefore become necessary regarding Jesus himself, and his aims in claiming the messiahship. A movement that recruited a high proportion of its leaders from the Zealots would seem likely to have had more in common with that movement than orthodox thinking allows.

Apart from linguistic considerations, there is also some interesting manuscript evidence to suggest that Judas Iscariot means "Judas the Zealot". We have already considered (p. 31) the intriguing passage (John 14:22–24) in which a disciple Judas, carefully distinguished as "*not* Iscariot", tries to persuade Jesus to take a more active political role. We decided that this passage originally *was* about Judas Iscariot, at a stage when he was being portrayed as an uncomprehending activist rather than as a traitor. Confirmation of this view and of the theory that Iscariot means Zealot appears in third- and fourth-century Coptic versions of the Gospel of John. Here the word "not" is missing in the phrase "not Iscariot", but instead of Iscariot we find the word *Kananites*. The complete designation of Jesus's interlocutor at this point in these Coptic versions is thus Judas the Canaanite. Now obviously neither Judas Iscariot nor any other disciple was a Canaanite, since this nation had ceased to exist many centuries before the time of Jesus. But easily confused with the name "Canaanite" is the Hebrew word *qan'ai*, which means Zealot. The tendency of the Gospel writers to confuse this word with Canaanite is shown elsewhere (Mark 3:18, Matthew 10:4), where Simon the Zealot is called Simon the Canaanite. So what the Coptic versions alone have preserved is that Jesus's interlocutor in John 14 was in fact Judas Iscariot (the "not" being omitted), and that an alternative name for him was Judas the Canaanite, i.e. Judas the Zealot. The "not" included in later manuscripts of John is thus an interpolation, inserted by some editor who realized that the role here assigned to Judas Iscariot was not reconcilable with the mature conception of his opposition to Jesus, and that therefore the speech ought to be attributed to the other, undiabolic, Judas.

There is further evidence that, at a period earlier than the final redaction of the Gospels, a person called Judas the Zealot was included in the records of the Church. A list of the apostles is given in Matthew 10:2–4. In this list we find only one person named Judas, namely Judas Iscariot. But we also find an apostle called "Lebbaeus, whose surname was Thaddaeus" in some manuscripts, or simply "Thaddaeus" (in others). We also find the name Thaddaeus in the list of apostles given in Mark 16–19. Who was this apostle, Thaddaeus? In the apostle-lists in Luke, we do not find the name Thaddaeus, but in the corresponding place we find "Judas the brother of James" (Luke 6:16). It has been thought, then, that Thaddaeus is another name for Judas, and some scholars have even suggested that it is a variant form of the word, though this seems unlikely. Most significant of all, however, is that in some early Latin versions of Matthew, we find Judas Zelotes in place of the name "Thaddaeus".

133

This confirms that "Thaddaeus" (whoever it denotes) was expressly substituted for Judas. We also find confirmed the name Judas the Zealot which appears (in the form of Judas the Canaanite) in the Coptic versions of John.[9] The probability that the name Judas Iscariot means Judas the Zealot thus increases.[10]

It may be argued, however, that Judas the Zealot was not Judas Iscariot, but the other Judas, referred to by Luke as the brother of James. This is the conclusion of some scholars, who also identify this second Judas with the "Judas, not Iscariot" of John 14:22. This is a possible solution, but not a likely one in my opinion. That there were two apostles, both called Judas, one nicknamed the Zealot and the other nicknamed Iscariot—a name that, to say the least, *could* mean Zealot—strains credulity. The whole appearance of the apostle-lists, which are so equivocal about whether there were two Judases or one, and whether there was even such a person as Judas the Zealot, shows a process of covering up. What are these lists trying to hide? I suggest the best hypothesis is that there was originally only one Judas, namely Judas Iscariot, and that when he was chosen for the mythic role of traitor, the good traditions about the historical Judas were shifted to a second Judas, who was at first assigned some of the sobriquets of the original, but was gradually differentiated from him by being given different designations.

There is thus both linguistic and textual evidence that Iscariot means Zealot, being derived from *sicarius*. Here, however, it only needs to be stressed that a plausible alternative exists to the derivation "man of Kerioth", usually regarded as the best theory, despite its acknowledged difficulties. Consequently, there is no need to be bound by the commonly-accepted scenario that Judas was an isolated Judaean in a band of Galileans. On the contrary, there is every reason to accept the obvious view (nowhere explicitly denied in the Gospels) that Judas, like the other apostles, was a Galilean.

It should also be pointed out that if Judas Iscariot means Judas the Zealot, there is no difficulty to be found in the fact that John calls him "the son (or brother) of Simon Iscariot". It was a strength of the "man of Kerioth" theory that it was able to explain this satisfactorily; two members of the same family would naturally have the same place-name sobriquet. (But if so, what happens to the "odd man out" theory? Two odd-men-out do not provide so neat an explanation of Judas's "alienation".) But the "Zealot" theory also explains satisfactorily the shared sobriquet: two ex-members of the same movement could easily bear the same sobriquet, especially if the correct translation is "brother of", rather than "son of". Indeed, once we assume that Iscariot means "Zealot", we may infer that Simon Iscariot and Simon the Zealot were the same person, just like Judas Iscariot and Judas the Canaanite (Zealot). In this case, we arrive at the conclusion that Simon the Zealot, the apostle, was Judas Iscariot's brother. For it seems unlikely that there were two Simons, one called Simon the Zealot, who was not Judas's brother, and the other having the equivalent name, Simon Iscariot, who was.[11]

Before we leave the subject, mention should be made of theories that derive the name Iscariot from the Hebrew and Aramaic root *shqr*, meaning "to lie, deceive". It has also been suggested that the name may be based on the root *sgr*, meaning "to hand over", used in Hebrew (in the Hiphil form) to mean "to hand over to an enemy". There are some linguistic difficulties about how the name Iscariot could have developed from these roots, but the main objection is that this explanation implies that the name Iscariot was not borne by Judas while he was an apostle, but only after his defection. Yet all the evidence suggests that he had this name from the beginning. This line of explanation is therefore unpersuasive; though there is certainly the possibility that, after his defection, the name Iscariot, originally having nothing to do with treachery, was *interpreted* this way. There are many examples in the rabbinic literature of such *post hoc* derogatory interpretation of names of people who played an evil role.

The notion that Judas Iscariot was, or had been, a Zealot has been dismissed by many scholars on what appear to be ideological grounds.[12] Taken together with suggestive information about other disciples, it might reinforce the conclusion that Jesus's movement had a good deal in common with the Zealots, and was not so other-worldly and pacifist as orthodox Christianity would wish to represent it. On the other hand, some scholars have accepted the proposed Zealotism of Judas Iscariot as a plausible reason for his defection. If Judas had been a Zealot, engaged in guerrilla warfare against the Romans, he might have retained a this-worldly, militaristic attitude that was foreign to Jesus. Attracted by Jesus's charisma, he left (on this theory) the Zealot movement, under the impression that Jesus was the true Messiah who would bring about, by miraculous means the downfall of the Romans. But it gradually dawned on him that Jesus had no intention of overthrowing the Romans, since he conceived his messiahship as purely spiritual. In disappointment and bitterness, Judas took revenge on Jesus for having misled him, and betrayed him to his enemies.

An alternative version is that Judas never lost faith in Jesus as the Messiah, but became impatient with Jesus's delays, and decided to force events to a conclusion by betraying Jesus, thus compelling him to exercise his miraculous powers to overthrow the Romans. In this version, Judas was not a villain, but a well-meaning disciple who did not understand that Jesus's reluctance to take political action was motivated by a spiritual idea of salvation to which the overthrow of the Romans was irrelevant. This version of events has proved popular not only with scholars but with authors of novels and film-scripts about Jesus and early Christianity, usually in combination with the "man from Kerioth" theory, by which Judas was in any case marked out from the other disciples by his Judaean origin.[13] This scenario gives Judas a comprehensible set of motives, suitable for fictional representation, rescues him from the unpalatable Gospel account of Satanic possession, and also gives Judas symbolic value as typical of Jews of the time who were looking for a political rather than a spiritual Messiah. Thus a degree of sympathy for Judas, as having a point of view and a sense of patriotism, is combined with criticism of him and the Jews as a whole for failing to appreciate the spirituality of Jesus and his mission of atonement on the Cross. It is hardly surprising that this amalgam has strong appeal for novelists and film-makers who wish to preserve Christian religiosity, while avoiding the grosser antisemitic implications of the story.

This theory, though it catches the hints in the narratives and variant readings of the Gospels pointing to the Zealot affiliation of Judas, accepts too readily the historicity of Judas's betrayal. It also too readily accepts the alleged other-worldliness, pacifism and suicidal aims of Jesus himself, and his alleged alienation from the Judaism of his time. The theory thus provides a more acceptable and less Satanic version of the usual account, in which Judas, in betraying Jesus, represents the failings of the Jews and their religion.

Another line of thought maintains that Judas never existed, but was entirely a fictional creation of the early Church. J.M. Robertson argued cogently that Judas Iscariot was invented as a propaganda device against the Jews and Judaism. This view was also argued with great force by William Benjamin Smith, A. Drews, G. Schläger, L.G Lévy and S. Lublinski. Others see the story as having no propaganda purpose, but rather as developing in a fictional way in order to fill puzzling gaps in the story, such as the question of how Jesus came to be arrested. Frank Kermode has put forward the view that the story of Judas supplies the narrative need for an Opposer; on this view, the story was invented, or crystallized, not to fill a historical lacuna but out of a narrative necessity, since it would not be felt to be complete without the element of Opposition (here he bases himself on the work of Vladimir Propp, who analysed a wide range of folk-tales, finding the Opposer to be an essential ingredient).

All these scholars have had important insights and have made valid points. They have been especially receptive to the aspect of *development*: the story's acquisition of new themes and motifs, from its first adumbration in Mark to its elaboration in John, and its accumulation of legendary detail in the Middle Ages. But it still remains to ask, "Who was the historical Judas?" It can be argued, as does J.M. Robertson, that this is an unanswerable question, since the original Judas—if there ever was such a person—has been so over-laid by myth that he is irrecoverable. Similarly, with regard to the question about the historical Jesus, there have been those who have denied that he ever existed (most recently, G.A. Wells) and those who have admitted his existence, but denied the possibility of knowing anything about him (as does Rudolf Bultmann). My own view is that the Gospels are composite works, and that beneath their upper layers they contain much material of historical value that later editorial activity failed to obliterate. This historical material can be recognized by the application of *tendenz* methodology, which began to be developed in the nineteenth century, but produced results that were so alarming to Christian belief (in displaying a Jewish Jesus and a Jewish Jerusalem Church) that it was replaced in the twentieth century by other more congenial methods, notably "form criti-cism".[14] By the use of *tendenz* methods, both the historical Jesus and the historical Judas Iscariot can, to some extent, be recovered.

One other approach to the problems presented by the Judas Iscariot story should first be considered, namely the psychological, or psychoanalytical, approach. The most thorough treatment from this standpoint is that of Sidney Tarachov, who has applied the method of Theodor Reik, the Freudian analyst and student of mythology. In his article, "Judas the Beloved Executioner",[15] Tarachov builds on certain Gospel indications (noticed by previous scholars too[16]) that Judas, before his defection, was not merely one of the disciples, but an especially favoured one. One such indication is that at the Last Supper, Judas seems to have been reclining next to Jesus. It has even been suggested, prior to Tarachov's work, that Judas Iscariot was in fact the "beloved disciple" mentioned by John; and one writer, C.S. Griffin, has even suggested that Judas Iscariot was the author of the Fourth Gospel (Griffin 1892).

Some authors, studying the lists of disciples to be found in early Church writers, have concluded that originally Judas Iscariot's name stood first in the list, not last as in the Gospels. Tarachov, basing his work on these suggestions, throws new light on the kiss of betrayal at the time of the Jesus's arrest. This kiss, Tarachov suggests, shows an erotic relationship, not necessarily conscious or overt. But even more important is the parallelism in the story between the two men. Judas Iscariot is the mirror-image of Jesus. (Some support for this idea can be seen in the *Golden Legend* account of Judas's childhood, in which he appears as Jesus's brother, with a claim to the same royal inheritance.) Jesus submits to a cruel death decreed by God the Father; Judas, on the contrary, brings death to God the Son. Judas represents the other side of the coin; while Jesus shows submission, Judas shows rebellion. Judas is the bad side of Jesus, evidencing the sadism that underlies Jesus's masochism.

The eroticism of the relationship between Jesus and Judas may be understood from this perspective as a sadistic-masochistic bond in which the deepest erotic act is one of murder and submission to murder. From another aspect, however, it expresses the *identity* between Jesus and Judas. Jesus's act of self-immolation is a way of resolving the ambivalence of the son's relationship with the father; he who (as Judas) wishes to destroy the father, accepts (as Jesus) his own destruction, thereby atoning for the Oedipal death-wishes of all mankind. When Judas destroys Jesus, this is really Jesus destroying himself. That is why a positive relationship of love exists between Jesus and Judas. Of all Jesus's disciples, Judas is the only one who understands what Jesus requires. This idea was perhaps hinted at by Friedrich Hebbel, when he wrote, in his sketches for a play he was planning to write about Jesus, "Judas war der allergläubigste"

138

("Judas was the most faithful disciple of all"), rather than (as has been suggested) that Hebbel had a "Jewish Zealot" scenario in mind for Judas.

We have already seen something similar in the Gnostic Cainite view of Judas as intending to bring about the salvation of mankind (see p. 93), and in the views of the modern Christian thinkers Léon Bloy and Charles Péguy. Even the Jewish writer Bernard Lazare was at one time attracted to the idea of Judas's mission of betrayal (see p. 95). The psychoanalytic version, however, takes the story out of the public realm and makes it relevant to every individual. The salvation offered by Jesus is not through "the body of the Church", as Paul puts it, but an individual salvation obtained through personal relationship to Jesus. This kind of explanation of the Judas story is valuable on its own level; but it does not cope with the communal level on which the Jesus myth functions, as the pattern for a whole society. On the communal level, the story demands an anthropological rather than a psychoanalytic treatment. We have to ask, "To what category of societal myth does the Christ-myth belong, and how does it contribute to the cohesion of Christian society?"

The answer suggested here (and in my previous book, *The Sacred Executioner*) is that the Christ-myth belongs to the range of myths that sprang from rites of human sacrifice, performed to save an existing tribe from impending disaster, or to inaugurate a new tribe (when the dangers of newness invite such disaster). The insights obtained on the psychoanalytic level all have their sociological analogue. In particular, the identity of sacrificial victim and sacrificer expresses the victim's willingness to die, and the common tribal identity of the victim and the community which commands and oversees the sacrifice. But this identity of sacrificing community and willing victim is usually concealed behind what Walter Burckert has called a "comedy of innocence". The community pretends that it did not command the sacrifice at all, and that it came about against their will. A ritual "washing of hands" takes place to express the innocence of the communal authorities, and the executioner, in reality a public servant, is disowned and sent into banishment. On the individual, psychoanalytic level, this disowning of the ritual takes the form of banishing from consciousness the murderous desire that underlies masochistic behaviour. But on the sociological, or anthropological, level, the disowning procedure leads to a societal institution; namely, the setting up of a caste of pariahs who eternally bear the guilt of the sacrifice, so that society can benefit from it without guilt. This pariah caste, in Christian culture, is the Jews, who are singled out to enact an eternal Judas-role. To reduce the Christian myth to a matter of individual psychology intended to cope with personal neurosis would be to miss this societal dimension and overlook the plight of the Jews in Christendom.

The psychoanalytic theory thus has the merit of regarding the Judas story as symbolic rather than as an account of actual historical events. Such an approach is essential in order to understand the development of the story and its power. But the symbolism would be too narrow if confined to the level of individual psychology. An analysis of the myth should provide an explanation of the viability and durability of Christian society, as well as accounting for the cruelty, hatred and oppression that have stained its record. Yet the story of Judas is not wholly symbolic. It has a historical core, and if we can gain further understanding of this, however limited, the distinction between fact and fantasy will become even clearer, and the ability to resist the process by which fantasy turns into cruel reality will be all the greater.

$$\Leftrightarrow 9 \Leftrightarrow$$

Prince Jude: A Reconstruction

We have demonstrated that the story of the betrayal by Judas Iscariot is a legend or myth that grew by accretion, that it fulfilled a need in a societal strategy for the exorcism and transfer of guilt, and that it can be paralleled in the mythologies of other societies in a similar context of guilt for a necessary and atoning murder. We must now ask what we can reasonably suppose to be the substratum of fact out of which this legend has been constructed.

The legendary character of the story should not be thought to prove, in itself, that Judas did not betray Jesus. A historical event may well acquire symbolic meaning and then accumulate imaginative elaboration which carries it far away from its original truth. The story of Jesus itself is a good example of this. That Jesus died by execution on a Roman cross may be a historical fact. But to say that this was an incident in a cosmic war between God and Satan, or that the death of Jesus functioned as a victory over sin and an atonement for mankind—these are mythical re-workings of an incident that, on the historical plane, had to do with the Roman occupation of Judaea and Jewish hopes of messianic liberation. Similarly, a follower of Jesus called Judas Iscariot, in one of the turns and twists of revolutionary politics, may have betrayed his leader to the Romans or to the quisling Jewish priests, and this incident may have gained symbolic significance and received legendary accretions after the development of a mythical cult based on the leader in question.

A strong objection, however, to this interpretation is that evidence exists that, for a period after the death of Jesus, the story of the defection of Judas was unknown. In the writings of Paul and in the Gospel of Peter it appears that after the crucifixion of Jesus, the disciples still constituted a united body of twelve, all of whom

141

mourned their leader's death. This consideration alone would not be enough to constitute more than a surmise. However, taken together with other information found in the Gospels, or in variant Gospel readings found in early manuscripts or translations, or in traditions transmitted in the early Church, the surmise turns into a probability, and a fairly detailed picture can in fact be obtained of the real life and career of Judas Iscariot.

That Judas did not betray Jesus is shown not merely by the evidence of the early Pauline source—not to mention the similar evidence of the fairly late source, the Gospel of Peter—but also by the internal contradictions of the story that is told in the Gospels. For one thing, it is never clear what the betrayal consisted of. Did Judas lead the Roman troops to a place where Jesus was hiding, of which Judas had special knowledge? But only John identifies this as the mechanism of treachery, and the lateness of its appearance seems to point to John's awareness of a puzzling lacuna in the story which he hereby endeavours to fill. Another important aspect of Judas's betrayal is the kiss by which he identifies Jesus to the arresting troops. But are we really supposed to believe that Jesus, after preaching in public in Jerusalem and the Temple for a whole week, was unknown to the authorities? A different explanation that appears to be part of the story is that Jesus, while well known to the authorities, could not be arrested in public because he had the support of the masses (Matthew 26:5; Luke 22:2). Therefore he had to be taken in some quiet spot, and Judas performed the task of discovering the best place for such an arrest and leading the way at the appropriate time. It hardly seems plausible, however, that it would be necessary to suborn a disciple for such a task. Surely the routine police procedure of "tailing" a wanted man, who was making no effort to avoid public areas or escape attempts to locate him by day, would suffice without elaborate arrangements that included bribing an intimate.

It seems, then, that while the narrative urgently required a traitor, the rationale and mechanism of treachery were inserted in a most perfunctory way. The prosaic questions asked above would not bother the audience for which this story was intended. Who asks closely what motives and means were deployed when Set destroyed Osiris, or Loki killed Balder? The important thing is the existence of a victim, and a villain to bring about his destruction, preferably by

142

cunning and treacherous means, inducing, perhaps, some relatively innocent person (Pilate, Hother) to perform the act of destruction itself.

The role of the Jewish masses in the destruction of Jesus is equally riddled with contradictions. At certain moments, they give Jesus their enthusiastic support, as on Palm Sunday, and later when the "chief priests" fear to act because of Jesus's popular support. Yet at the climactic moment, the Jewish masses call for his crucifixion, and bring a curse on their own heads. When popularity is needed for some narrative purpose—to set the scene of Jesus's Triumphal Entry (or in mystery-religion terms, his Hilaria), or to explain the "chief priests'" reluctance to act—then popularity is granted. When the guilt of the Jewish people needs to be stressed, Jesus's popularity disappears. The explanation that Jesus lost popular support because of his arrest and perceived failure makes little sense; Barabbas too had failed and was in prison, but did not thereby lose support; moreover, imprisonment by no means signified failure, since Jesus, a noted miracle-worker, would be confidently expected to break out of prison by supernatural means, as was later said of Peter (Acts 12:6–10). Nor can it be said that Jesus had lost popularity because of his pacifist, self-immolatory conception of messiahship, since this conception (if he had it) was not known to the Jewish masses. They would have been more likely to assume from his Triumphal Entry that he was a messianic claimant in the normal sense; indeed, the Gospels make clear that even Jesus's disciples did not understand Jesus's alleged suicidal intentions at this stage.

The accounts of Judas's treachery thus suggest not so much an historical event but rather an overwhelming narrative necessity, having no need of consistency. The evidence in the sources that the treachery story was unknown up to about AD 60 gives added confirmation to what is already a probable hypothesis. Further evidence, now to be adduced, of Judas's historical identity will add even more credence to the view that Judas did not, in historical reality, betray Jesus.

As we have seen, the most probable source for the name "Iscariot" is the Latin *sicarius*, meaning a Zealot. If this is so, it means that Judas was of Zealot background. We have already considered, and rejected, the possibility that such a background might have provided a motive to Judas for betraying Jesus, either through disillusionment with Jesus's alleged pacifism and quietism, or in order to spur him into exercising his miraculous powers to overcome the Romans. On the contrary, Judas would not have been isolated in Jesus's band of apostles because of his Zealot background, for there were others who had the same background, and the aims of Jesus himself were not too far removed from Zealotism. Indeed, if anything Judas's Zealotism, or previous Zealotism, provides an argument *against* his alleged treachery, and not for it.

As we have noted, the New Testament itself explicitly reveals the Zealot background of one of the disciples; namely, Simon the Zealot (Luke 6:15). Yet there was evidently some embarrassment about this admission, for we find in other Gospels an apparent attempt to disguise the matter by calling this disciple "Simon the Canaanite" (Mark 3:18, Matthew 10:4). This is an interesting example of the usefulness to modern scholars of the fourfold attestation to the story of Jesus in the Gospels, since what one or more editors have decided to suppress may be allowed to slip through by another editor. If (supposing the absence of Luke's testimony) some modern scholar were to conjecture that "Canaanite" in Mark and Matthew is a cover-name for "Zealot" (Hebrew, *qana'i*), he would no doubt be laughed to scorn, and the very idea that one of Jesus's disciples could have been a Zealot or ex-Zealot would have been discounted. Luke's testimony, however, establishes the identity of "Canaanite" and "Zealot" beyond doubt.[1] It also justifies our asking whether any other names, or nicknames, belonging to members of Jesus's band may indicate affiliation with the Zealot movement.

They do indeed. Simon Peter himself is at one point called "Bar-Jonah" (Matthew 16:17). The word *bar* means "son" in Aramaic; so this expression could simply mean "son of Jonah". Yet there are some objections to this interpretation. The expression is not written in Matthew as two words, but as one, *bariona*. Further, we find in the Gospel of John that Peter is called "Simon (son of) John" (John 1:42; 21:15, 16, 17). This could be a confusion for "son of Jonah", but in some early Latin versions, we find *bariona* even in John. So the most likely theory is that this, the earliest form, was later translated into "son of Jonah" and finally corrupted into "son of John"—each step taking us further away from an early sobriquet that had perhaps become puzzling, or even embarrassing. The most challenging question, is why, if Bar-Jonah means "son of Jonah", was *bar* left in the

Aramaic. The usual New Testament way of expressing "son of" is to put the second name in the genitive case; why not here? (We do find names in which the first syllable is *bar-*, e.g. Barabbas,[2] Barnabas, Barjesus, but these are all first names, not patronymics.)

The right conclusion seems to be that Bar-Jonah is not a patronymic but a sobriquet or nickname by which Simon Peter was known. What could such a nickname mean? The answer is that *bariona* means, in Aramaic, "Zealot". The name Abba Sikra, meaning Abba the Zealot (*sicarius*), found in the rabbinic writings, was quoted above to show that Iscariot means Zealot. But the complete phrase about this personage, Abba, runs as follows: "Abba Sikra, chief of the rebels (*resh barionei*)" (b. Gittin, 56a).[3] The singular form of this last word is *bariona*, which means "outlaw, rebel, or freedom-fighter"—in other words, a Zealot. It seems then that Simon Peter, like Judas Iscariot and Simon the Zealot, was previously a member of the Zealot party and retained a nickname to mark this affiliation. This makes three members of the band of twelve with Zealot associations.

But this may not be all. The two brothers John and James, the sons of Zebedee, had the nickname "Boanerges" (Mark 3:17), given to them by Jesus himself. This nickname is preserved only by the earliest Gospel, Mark, and was dropped from the record by later Gospels, a fact that may reveal that some embarrassment was felt in the matter. The name is translated by Mark to mean "sons of thunder", and if, as most scholars believe, the derivation is from the Hebrew *benei ra'ash*, the translation is fairly correct (though this Hebrew phrase would be more accurately rendered, "sons of earthquake"). It hardly seems a suitable name for men of peace, nor is it the kind of name that Jesus would bestow on disciples if he were as pacific as orthodox Christianity insists.[4] The name seems suitable for redoubtable warriors, and suggests that the two brothers had a background of violent resistance to the enemies of their country for which Jesus respected them.

Nicknames often occur among bands of men bound together in comradeship in a cause requiring heroic action and endurance. An instance in Jewish history is the band of the Hasmoneans, who fought against the Seleucid Greeks in the second century BCE, led by the heroic Judas Maccabaeus. The name "Maccabaeus" (Maccabee) is itself a nickname, meaning perhaps "the Hammerer", and all the other members of the band had nicknames too (see Josephus, *Antiquities*, xii. 266). Nicknames seem inappropriate to the usual conception of Jesus's band of disciples as engaged on a pacifist, otherworldly religious cause, but they seem perfectly compatible with the camaraderie of men aiming at the overthrow of an occupying power and the restoration of national liberty.

I am not suggesting that Jesus was himself a Zealot. But he was the leader of a band in constant danger of arrest and execution. This had already happened to John the Baptist, who was also not a Zealot. Jesus was primarily a wonder-worker, whose healing miracles had aroused the hope that he would be able to overcome the Romans not by force of arms, but by a divine event as Zechariah had prophesied. His charisma attracted men who had previously belonged to armed bands engaged in guerrilla resistance. Jesus's aims were the same as theirs: to remove Roman rule, restore the independence of Israel under its royal Davidic house, and institute the world-wide Kingdom of God, in which there would be no more military empires, and the rule of the sword would cease. Even in the Gospels, with all their editorial accretions, it is clear that this is how Jesus's disciples saw him,[5] though he is represented as seeing himself differently, as an other-worldly, self-immolating messiah.

We therefore have a picture of Judas Iscariot, not as an isolated Judaean among a band of Galileans, or even as an isolated Zealot among a band of pacifists, but as not being isolated at all. He is a Galilean among Galileans, a Zealot among Zealots, a wanted man among wanted men, bound to the others by ties of danger and shared hope. But there may be another kind of tie that may have made Judas Iscariot even more at home among the other apostles. We have seen that Jesus's band was similar to that of Judas Maccabaeus, in its hopes, in its companionship and in its use of nicknames. But the Hasmoneans also had a deeper tie, which give their companionship the solidity of rock: they were all brothers. I will now argue that the bond of brotherhood was an important factor in the company of Jesus as well: and that in fact Judas Iscariot was Jesus's brother.

We may begin by recalling that in Luke's list of the twelve disciples there is "Judas the brother of James" as well as Judas Iscariot (Luke 6:16). In Matthew, there is no second Judas, but it has been thought that "Lebbaeus, surnamed Thaddaeus" (Matthew 10:3), is another name for the same person. In Mark, there is again no second Judas, but Thaddaeus is named (Mark 3:18). In John there is no list of twelve disciples, but a second Judas does appear (John 14:22), carefully labelled "Judas, not Iscariot" (though, as we have seen, there are variant readings that would make this "Judas the Zealot"). Thus the picture that emerges from the lists of the apostles in the Gospels is far from clear. Why the name Thaddaeus should have been an alternative for Judas has never been explained. If our knowledge were restricted to Mark and Matthew, we would never know that there was a second Judas at all, since it is only in the light of Luke's testimony that a search was made in Mark and Matthew resulting in the selection of Thaddaeus as the only possible candidate.

Yet it would have been impossible to hide the existence of another Judas, since we know about him from other sources. In the Epistle of Jude, a canonical work of the New Testament, the author is described as the "brother of James". The Greek here does not leave us in any doubt about whether James is the brother or the father of Jude (as in Luke 6:16), since it says "brother" (*adelphos*) explicitly. Indeed, the specificity enables us to settle the doubt in Luke 6:16, and conclude that here too "brother", not "father", is meant. The James referred to in this way can only be the leader of the Jerusalem Church, and we know that this James was the brother of Jesus himself. It therefore follows that Judas was also the brother of Jesus. As it happens, we have a list of Jesus's brothers which includes a Judas. The full list (Mark 6:3, Matthew 13:55) consists of James, Joses, Juda, Simon; sisters are also mentioned, but not named. Whether the Epistle of Jude was actually written by Judas the brother of Jesus is not the point; it testifies to the existence of such a person, and as we shall see, there are other testimonies to this fact.

We now see that at least two people who were brothers of Jesus were prominent in the Jerusalem Church after Jesus's death. If we accept that Luke's "Judas of James" is the same person as the Epistle of Jude's "Judas the brother of James", then one of Jesus's brothers was actually one of the twelve, and took part in the Last Supper. But these data constitute a problem. For what the Gospels tell us is that Jesus's brothers were hostile to him. John tells us that "his brothers had no faith in him" (John 7:5), while Mark tells us that his family thought that he was out of his mind (Mark 3:21). Moreover, we are told elsewhere that Jesus refused to have any special relationship

147

with his mother and brothers, or to allow them any special access to him (Matthew 12:46, Mark 3:31, Luke 8:19).

So far there is a contradiction between the Gospel picture of Jesus's relationship with his brothers and the fact that, after his death, at least two of his brothers were prominent in the Jerusalem Church. This contradiction did not go unnoticed by early Church commentators on the New Testament. The theory developed that James was hostile or indifferent to Jesus during his lifetime, but became converted to faith in him by a special resurrection-experience. As for the apostle Judas, the Luke listing was understood as referring to yet another Judas, called "Judas, the *son* of James" (rather than the "brother of James"); a translation now adopted by the NEB translation, presumably for the very reason that it seems difficult to suppose that one of Jesus's brothers was actually a member of the twelve. This Church interpretation of the matter, however, is full of difficulty. Why should James, after ignoring his brother Jesus during his lifetime, have been elected as leader of the Jerusalem Church, over the heads of all the Apostles, merely because of a late conversion? One would have thought that he would have had a humble position in the Jerusalem Church, as befitting one who was not one of the twelve during Jesus's lifetime. It does seem that the Gospel picture of Jesus's estrangement from his brothers may require adjustment, and possibly reflects some special motivation that should be discounted in the interest of historical truth.

There is one curious passage in the Gospels that is inconsistent with the picture of estrangement between Jesus and his brothers usually presented in the Gospels:

As the Jewish Feast of Tabernacles was close at hand, his brothers said to him, "You should leave this district and go into Judaea, so that your disciples there may see the great things you are doing. Surely no one can hope to be in the public eye if he works in seclusion. If you are really doing such things as these, show yourself to the world." For even his brothers had no faith in him. Jesus said to them, "The right time for me has not yet come ..." (John 7:2–6.)

While this passage does contain a degree of alienation between Jesus and his brothers, it presents them in a light that is startlingly inconsistent with the rest of the Gospel account. Here Jesus's brothers are shown in an advisory role. Instead of ignoring or opposing his mission, they accept it, and, however misguidedly, seek to further it. The significance of the passage becomes even greater if we juxtapose it to another, which we have already considered in other connections. At first sight the passage does not seem to concern Jesus's brothers at all:

> Judas asked him—the other Judas, not Iscariot—"Lord, what can have happened, that you mean to disclose yourself to us alone and not to the world?" (John 14:22.)

The striking coincidence of language between these two passages strongly suggests that they are two versions of the same incident. When we discussed the light the latter passage throws on Judas Iscariot, we concluded that the parenthesis "not Iscariot" should not be taken at face value. But in the present context, we need only to note that an apostle called Judas is presented here as having the very same argument with Jesus that is elsewhere attributed to Jesus's brothers. Thus the passage reinforces a view which holds that Judas the brother of Jesus and Judas the Apostle were indeed the same person.

Further, the impression of Judas the Apostle given in this passage is somewhat unusual. Here we have not a null, faceless Judas, but one who urges Jesus to adopt a policy of activism and self-promotion. There is rather less sense of confrontation than in the parallel passage about the "brothers", but there is still a tension between Judas's question and the allegedly pacifist and quietist stance of Jesus himself. We may be justified in concluding, therefore, that this passage represents a stage in the development of the character of Judas that for some reason was omitted by the other Gospel-writers.

What happened to the activist Judas? The answer, I suggest, is that he developed into the much more evil character of Judas Iscariot. At first, there was only one Judas, who was not an evil character, but simply one of the Apostles. Then, like Peter, and the brothers John and James, he began to be represented as failing to understand Jesus's pacifism and plan for self-immolation. At this stage, Judas Iscariot was simply one of the "uncomprehending disciples", who were introduced into the Pauline Gospels as part of their campaign against the Jerusalem Church. For the Jerusalem Church did not share the Pauline view of Jesus as an otherworldly Messiah. They thought of Jesus as a human deliverer, who would shortly return to complete his mission of liberating Israel, overthrowing the Romans, and inaugurating the age of peace and prosperity for the whole world prophesied in the Hebrew Bible. For the Pauline Church, this attitude was mere incomprehension, and since the difficulty had to be faced that the Jerusalem Church, being led by former disciples of Jesus himself, could claim more authority than the Pauline Church, these disciples had to be denigrated as having misunderstood Jesus from the first. Thus we have the pervasive theme in the Gospels of the "stupidity of the disciples". Part of this "stupidity" is apparently their desire that Jesus should behave like an aspirant to the Jewish throne, and pursue an activist policy to this end. The plea of Judas, here preserved only by John, is part of this demand.

But Judas was soon required for another, more evil, role. Consequently, the stories that made him similar to Peter, John and James in his demand for activism were suppressed, and this role was left to other apostles. Judas, perhaps simply because of his symbolic name, became the required Betrayer, and the previous stage of his character, in which he was not evil but merely stupid and uncomprehending, was preserved only in the anomalous passage of John—who, however, is careful to dissociate this character from Judas Iscariot by the phrase "not Iscariot", since the old uncomprehending Judas is not consistent with the new evil Judas. However, now that Judas Iscariot had become so evil, the traditions about him that survived from his innocuous period became a problem. Mark and Matthew simply ignore this problem, since they include only one Judas in their apostle-lists. But Luke splits Judas into two: the evil Judas and the innocuous "brother of James". The name Iscariot is allotted to the evil Judas. From now on, there are two Judases.

Part of this evolution is the suppression of historical facts such as the apostles' family relationships with Jesus. It becomes inconvenient to the Pauline Church to admit that any of the apostles were Jesus's brothers. This is partly because of the need to portray Jesus as isolated from his Jewish surroundings. Jesus has to be shown as a visitant from outer space, rather than as a Jew with normal family ties: consequently, he shows indifference to his mother and brothers, regarding them as having no special kinship with him. Further, the developing myth of Mary's virginity makes it awkward to admit that Jesus had brothers. Mary would have had to have sexual relations with Joseph after the birth of Jesus, and this was felt to be inconsistent with the dignity of one whose first child was conceived through the Holy Spirit. Consequently a doctrine developed of the "perpetual virginity" of Mary. Even though the New Testament still retained evidence that Jesus had brothers, this is reduced to a minimum, and is suppressed completely as far as the apostles were concerned. The Church endeavoured to nullify what evidence remained in the New Testament by the theory that these brothers were not really brothers in the full sense. According to the Eastern Church, they were half-brothers, being the children of Joseph by a former marriage. According to the Western Church, they were cousins.[6]

Our conclusion, then, is that there were in fact relations of brotherhood between Jesus and at least some of his apostles. The pattern of contradictions in the Gospel remarks about Jesus and his brothers can be explained in evolutionary fashion.

In the earliest phase (corresponding with historical reality), Jesus and his brothers had a loving relationship, in which the brothers supported Jesus's claim to messiahship and gave him friendly advice. This explains why John 7 preserves a picture of co-operation between Jesus and his brothers, though this friendly relation is already beginning to sour. This support for Jesus in his lifetime accounts for the prominence of Jesus's brothers in the movement after his death, without the need for explanations based on sudden late conversions, as in Church tradition. In this phase, Jesus's brothers James and Judas were actually included in the number of his twelve Apostles.

In the second phase, Jesus's brothers began to be represented as hostile to his more "spiritual" aims—specifically his intention to abandon any thought of political success and to die on the cross as an atoning sacrifice. Representative of this phase is the episode in John 14 where Judas ("not Iscariot") criticizes Jesus for failing to "show himself to the world" as a serious claimant of political power. Judas is not represented here as Jesus's brother, but the parallel passage in John 7—based, as we have seen, on the same incident—reveals that the criticism in question derived from Jesus's brothers. We can see, therefore, that between the redaction of John 7 and that of John 14 a trend has developed to make Judas into the leader of the brothers' dissent against Jesus's "spiritual" aims.

In the third phase, this role of anti-spiritual leader has passed to Peter, since Judas is now reserved for a more diabolical part, and a distinction is introduced between Judas the Apostle and Judas Iscariot, the Betrayer. Peter thus becomes the representative of the Jerusalem Church in its rejection of Pauline doctrine (though Acts portrays his gradual redemption and reconciliation with Paul). At this stage, the memory that Jesus was supported by his brothers in his lifetime is suppressed, mainly because the growing status of Jesus as a divine, virgin-born figure is inconsistent with his having brothers at all. Only Mark 6:3 and Matthew 13:55 carelessly fail to suppress mention of their names.

Thus Judas Iscariot did not suddenly spring into existence as the betrayer of Jesus, but developed through several phases. First, he was a brother of Jesus and an apostle who criticized Jesus for being too unworldly; then he became the leader of this opposition within the movement. Then he lost his status as Jesus's brother; and finally he was differentiated from the blameless Apostle, also called Judas, by being given the sobriquet Iscariot (a name that belonged to Judas from the first, but was now reserved only for the "evil" Judas). In other words, there was originally only one Judas, who was split into two, the good and the bad. The real Judas did not oppose Jesus at all. He did not criticize Jesus for lacking political aims, because the historical Jesus did have political aims, intent on becoming the King of Israel. The episode in which Judas criticizes Jesus on these lines was inserted into the Gospels as part of the campaign by Pauline Christianity against the Jerusalem Church, which retained the political aims of Jesus himself, and hoped for his return and ascension of the Jewish throne in Jerusalem.

The above considerations solve the problem of why it was James, and not Peter, who became leader of the Jerusalem Church after Jesus's death. Since it was Jesus's aim to become the Jewish King, his movement was political and monarchical as well as religious. The Jerusalem Church was not in fact a Church at all in the usual sense, but a messianic, political movement which regarded Jesus as the rightful King, who would soon return (having already been brought back to life by a miracle of God). Meanwhile, the leader's office was assumed by James, his nearest relative.[7] James was thus not Bishop of Jerusalem, but Prince Regent, occupying the Pretender's throne until Jesus's return. This also explains why Peter (later regarded as the first Pope) did not become leader after Jesus's death. When Jesus gave Peter the title "Rock" (Matthew 16:18), and said, "I will give unto thee the keys of the kingdom," he was not making him Pope, as the Church later thought. If so, he would undoubtedly have been the leader of the Jerusalem "Church" rather than James. Jesus, as Jewish parallels show,[8] was making Peter his Chief Minister, and the "kingdom" in question was not the celestial one of Heaven but the kingdom of Israel. Therefore, when Jesus died, his successor was not his Chief Minister, but his eldest brother, whom Peter continued to serve in the same capacity.[9] Further, the Prince Regent, James, was probably not a late adherent of Jesus converted after the Crucifixion, as the Gospels indicate. He had previously been one of the twelve, and he appears in the Gospel lists, in somewhat disguised form, as "James (son of) Alphaeus". The probability is increased by a surviving fragment of the Jewish-Christian "Gospel of the Hebrews" in which James the brother of Jesus is said to have been present at the Last Supper.

The two Judases, then, are one Judas. He was the brother of Jesus, and possibly the author of the Epistle of Jude. This means further that Judas was regarded in Jesus's movement as a royal personage, a prince of the House of David. Judas Iscariot the Betrayer of Jesus never existed. He was a fictional character used to displace a real person of the same name who was not only loyal to Jesus, but was an honoured member of the Jerusalem Church and the possible author of a canonical work revered by Christians to this day.

What do we know about this Prince Judas? We can begin by noting that before he joined the Jesus movement, Judas had been a member of the Zealot movement, as his nickname "Iscariot" shows. Indeed, in one variant text he is plainly called Judas the Zealot, supposedly a reference to the "other" Judas. As we saw in the case of Simon the Zealot and Simon Peter Bariona, there was nothing surprising in such a background. The Zealots were a deeply religious movement, dedicated to liberating the Holy Land from the militaristic Roman idolaters. The Zealots, like both the biblical Gideon and the post-biblical Hasmoneans, believed they had only to show faith and the courage to fight, and God would help them. Jesus had the same outlook, as is shown in the extraordinary scene where he equips his disciples with swords (Luke 22:36). This occurs at the climactic moment of his life, when he goes with his disciples to the Mount of Olives to pray for the miracle that was prophesied to happen there (see Zechariah 14:4).[10] Jesus's alleged pacifism, recorded in the Gospels, is inconsistent with this incident of the swords, which has been preserved only by Luke. Such an incident, flatly contradicting the general *tendenz* of the Gospel narrative, must be a survival from an earlier tradition, and is therefore highly likely to be accurate historically. If so, the difference between Jesus and the Zealots was simply that Jesus relied more on God. "Two swords", Jesus says in Luke 22:38, would be enough to defeat the Romans. His faith in his own destiny as Messiah was enough to make the military preparations of the Zealots unnecessary in his eyes. But he still knew that a token show of force would be needed on the part of his followers. On this view, there was no great change in ideology involved in moving from the Zealots to Jesus's messianic movement. It is therefore understandable that Jesus's disciples retained their Zealot nicknames, which, on the orthodox understanding of Jesus's ideology, is very difficult to explain.

We must now ask what else is known about the life of Judas, or Jude, the apostle and brother of Jesus, who was also, if our argument is correct, no other than Judas Iscariot. There is less information than we would like about this apostle; indeed, the sparseness is such that, at some later time, he acquired the appellation "Jude the Obscure". Even the embroidery of legend is mostly lacking in this case.[11] Yet the amount of information that can be gleaned from various sources is not entirely negligible.

It has been argued above that the status of Judas in the Jerusalem "Church" was that of a Prince. This is indirectly confirmed in Paul's reference to "the brothers of the Lord" as a group having special authority, separate from that of the "apostles" (I Corinthians 9:5). There is also some interesting direct confirmation in a document of the early third century, the *Letter to Aristides* of Julius Africanus, preserved by Eusebius (*HE* 1:7:14). He writes about the relatives of Jesus that they travelled through Palestine, and that everywhere they went, their main message was to explain their own genealogy:

From the villages of Nazareth and Kokhaba they travelled around the rest of the land and interpreted the genealogy they had and from the Book of Days as far as they could trace it.

154

It would be hard to understand the above tradition, which comes from a very early Palestinian source,[12] on the usual interpretation of the concerns of the Jerusalem "Church". Why should Jesus's family travel around explaining their family tree? Surely such personal matters should have taken second place to teaching about the salvation to be secured through belief in the sacrificial death of Jesus? But in fact, the family tree was the first consideration. For what was being preached was the messianic royal claim of Jesus, and his imminent return to assume the throne of Israel. By proving their own Davidic descent, the relatives of Jesus were proving *him* to be the promised Messiah, in the Jewish, and not the Pauline, sense of the word. Though the followers of Jesus regarded him as King and his family as princes, this was not the general belief of the Jewish people, who regarded Jesus's claims as have been refuted by his death. Thus a campaign was necessary to re-assert Jesus's claim to royalty.

A strong confirmation of the royalist orientation of the Jerusalem Church is the fact that after the death of James, the brother of Jesus, in 62 CE, the next leader to be appointed was another relative of Jesus. Symeon the son of Cleopas (or Clopas), was Jesus's first cousin. It should be noted that the death of James came about through the action of Ananus, the Sadducee, pro-Roman High Priest, for political, not religious reasons. This is shown by the fact that the Pharisees were outraged by the execution, and protested about it (Josephus, *Antiquities*, xx. 200–201). The incident sheds light on the execution of Jesus himself, who, contrary to later Church teaching, fell foul of the political, not the religious, authorities. (Compare the trials of both Peter and Paul, who were saved from the High Priest by the Pharisee members of the Sanhedrin.) Later, Symeon was himself executed, on the charge (according to Hegesippus) of "being of the house of David and a Christian". This charge is revealing, for it shows that claim to Davidic descent, rather than heretical views, was the deciding factor; such a claim constituted a *prima facie* presumption of sedition against Rome and the quislings led by the High Priest.

But what is particularly interesting, for our purposes, is that Symeon's successor as leader of the Jerusalem "Church" was no other than "Judas of James", according to *Apostolic Constitutions* 7:46. The common view of later commentators, such as Ephraem, was that he was Judas, the brother of Jesus, and author of the Epistle

155

of Jude. If this is true, then Judas was actually the third "Bishop" (or more correctly Vice-Regent) of the Jerusalem "Church". Such an appointment is only what one would expect, given the royalist position of the group. What better candidate for leadership, pending the return of King Jesus, than his brother, Prince Judas Iscariot?

This attractive version of events is open to certain objections, however, although the first, a chronological objection, is perhaps not very formidable. We are told (also by Hegesippus) that Symeon was ,120 years old at the time of his martyrdom. Some time before, in the reign of Domitian, the "grandsons of Jude" were arrested on a charge of being descendants of David, but were released (Eusebius, *Hist.* 3:19). The execution of Symeon, we are told, took place in the later reign of Trajan (99–117). It seems from Hegesippus (as quoted by Eusebius) that only the "grandsons of Jude" were still alive at this time, not Jude himself. (However, another source, Epiphanius Monachus, speaks of the "sons of Jude", not his grandsons, as living at this time). But the age of Symeon is obviously exaggerated, in order to link him with figures like Moses, Hillel, Johanan ben Zakkai and Akiba, all supposed to have died at the same advanced age. In order to lend colour to this account, the execution of Symeon was no doubt postponed till the reign of Trajan. If it took place about 40 years earlier, at the more credible age of 80, it would have been possible for Judas to succeed him.

A stronger objection is that Eusebius, in his lists of Bishops of the Jerusalem Church, calls the third Bishop Justus, not Judas. On the other hand, in the list given by Epiphanius, the third Bishop is again Judas. The evidence is thus somewhat contradictory, though it is quite possible that Justus, a Roman name, is simply a convenient equivalent for Judas, just as Jason, a Greek name, was often used for Joshua. We may conclude that it is at least possible that the third Bishop was Judas the brother of Jesus, as many early commentators thought. It is a little difficult to explain why Judas was overlooked in favour of the more distant relative Symeon as second Bishop. But there may be good reasons for this: for example, at the time of the execution of James, Judas may have been a wanted man, who had to remain in hiding.

The story given by Hegesippus (Eusebius, *Hist.* 3:19:1–3:20:7) of the prosecution of the grandsons (or sons) of Jude "as being of the family of David" shows again that the messianic royal claim was at the centre of the programme of the Jerusalem "Church". The grand-sons are shown as pleading that Christ's kingdom was "not earthly", and it is said that the emperor Domitian accepted this plea and acquitted them. But this aspect of the story (as Bauckham argues) is probably unhistorical, forming part of the Christian propaganda of a later time, directed to proving the non-political nature of Christianity. At any rate, the story shows again that Jude was regarded as belonging to a royal family.

Further confirmation may be found in the story, also quoted by Eusebius from Hegesippus (*Hist.* 3:12), that "Vespasian, after the taking of Jerusalem, gave orders that all the members of the family of David should be sought out, so that none of the royal tribe might be left among the Jews". This is told in a context of persecution of the family of Jesus.[13]

No authentic tradition exists about the death of Judas. We are told by Hegesippus that his grandsons (or sons) made their living as farmers by the toil of their hands. It is probable, therefore, that Jude himself, despite his princely status, did the same. He was not the first or last member of a royal family who had to nurse his hopes in a humble state of life; but his high status and the reverence accorded to him in the Jewish-Christian community must have given him solace. The late legends about the martyrdom of Saint Jude the Apostle have no historical value. A work called "The Passion of Simon and Jude", reckoned among the New Testament Apocrypha, describes the martyrdom of Jude, together with that of Simon the Zealot, in Persia. Consequently, Saint Jude shares a feast-day with Saint Simon in the Catholic Church. Another legend, however, claims that Jude suffered martyrdom in Syria, while yet another claims it for Armenia.

One aspect of Judas's life is subject to conjecture and argument. Was he in fact the author of the Epistle attributed to him in the New Testament? Most scholars have rejected this ascription, but a recently published book by Richard Bauckham has argued persuasively for its authenticity.[14] If this is correct, then Prince Judas was at the least a man of learning and eloquence.

The later history of the Jerusalem Church is shrouded in mystery. According to a Church legend, the whole Jerusalem Church, warned by a prophecy, left Jerusalem shortly before the outbreak of the Jewish War in 66 CE and settled in Pella, in Transjordania, thus avoiding the horrors of the war. This would have been during the leadership of Simeon Cleopas. Modern scholars, however, have shown that this legend is unhistorical.[15] It was devised at a later period in order to provide an appearance of continuity for the Gentile Church of Jerusalem which was set up in 135 after the Hadrianic war. Since many members of this Gentile Church came from Pella, it was considered necessary to provide a link between this city and the Jerusalem Church of earlier times. In historical fact, the Jewish-Christians of the Jerusalem Church remained in Jerusalem throughout the Jewish War (66–73) and shared in the fight against Rome and in the disaster. After this, the Jerusalem Church no longer existed in the capital, and evidently its strength was shattered, since it ceased to have central importance for the churches of the outside world. Thus, Judas, the third leader, presided over a much depleted and scattered community. Some Jewish Christians left Palestine after the Jewish War, and settled in Beroea (now called Aleppo) in Syria, while others lived in Damascus. They began to be known as Ebionites, from the Hebrew word *ebyon*, meaning "poor", probably because of their stricken state. After the Hadrianic War, they formed such a weak minority that they lost all respect among the Gentile Christians, who condemned their observance of Jewish law as heretical.

Eusebius gives his complete list of the leaders of the Jerusalem Church before 135 as: James, Symeon, Justus, Zacchaeus, Tobias, Benjamin, John, Matthias, Philip, Seneca, Justus, Levi, Ephres, Joseph and Judas. (Since Eusebius puts the death of Symeon at 106, a date criticized above, he has to crowd thirteen leaders into a space of 29 years.) These, says Eusebius, were all observant Jews, and the last fourteen of them are supposed to have officiated in Pella. In 135, the first Gentile leader of the Jerusalem Church, Marcus, was appointed. The historical fact is probably that the Jewish leaders officiated at various centres in Judaea or Galilee, and the appointment of Marcus represented the setting-up of a new Gentile-Pauline Church in Jerusalem with no connection with the earlier Jewish Jerusalem Church. We have no information about the successors of Judas (whom Eusebius calls Justus) apart from their names. It would be interesting to know whether they all belonged to the family of Jesus, but no source has anything to say about this.

The future of Christianity lay with the Pauline Gentile Church, which turned Jesus into a deity, and gave Judas the role of archetypal traitor. The Christians of the Jerusalem Church, who followed the teaching of Jesus himself and his immediate disciples (including his brothers), became a persecuted minority, and eventually disappeared, either by returning to Judaism or, in some cases, joining the Pauline Church. Traces of them can still be discerned as late as the tenth century, but as an organized body they did not last longer than the fifth. Their writings were mostly suppressed by the Church, but some fragments of them are still extant.[16]

The Judas Myth

The arguments of the last chapter constitute a considerable chain of circumstantial evidence. It may be concluded with a very high degree of probability that there was no defection of Judas in historical fact. This being so, we are left with a character, Judas Iscariot, about whom we have only mythical data. At the same time, we have *another* Judas, who is not called Iscariot, but is also an apostle; whose name is suppressed from some of the lists but retained in others; who is a null character in some accounts, but shows militant features in others; who appears as Jesus's brother in some accounts, but not in others; who has a blameless and loyal career as a follower of Jesus; who may even have eventually become the elected leader of the Jesus movement. It seems probable that this is the real Judas Iscariot, whose sobriquet was given to the mythical Judas who was split off from him; who could not be entirely suppressed from the record because traditions persisted about his loyalty and prominence in the early Church; and who therefore survives in the background as "Jude the Obscure", while the foreground is occupied by the garish, nightmare figure projected over him in the Pauline Church (though after the death of Paul himself).

In order to arrive at this result it has been necessary to engage in detective work. Particular attention has been paid to anomalous data—details of the Gospel narrative, whether in the generally accepted text or in manuscript variations, that stand out in contradiction to the usual trend of the narrative. Some may complain this process is "selective", and builds up too much on too little. Why highlight some details as more significant than others? The same criticism might be directed against any detective, who would explain that it is the anomalous detail that provides the clue. Similarly, Freud showed in his *Psychopathology of Everyday Life* that it is not in

160

ordinary conversation that we learn a person's inner feelings, but in his slips of the tongue. In our analysis of the New Testament, it is the Freudian slip—the inadvertent lapses of the various authors—that has provided the significant clue to the hidden historical truth. These discordant particulars could not have been added at a late stage, since they contradict the prevailing policy of the final editor: they must have been left over inadvertently from an earlier stage. Some of the examples we have already noted are the passage in Luke in which Jesus checks that his disciples are equipped with swords (contradicting the general picture of Jesus's pacifism); the passage in John that reveals that Jesus's brothers took an interest in his career and gave him advice (contradicting the picture of their total hostility); and the evidence from certain manuscripts that there was a Judas called Judas the Zealot (a detail suppressed in the main textual tradition). This method has been applied to ancient historical writings since their scientific study began, but was applied much later to the New Testament because of its canonical status. The method involves the abandonment of complicated harmonizing interpretations, intended to preserve Scripture from the charge of self-contradiction. Instead it adopts simple explanations based on the acceptance of the fact that real contradictions exist in the texts, which developed by a process of accretion and editing.

Nevertheless, the view that Judas Iscariot and Judas the Apostle were historically the same person remains a hypothesis. It is offered as a probable solution to the manifest difficulties of the Judas Iscariot story as it appears in the New Testament. The theory has advantages over other views about Judas, but it does not have the urgency and importance of the main argument, which concerns the tragic consequences of the Judas myth. That the Judas myth has functioned, and still functions, as a vehicle of antisemitism is not a theory but an incontrovertible fact.

Every time the word "Judas" is used to mean "traitor"—that is, when the accusation of treachery is being put forward with particular venom—the antisemitic conviction latent in the expression is made manifest. To call someone a Judas is to say, "You are as bad as the Jews when they betrayed Jesus." Jewish evil is thus established as a universal benchmark for the ages. The expression is antisemitic, therefore, even when used to characterize a non-Jew in a totally non-Jewish context. For throughout history, Judas has not been

161

regarded merely as an individual who betrayed Jesus. He has been regarded, always and from the beginning, as the eponymous representative of the Jewish people as a whole.

If the opprobrious use of a word such as "nigger" has been abandoned by all decent people, what should be done about the Judas myth, and the use of the word Judas? A word that has been the focus not only of contempt, but of hatred and violent oppression should be outlawed, not by legislative action, but by the common consent of people of good will. The word Judas expresses prejudice in a more subtle, subliminal way than "nigger", or "kike". It is possible for a person to use the word without being consciously aware of what gives this word its special charge of loathing. But it is not sufficient simply to eschew conscious antisemitism. It is necessary to extend conscious awareness, and if possible to gain control of the unconscious and irrational processes by which a culture can propagate hatred.

Yet, unfortunately, it is not enough merely to attack the Judas myth in isolation. For the story is part of a larger myth, which gives to Jews an archetypal role as being people of the Devil. The Christian myth itself has made the Jews into the pariah people of Western civilization. It is here that the technique of bringing unconscious processes to consciousness is particularly required. For many, perhaps most, people today believe themselves to have outgrown the Christian myth. But it is just at this point in the development of culture, when a myth is renounced on the conscious level, that it can take hold even more strongly on the unconscious level.

Jung has familiarized us with the concept of archetypes: symbolic entities, such as the Serpent, or the Eye of God, appearing often in dreams, and acting as basic constituents and parameters of the unconscious mind. Such archetypes, in Jung's theory, are not socially conditioned, but are hereditary, being part of the collective unconscious. Here, however, we are concerned with a socially formed archetype that arises out of a particular society's foundation-myth, and has been deeply imprinted by centuries of repeated indoctrination, much of it inarticulate, being conveyed by tone of voice, gesture and eye, rather than by explicit education.[1] Such an archetype is very difficult to dislodge, but not impossible. What has been created by social conditioning can be eradicated by the same means, though quick results are not to be expected. Harmful unconscious

162

fantasies can be exorcized by techniques bringing them into consciousness. In the case of an individual, this may mean the use of hypnotism or free association. In the case of a society, the chief instrument for transforming the unconscious into the conscious is education in the form of books, articles and public discussion. Once the diagnosis receives some measure of general acceptance by formers of opinion, attention can be turned to the institutions which continually reinforce the archetype, ensuring its survival from generation to generation. Modern Christians, shocked by the Holocaust, and aware at last that Christian teaching was mainly responsible, often make strenuous efforts to counter the effects of the Christian myth by interpreting it in innocuous ways, and importing such interpretations or minor bowdlerizations into school textbooks. This kind of effort is merely cosmetic. It is the sheer power of the myth itself, moulding the minds of children too young to be affected by well-meaning interpretations, that implants the archetype of the Jew for life. Only a solution that prevents this imprinting of infants can work on a large scale. In the case of post-Christians, who receive no religious education, but imbibe the archetype just as effectively through literature, casual conversation or the bias of the media, a more complicated process of re-education is necessary, beginning with the difficult realization that a problem exists.

Throughout the Middle Ages, the Jews were regarded as the agents of an unexpungeable evil. The Passion Plays instilled a loathing and contempt for Jews that finally acquired the force of instinct. The influence of Church art, and the constant antisemitic preaching of the lower clergy—never effectively restrained by higher religious authorities—made the common people, who often in earlier centuries had resisted antisemitic pressure, into fully indoctrinated and unthinking Jew-haters. The Reformation made little difference, as Luther was even more virulently antisemitic than his Catholic forerunners. In his pamphlet *Against the Jews and their Lies*, he called the Jews "venomous serpents, desperate enemies of the Lord", and advocated that their synagogues should be burned, and that they should be expelled from Christian lands. In a later pamphlet, *Shem Hamephoras*, he included the inevitable reference to Judas Iscariot, elaborating it in his own inimitable way: "Cursed *goy* that I am, I cannot understand how they manage to be so skilful, unless I think that when Judas Iscariot hanged himself, his guts burst and emptied. Perhaps the Jews sent their servants with plates of silver and pots of gold to gather up Judas's piss with the other treasures, and then they ate and drank his offal, and thereby acquired eyes so piercing that they discover in the Scriptures commentaries that neither Matthew nor Isaiah himself found there, not to mention the rest of us cursed *goyim*." It is not surprising that Luther was Hitler's favourite reading.

The Enlightenment ostensibly revolutionized the position of the Jews in Europe. They were gradually, and after many false starts, accepted into Western society. They were allowed into the professions, instead of being channelled into money-lending and then vilified as money-lenders. They were finally even given citizenship, allowed to vote and to attain positions of leadership. Many Jews accepted these developments with the highest enthusiasm. They jettisoned their religious beliefs and adopted current rationalist systems. They became fervent citizens of the nations to which they had been admitted, embracing the national culture. There was a pathetic willingness among Jews to believe that the Age of Reason had arrived and that the irrational, or mythic, element in social life was a thing of the past.

But this new integration of Jews into Western society led to explosions of antisemitism that were, if anything, worse than before. This was not because there were any new compelling proofs of Jewish evil; although such proofs were offered. It was because underneath the veneer of enlightenment, the old, deeply instilled myth continued to assert that the Jews were not like other human beings. Few "enlightened" antisemites, however, were able to admit that their hatred for the Jews arose from a remote theological doctrine. So they invented new scenarios in which the Jews continued to act as agents of the Devil, and all the other props and scenery of the medieval Passion Play were given modern analogues. Right-wing antisemites substituted a drama based on nationalism, in which the Jews were eternal aliens and archetypal traitors, working like rats or voracious insects to undermine the fabric of the holy nation; at its most extreme, this became a fascist doctrine in which the Jews were bacilli poisoning the blood-stream of the master race. Indeed, beyond deploying the whole medieval and Reformation armoury of antisemitic accusations, even re-creating medieval antisemitic art and caricature, the Nazis reinstated the medieval doctrine

164

of the Millennium, an apocalyptic fantasy in which the Jews, led by the Antichrist, would be annihilated, to the last man, woman and child, by a Christian army led by the risen Christ himself, who would then reign for a thousand years. Hitler's "thousand-year Reich" was a plain echo of millenarian slogans, and he himself was a modern racialist version of the Triumphant Christ.

The Left developed an equally archaic scenario. Karl Marx, a Jew by descent but a Christian by baptism and upbringing, was an antisemite, and in his economic theory of politics and history, the Jews were the arch-representatives of a capitalist Devil. Indeed, according to Marx, Judaism was merely capitalism in a pseudo-theological form, and ought to be called "Hucksterism". Further, the Communist millennium would result in the "disappearance" of the Jews. Even when Communism shed its early form of internationalism, when Lenin permitted nationalistic aspirations within the Soviet Union, Jewish nationalism was still not allowed because the Jews were not a nation in Communist theory, but only an economic class scheduled for extinction. This form of antisemitism became endemic among today's New Left, for whom the Jews and Zionism are the supreme representatives of Western imperialism, capitalism and Third World exploitation. Ironically, however, the Jews were also elected by the Right as being archetypal Communists, inspiring the Russian Revolution and seeking the downfall of all established governments and especially of capitalism. Every political system that has a concept of an active principle of evil in the world elects the Jews for the diabolic role. The resultant roles ascribed to the Jews may be contradictory, but they are all consistent in one thing: they continue the diabolization of the Jews contained in the Christian myth.[2]

These facts illustrate that myths do not die as easily as dogmas. Both Nazis and Communists considered themselves to have outgrown Christianity, but the furniture of their minds remained stubbornly Christian. The myth upon which a religion is based may be more deeply influential than its creeds. It is the myth that determines the temper of the culture to which the religion gives rise, and this temper may survive the death of belief in the creeds by many generations. Bertrand Russell once said, "There is a great difference between a Catholic atheist and a Protestant atheist." This is very true, and I would say that there is an even greater difference between

165

a Christian atheist and a Jewish one. For there is one thing that is likely not to differ between Catholic and Protestant atheists: they will retain a predisposition to antisemitism. Perhaps it is sufficient proof to note that although both fascism and communism have been defeated in this century, antisemitism, which coexisted easily with both, continues to thrive. Recent developments in Eastern Europe prove once more how resistant to change antisemitism is. The removal of Communist restraints on religion have brought out varieties of antisemitism that have retained their full paranoid flavour from Tsarist days. In Poland the Jews continue to be blamed for economic ills in spite of the fact that there is hardly a Jew left in the country.

A Christian, however, knows that he is influenced by his beliefs, including the dogmas of his myth. The difficulty with secular antisemitism is that the post-Christian prides himself on being a rationalist, and must first overcome this very typical modern intellectual pride in order to find out how paranoid he really is. Further, the post-Christian antisemite is peculiarly dangerous to the Jews because of his optimism. He really thinks that he can make the world *Judenrein*.[3] Christians, on the whole, do not think this, because they believe in the necessity of the Devil, at least until the millennium. Only when in the grip of millenarian fervour do Christians think of Satan and his Jewish henchmen as dispensable.

Some post-Christians are not millenarians, and may inherit everyday Christian (or Judaeo-Christian) traditions of charity and social ethics, as in the case of the Utilitarians, such as Bentham and John Stuart Mill. But post-Christians with a more radical political philosophy tend to be influenced mainly by Christian millenarian patterns. Consequently, post-Christians are prone to reproduce a millenarian scheme in which the Jews are scheduled for annihilation.

Exorcizing Judas from the Western mind will therefore not suffice, though a resolution not to use the word Judas in its pejorative sense would certainly be a positive development. The real and only permanent solution to the problem of antisemitism is to dismantle the Pauline Christian myth of atonement. When Jesus is revered as a teacher, rather than worshipped as a sacrifice—when he is valued for his life and deeds, and not for his death and mythic resurrection—antisemitism will cease. For then the Jews will no longer have to function as his executioners and be held indispensable for salvation—and hated all the more for that. The shock of the Holocaust has made many Christians re-appraise Christian doctrine. Catholic teaching, since Vatican Council II's *Declaration on the Relation of the Church to Non-Christian Religions* (or *Nostra Aetate*) of 1965, has changed considerably, though as yet without any recognition that antisemitism is caused by the central Christian myth rather than by "popular misinterpretations" of it. The recent unregenerately antisemitic utterances of Cardinal Glemp were sharply disciplined by the Pope, and the Cardinal was forced to retract. Some Christians have even come to realize that the Christian atonement myth is deeply flawed; the publication of *The Myth of God Incarnate* (ed. John Hick, London, 1977) was a milestone in this respect. Christians, however slowly, are on the move; the deeper problem may be to dissolve post-Christian antisemitism, with its unconscious absorption of the most extreme elements of the Christian myth.

One response obstructs progress: the idealization of the Pauline Christian myth in its own mythological terms. Many people are quite prepared to admit that there is no historical truth in the atoning aspect of the events related in the New Testament; but they retain respect for it as the expression of a "beautiful myth". This kind of post-mythological respect may take two forms. One is typified by Joseph Campbell; the adoration of myth as the crystallization of mystic truths, the deliverance of the collective unconscious which cannot lie. The other is typified by Frank Kermode; the reverence for myth as pure story, taking shape with the inevitability of art. Both these reactions, the mystical and the aesthetic, are a kind of revival of fundamentalism on the non-literal plane (see p. 17). The myth cannot be criticized any more than when it was taken as literal truth, because it is regarded as a perfect expression of mysticism (Campbell) or literary art (Kermode). In this way, the evil in the myth is overlooked. Myth must be criticized, however, not on the grounds of historical fact, but on the grounds of its moral value and effects. Certainly, every society is based upon a myth; but no society is an ultimate value in itself. Any society can and must be criticized, if its stability and even its beauty are based on the scapegoating and suffering of a pariah class.

One welcome result of the criticism and dismantling of the Christian myth of atonement will be the rehabilitation of Judas Iscariot.

Whether he was identical with Jude the Apostle, as I have argued, or was a separate apostle, he has been saddled with a degrading myth that is an insult to his loyalty and integrity and the liberating mission on which he embarked in support of his martyred leader, Jesus. And the rehabilitation of Judas Iscariot too will have its effect: the restoration of honour to the name Judas, and to the people of Judah who still bear this name.

Notes

CHAPTER ONE

1 The lack of a death-account of Judas in Luke cannot be regarded as a gap, since Luke and Acts are by the same author.
2 In Nikos Kazantzakis's *The Last Temptation of Christ*, Judas is portrayed as a zealot or political realist who is nevertheless the closest thing Jesus has to a friend or equal. I do not wish to deny the value (literary or historical) of such a portrayal, though I consider that, historically speaking, it has the grave defect of taking for granted that Jesus himself was neither a zealot nor a political realist, and, morally speaking, that the quietism and other-worldliness attributed to Jesus was morally superior to the this-worldly messianic Utopianism of Judaism. The main point, however, is that it is wrong to think that such a portrayal is a valid interpretation of the Gospel narrative itself, which is a myth about good and evil, and neither a realistic novel nor a historical treatise.
3 Shakespeare's Shylock is in the popular tradition of the medieval "Jew's Beautiful Daughter" stories, in which a miserly Jew is robbed of both his treasure and his daughter by a young Christian. See Maccoby, "The Figure of Shylock" (1970) and "The Delectable Daughter" (1970). Scott's Isaac, in *Ivanhoe* (though somewhat more sympathetic) is in the same tradition. Dickens's Fagin is a compendium of Jewish stereotypes, including miserliness. The Oxford English Dictionary includes the term "grasping" in its list of the colloquial meanings of "Jewish".
4 Mishnah, Gittin, 5:8.
5 Oddly enough, the Japanese, who uncritically accepted much of the antisemitic mythology of their Nazi allies, have regarded this mythical financial skill with *admiration*.
6 "Moreover, for the two characteristic occupations of the Middle Ages—fighting and building—Jewish aid was at this time [eleventh to thirteenth centuries] indispensable. The Crusades, fatal as they were to

the Jews, would not have been possible on the same vast scale but for the capital which they had to provide. Even ecclesiastical foundations had recourse to them when any important undertaking was contemplated: thus Aaron of Lincoln, the great Anglo–Jewish financier of the twelfth century, is thought to have assisted in the construction of no less than nine of the Cistercian monasteries of England, as well as of the great Abbey of St. Albans and even Lincoln Minster." (Roth, 1943, p. 231.)

7 Frazer (1957), vol. 2, pp. 795–874.

8 See Brandon (1967), pp. 155–156.

9 The annual Bouphonia (Bull-slaying Feast) at Athens represented the sacrificial slaying of Zeus in the form of a bull. The custom was that the priests, after sacrificing the bull, fled from the altar in mock panic, crying out a formula absolving them from the guilt of having slain the god. Afterwards, in a special chamber of the temple, a trial was held, in which the blame for the slaying was attributed to the knife that slit the bull's throat. The knife, having been found guilty, was punished by being thrown into a river. See Yerkes (1953), pp. 68–74.

10 This is an example of what Walter Burkert calls "the comedy of innocence", which, he argues, forms part of all Greek sacrifice. See Burkert (1983).

11 Christians usually deny that they have shifted responsibility for the Crucifixion to the Jews, arguing that all mankind was responsible for this crime, the Jews merely acting as representatives of mankind. This claim often takes the form, "If we had been there, we would have done the same." The unspoken words, however, are, "Thank God we *weren't* there." A generalized guilt is not hard to endure, as long as there is some specific scapegoat to bear the main burden. It hardly helps the situation of the Jews to be regarded as the paradigm of human evil, rather than as inhumanly evil.

12 Tierney (1989).

13 The name "Cain" (Qayin) is the basis of the tribal designation "Kenite" (see Numbers 24:22, Judges 4:11). The influence of Kenite religion on Israelite religion is preserved in the Bible in the story of Moses's father-in-law and adviser, Jethro, who is identified as a Kenite (Judges 1:16 and 4:11). For full discussion, see Maccoby, *The Sacred Executioner* (1982), pp. 11–70.

14 The Greco-Roman mystery cults, among which Christianity should be reckoned, were spiritualized versions of sacrificial cults stemming from prehistoric times. See Campbell (1959) and Burkert (1983).

15 A human sacrifice was often thought of as also a divine sacrifice. The sacrificed person usually became divine after death. The mystery-

religion gods Osiris, Attis, Adonis and Dionysus were all human-divine figures. Frequently the necessary mixture of human and divine in the sacrifice was achieved by the arrangement that one parent of the victim was human and the other divine.

16 See Maccoby (1989), pp. 90–93. The rabbinic theory is that the sin-offerings apply only to unwitting sins. By repentance, deliberate sins acquire the status of unwitting ones, and thus a sin-offering becomes applicable. This doctrine is to be found in the Bible itself (see Leviticus 4, 5:1–19, 5:20–26).

17 See particularly Hebrews 9:11–14 for the Christian view of the relation between the death of Jesus and the Jewish sacrificial system.

18 Nazism can be seen more easily as deriving from Romanticism, which was a *völkisch* reaction against Enlightenment rationalism and individualism. But Nazism's pseudo-scientific appeal to biology and eugenics, as well as its unrestrained social engineering and its emphasis on technology, derive from Enlightenment attitudes. See Berlin (1979), Talmon (1960), Horkheimer and Adorno (1973).

19 Millenarianism influenced the People's Crusades of the twelfth and thirteenth centuries (Pastoureaux), the Peasants' Revolts in England (fourteenth century) and Germany (sixteenth century), the Taborites (fifteenth century) and the Anabaptist movement (sixteenth century). Prominent millenarian leaders were John Ball, Martin Huska, Thomas Müntzer, Jan Matthys and Jan Bockelson.

20 See Bousset (1896), Cohn (1957). See also Cohn (1967) for the influence of Christian millenarianism on Nazism.

21 The Talmud does envisage the possibility that the "evil inclination" will eventually be abolished. But this is regarded not as a solution to the human dilemma, but as a reward for the long struggle with it. It takes place in the World to Come, when the time for reward arrives. But the rabbinic attitude to this cessation of the moral fight is equivocal. Consider the saying: "One hour of the tranquillity of the World to Come is better than all the life of This World; but one hour of repentance and good deeds in This World is better than all the life of the World to Come." (Mishnah, Abot, 4:17). Reluctance to accept the idea of cessation of human effort, even as a reward, is also shown in the rabbinic saying: "There is no rest for the disciples of the wise, either in This World or in the World to Come." (Babylonian Talmud, Berakhot 64a). The impression one receives is that the rabbis regard the World to Come as something of a bore.

22 Kermode (1979).

23 The enormous increase in Muslim antisemitism because of the rise of Israel is due to the peculiar character of the Muslim antisemitic myth.

This is based not on deicidal fantasies, but on the concept of the Jews as a defeated people, humbled once and for all by the Prophet in battle. Muslims can thus be tolerant to Jews as long as they remain defeated and despised. However, when Jews have the audacity to meet Muslims in battle and even defeat them, the toleration disappears and is displaced by furious hatred, along with accusations of Satanic influence. Muslims have now taken over from Christian and post-Christian sources the complete battery of antisemitic calumny, previously alien to Muslim tradition. Such a reaction cannot be explained in political terms, but is again a matter of religious myth, although a different one.

24 See Maccoby (1976).

25 In *Moses and Monotheism*.

26 In *Bluebeard's Castle* (1971). A more popular version of this theory is also to be found in Prager and Tolushkin (1987).

27 The idea that the demands of the Jewish morality are cruel crops up continually in certain expressions that appear continually in the press. If Jews ever ask for justice, or act in self-defence, this is represented as "revenge" and "an eye for an eye", though these expressions are never used in similar circumstances about other nations. This antisemitism is hardly conscious. Rather it is an automatic response, conditioned by Christian theology, which represents Jesus as substituting the law of love for that of revenge—a total travesty of Jewish moral thinking. The biblical expression "an eye for an eye" is not concerned with cruel revenge but with justice, which demands compensation for injury that shall be adequate but not excessive. It was never taken literally, as the Bible itself shows, when it explains the various heads of monetary compensation for an injury (Exodus 21:19).

CHAPTER TWO

1 Moreover, it is probable that the Jerusalem Church never regarded Jesus as divine, and did not practise the Eucharist. See Maccoby (1986) and Maccoby (1991). For the general standpoint of the Jerusalem Church, see also Brandon (1951). The view that there was irreconcilable conflict between the Jerusalem and Pauline Churches was first argued by one of the founders of the scientific study of the New Testament, Ferdinand Christian Baur, and his followers of the "Tübingen school" (see especially Baur, 1845). Baur's work, however, contained many flaws, including errors of dating and the inadmissible introduction of Hegelian philosophical concepts. His brilliant insights were buried by subsequent criticism, and by the growth of "form criticism", which

fostered the view that Acts was totally unhistorical and gave no reliable information whatever about the Jerusalem Church. This radical scepticism (which was applied also to the Gospels with the conclusion that nothing authentic could be gleaned about the historical Jesus) served a pious purpose; for the essential Jewishness of the Jerusalem Church, as disturbingly proved by Baur, could now be discounted as deriving from a later stage of "re-judaization" in the sources. Ultra-scepticism thus led back to a conventional picture of Jesus and the Jerusalem Church as rejecters of Judaism, and this is still the ruling doctrine of New Testament scholarship. An exception, however, is S.G.F. Brandon, who, in a number of outstanding works, revived the concepts of Baur but without his errors of methodology (see especially Brandon, 1951). Brandon, however, was largely ignored. Recently growing awareness among scholars of the arbitrary nature of "form criticism" and of its roots in theological apologetics must lead eventually to a thoroughgoing reassessment of the work of Baur and Brandon.

2 Paul uses the verb in this neutral sense in Romans 11:35. Even more striking is the parallel phrase in Romans 4:25, where all translators agree that the meaning is "he was delivered" or "handed over", not "betrayed".

3 It is puzzling that Matthias is elected, according to Peter, "to be a witness with us of his resurrection" (1:22), when it is quite clear from the previous narrative that Matthias was not present when Jesus showed himself to the eleven Apostles for forty days (1:3). How could Matthias be witness of what he had not seen? The answer (as far as the author of Luke/Acts is concerned) may be that Matthias was one of those who, together with the eleven Apostles, saw the resurrected Jesus at an assembly in Jerusalem (Luke 24:34, which says, "... the eleven gathered together, and them that were with them ..."). This, however, is not a complete answer, because there is some difficulty in explaining the account of the resurrection-appearance in Luke 24 in relation to that in Acts 1. Are they separate resurrection-incidents, or is the second an enhanced version of the first? If the latter, the author, in elaborating his account in Acts, has failed to provide a resurrection-incident for Matthias to "witness".

4 Of course, it is always possible to concoct some harmonizing or smoothing explanation of the conflict between Paul and the later writers; such as that Paul differed from them only in thinking that Matthias was elected before, not after, the Apostles' resurrection-experience. But such explanations are discredited by the whole course of modern New Testament scholarship, which achieved scientific status only by eschewing the ingenious but unconvincing harmonizations that

173

were the rule in the ages of faith. The fact is that Paul does not mention either the defection of Judas or the election of Matthias, and makes a statement that is hard to reconcile with either. It is implausible to import a knowledge of these alleged events into his writings, simply in order to reconcile his story tortuously with the later accounts.

5 For Paul as the creator of the Christian sacrificial myth, see Maccoby (1986).

6 See Maccoby (1986) and Maccoby (1990).

7 See Pearson (1971), for arguments showing the lateness of this passage.

8 See Maccoby (1980). The Jerusalem Church, on the other hand, showed loyalty to the Jewish cause by sharing in the fight against Rome, thereby suffering great losses. The Pauline Church originated the story that the Jerusalem Church, warned by an oracle, left Jerusalem just before the war and emigrated to Pella, in Transjordania. The legendary character of this story has been fully proved by modern scholars (see Brandon, 1951, pp. 168–73, and Lüdemann, 1980). The Pella legend was part of the Pauline Church's campaign (initiated by the book of Acts) to cover up the split between Paul and Peter, and construct a fictional continuity between the Jerusalem and the Pauline Churches.

9 See especially Matthew 23:31–37; Acts 7:51–53. For antisemitism in the Gospels, see Ruether (1974), Gager (1983), Sanders (1987).

10 Among the writers who have seen a deliberate connection between the name "Judas" and the Jewish people, such that Judas was intended from the first as the symbol and archetype of alleged Jewish treachery, may be mentioned the following: J.M. Robertson (1910), p. 110f.; W.B. Smith (1911), p. 308; A. Drews (1921), p. 249; L.G. Lévy (1909), p. 539; S. Lublinski (1910), p. 146: "er wird Judas genannt, weil er duch dieses Synonym als Vertreter des gottesmörderischen jüdischen Volkes bezeichnet werden sollte"; F.K. Feigel (1910) p. 50.

11 The trial of Peter and his companions resulted in their acquittal, owing to the support of Gamaliel and the rest of the Pharisees (Acts 5). This incident contradicts the usual picture in Gospels and Acts of Pharisees hostile to Jesus and his followers. Incidents that go against the usual trend of the narrative are likely to be historically true. They cannot have been added at the time when the narrative took final shape under Pauline editorship, and must therefore be survivals from the earliest accounts. This is the basic principle of what is called *tendenz* criticism.

12 A passage expressing the Pauline attitude to the Jerusalem Church is that in which Jesus rebukes the disciples for wanting high positions in his kingdom (Luke 22:24–27). Jesus then admonishes Peter: "Simon, Simon, take heed: Satan has been given leave to sift all of you like wheat; but for you I have prayed that your faith may not fail; and when

you have come to yourself, you must lend strength to your brothers." This embodies the Pauline version of events: that Peter eventually came round to accepting Paulinism. This version is propagated in the book of Acts, but contradicts other evidence that Peter remained unreconciled with Paul after their quarrel in Antioch (Galatians 2:11–14). For the full argument supporting the view of the Jerusalem Church given here, see Maccoby (1986), pp. 119–155.

13 The reading found in third- and fourth-century Coptic versions is "Judas the Canaanite said to him . . ." The meaning of "Canaanite" will be examined later (p. 133), and it will be argued that it is equivalent to "Iscariot". At the present stage, it is enough to point out that the word "not" is here missing, a confirmation of the suspicion that it was added by an editor.

14 Some commentators, however, deny that this Judas, or Jude, was the brother of Jesus; this would mean that there are *four* Judases to consider: Judas Iscariot, Judas son of James, Judas, Jesus's brother, and Judas the author of the Epistle of Jude. This proliferation of Judases is itself a curious phenomenon.

CHAPTER THREE

1 Support for this was found in I Peter 5:13; but this Epistle is now regarded as spurious, because of its highly developed Pauline theology. See Kümmel (1975), pp. 421–24.

2 In order to cope with this difficulty, early commentators on the New Testament suggested that Thaddaeus, who is included in Mark's list, was another name for Judas.

3 On the relationship between these two themes see Maccoby (1991), pp. 90–129.

4 This calculation is based on the Mishnah's provision of 75 silver shekels as food allowance for one year (plus 25 shekels for clothing) as statutory settlement for a divorced wife (see Mishnah, Ketubot 1:2 and Talmudic commentary). The value of a shekel is not likely to have changed much during the course of ancient times.

5 Kermode unaccountably says, "When Jesus prophesies that one of the Twelve will betray him, Mark makes them all ask, 'Is it I?' In Matthew it is Judas alone who asks the question . . ." (Kermode, 1979, p. 90). The author has overlooked Matthew 26:22.

6 For Cain and Abel as a sacrificial brother-pair, see Hooke (1947), p. 41–42; Maccoby (1982), pp. 11–40. For the mythical conflict between twins or brothers, leading to fratricide, see Kluckhohn (1968), Girard (1977), pp. 59–62.

7 I call these elements non-Jewish because they imply the holiness of evil. It is characteristic of Jewish religion that it refuses to accept ambivalence in an action. Endless discussion may take place about whether an act is right or wrong; but once the matter is decided, it becomes wholly right or wholly wrong. The Talmud expresses this, for example, by the ruling that if it is decided that it is right to desecrate the Sabbath in order to save a life, the desecration should be performed not by an insignificant person, but by a rabbi, or the most distinguished person present. The Hebrew Bible shows the same thought when it directs that an execution must be performed by the prosecuting witnesses and the "whole congregation" (Deut. 17:7). There must be no untouchable Jack Ketch figure to perform such work. If the community requires it, the community must do it, with a good conscience. This basic difference between Judaism and Christianity can be seen in their attitudes towards the "Just War" (i.e. a war of self-defence). Christianity allows it, but feels guilty about it; it is a matter of doing evil for the sake of good. Judaism regards a war of self-defence as a positive duty (*milhemet mitzvah*), with no admixture of evil. These Jewish attitudes constitute a deliberate rejection of what has been called "transgressional sacralism", i.e. the holiness of a wicked, usually forbidden act, often associated with the idea of the magic power of the forbidden. For "transgressional sacralism" as an element in Hindu religion, and as throwing light on Christian concepts of *felix culpa*, see Hiltebeitel (1989).

8 Kermode (1979), p. 87.

9 The "valley of Hinnom" (Gehinnom, later rendered as Gehenna), though at first an actual valley containing burning heaps of rubbish, later became the symbolic name of hell-fire.

10 See Chrysostom, Homily III on Acts of the Apostles 1:15–22. See Appendix, 3, for a translation of this passage.

11 The Targum is the Aramaic translation of the Bible, and the Peshitta the Syriac translation. Both date from the ancient world, whereas the earliest manuscripts of much of the Hebrew Bible are medieval. Like the Septuagint (the ancient Greek translation), the Targum and the Peshitta can sometimes be used to correct the text, since they provide evidence of early readings.

12 See Montefiore (1927), II, p. 342.

13 In this case, his later introduction of the potter in the phrase "potter's field" owes nothing to Zechariah 11:13, but is derived, as explained above, from Jeremiah 19, with, in addition, a conflated reminiscence of Jeremiah 18:2 ("the potters's house") and Jeremiah 32:6–15 (Jeremiah buys a field). Another possibility is that there was actually a burial-ground in Jerusalem called Blood Acre, which had previously been

called Potter's Field, and for which Matthew is giving a Christian aetiology. There is no evidence, however, in intertestamental or rabbinic literature of such a burial-ground. The name "Potter's Field" is unknown. The name "Blood Acre", or "Aceldama" (Acts 1:19), seems reminiscent of the place-name Ephes Damim (I Samuel 17:1), also called Pas-Damim (I Chronicles 11:13). The Aramaic translation of this name was *haqal sumaqta* ("Red Field"), see Palestinian Talmud, Sanhedrin, II, 20b. Ephes Damim, however, was not a burial-ground but a small town, about 16 miles south-west of Jerusalem. Possibly also hovering in Matthew's mind was the fact that *damim* can mean "price" in rabbinic Hebrew (in this meaning it is derived not from *dam*, "blood", but from the verb *damah*, "to be like, or equivalent"). The pun on "blood" and "price" may have suggested to Matthew unconsciously a new meaning for the old name Ephes Damim—the "field of the blood-price", causing him to attach this biblical echo to his story.

14 A connection between Judas and Ahitophel was also seen by Christian commentators in the incident of the Last Supper when Jesus gave a sop of bread to Judas. In accordance with John 13:18, this was regarded as a fulfilment of the biblical verse, "Yea, mine own familiar friend, in whom I trusted, which did eat of my bread, hath lifted up his heel against me" (Psalms 41:9). The verse in the psalm was seen as referring to Ahitophel as a prefiguration of Judas.

CHAPTER FOUR

1 See pp. 146–149. See also p. 32.

2 The solution found by early Church commentators to the problem of the absence of a second Judas in Mark and Matthew was to identify him with Thaddaeus (alternatively called Lebbaeus), (Mark 3:18, Matthew 10:3). No reason, however, was given to identify them except that they occupy a corresponding place in the lists.

3 There is some doubt among translators whether the Judas newly introduced by Luke was "son of James" or "brother of James" (the Greek has simply "of James", which can be validly interpreted as either). Elsewhere in the New Testament, Judas (Jude), the author or alleged author of the Epistle of Jude, is called in the superscription "brother of James" (here the word "brother" appears explicitly), and this is understood by all scholars to mean "brother of James, the brother of Jesus" (i.e. the James who was leader of the Jerusalem Church). Whether the Epistle of Jude is genuine or not, it provides evidence (and there is more elsewhere, in Eusebius, *Eccl. Hist.* iii. 19 ff. that

the early Church contained a figure known as Judas, brother of James, brother of Jesus. There is thus a *prima facie* likelihood that AV is right in translating "brother of James" in Luke, and that the NEB "correction" to "son of James" is wrong. We shall find other occasions when the decision between "son of" and "brother of" (in translation of the bare Greek genitive) will be of importance in reconstructing the historical facts. The NEB "correction" is motivated, in fact, by the difficulty found in reconciling the AV translation with the normally accepted doctrine about the Apostle Judas, which cannot allow him to be Jesus's brother.

4 See Brandon (1951); Maccoby (1986).

5 A valiant attempt was made by Thomas de Quincey (*Works*, 6, pp. 21–25), whose harmonization of the two accounts is a monument of implausibility.

6 Romulus, for example, was purified and absolved for his slaying of Remus, a lightly disguised foundation sacrifice.

7 This belief is based on the prophecy of Paul in Romans 11:26.

8 In the Synoptic Gospels, Jesus's death is bloodless, except that his flogging before crucifixion must have left him bleeding. Crucifixion itself, though a long-drawn-out agony, was a bloodless death. It is only John who introduces blood-shedding into his narrative of Jesus's death by having a soldier pierce his body with a spear (John 19:34), causing an effusion of blood and water. This unhistorical incident may have been intended to enhance the sacrificial character of Jesus's death, with the principle in mind, "Without shedding of blood there is no atonement" (Hebrews 9:22, quoting Leviticus 17:11). Luke's version of the eucharistic words of Jesus (in the Longer Text) include the words, "This cup is the new testament of my blood which is shed for you" (Luke 22:20), though Luke does not provide any effusion of blood in his account of the Crucifixion.

9 See Hooke (1947), pp. 40–41; Leach (1969), p. 18.

CHAPTER FIVE

1 The reading, mentioned earlier, "Judas the Canaanite" instead of "Judas, not Iscariot", supports this exegesis. "Canaanite" is equivalent to Zealot, and the appellation is appropriate to someone urging activism. It seems that John portrayed the "other" Judas as a Zealot, and some later editor of the Gospel, fearing that this did not sufficiently mark this Judas off, changed "the Canaanite" into "not Iscariot". It will be argued later, however, that "Canaanite" and "Iscariot" are equiv-

alent terms, and that therefore, in a still earlier version, it was Judas Iscariot himself who was the advocate of activism.

2 John mystifyingly changes the anointing of Jesus's head to an anointing of his feet. This is probably the result of a further conflation: this time with the story (Luke 7:36–50) of an unnamed sinful woman who wets Jesus's feet with her tears and dries them with her hair. In John's story, however, neither the anointing nor the wiping makes sense.

3 For discussion of the Eucharist as the creation of Paul, see Maccoby (1986), pp. 110–118, and, in greater detail, Maccoby (1990), pp. 90–128. The Jerusalem Church did not practise the Eucharist, and the earliest mention of it is in Paul's Epistles (I Corinthians 11:23–26), where Paul claims that he was instructed about it in a vision of the heavenly Jesus. The accounts in the Gospels of the institution of the Eucharist by Jesus are additions to the narrative of the Last Supper and stem from Paul's account.

4 The expression "good for that man if he had never been born" can be paralleled in Jewish sources (e.g. Mishnah, Hagigah, 2:1), but never in connection with deeds that were regarded as fated and necessary. A use of the expression in a way compatible with Judaism is found in Matthew 18:7, probably a genuine saying of Jesus, in which the element of necessity is merely that human beings in general cannot escape sin, but must nevertheless suffer punishment for it. Here, however, the thought is that the *particular* sin of Judas was foretold and fated, and is essential for mankind's salvation; yet Judas is to suffer untold punishment for it.

5 In the ransom theory of atonement (advocated by Hilary of Poitiers, Augustine and others), Satan was tricked into thinking that Jesus was only human. He accepted Jesus's death as a ransom for humanity, over whom he had acquired rights through the fall of Adam. He did not realize that Jesus would escape death by resurrection.

6 Actually, verse 23 contradicts such an interpretation, actuated no doubt by the fact that the beloved disciple did die.

7 Another such authentic detail is John's geographical reference "the Kedron ravine", unparalleled in the other Gospels.

CHAPTER SIX

1 Maccoby (1980).

2 For an excellent study of Jewish-Christian relations in this period, see Simon (1986). In the first century, Christian writings (later collected into the New Testament) were concerned to demonstrate that Christianity

was not a variety of Judaism, and was uninvolved in Jewish rebellion against Rome. In the second and third centuries, much Christian writing was aimed at preventing a drift back into Judaism. In the fourth century and onwards, a triumphal note enters as Christianity becomes the dominant religion.

3 Author's translation. The first two sentences are found in Oecumenius. The rest is found in Theophylact, who begins by quoting the sentences from Oecumenius, and completes the remarks of Papias from some other source. For discussion of the text, see Kürzinger (1983), pp. 104f, Körtner (1983), pp. 59–61, Klauck (1987), pp. 110–111.

4 Linguistically, *prenes genomenos* ("becoming headlong") is an unnatural expression, while *presthes genomenos* ("becoming swollen") is intelligible, though not elegant, Greek. There is also evidence in 5th-century Georgian and Armenian versions in favour of the amendment.

5 Acts 12:23, though Josephus, *Antiquities*, xix. 346, describes violent stomach pains but no worms.

6 Another figure who may have contributed to Papias's conception of the death of Judas is Antiochus Epiphanes. His death too involved both worms and a noxious smell (see II Maccabees 9:9). More doubtful connections have also been seen with the punishment under ordeal of the adulterous woman (Numbers 5:22); Nadan, in the Achikar story; Pheretime, as related by Herodotus; Cassander, as related by Pausanias; Catullus, as related by Josephus; Galerius, as related by Lactantius and Eusebius.

7 Irenaeus (*c*. 130–195) was Bishop of Lyons. He wrote a work in five books called *Against Heresies*, mainly directed against the Gnostics, but giving also the first systematic exposition of Catholic belief. His hostility to the Jews is expressed in Book IV; but he transmits certain beliefs of a Jewish character which mainstream Christianity rejected. These beliefs were no doubt derived from the Jerusalem Church.

8 There is no real basis to the theory of Joseph Klausner that the sceptical disciple is intended to be Paul.

9 Gamaliel's argument is that if something similar can be found in this world to the wonders of the world to come, there is no infringement of the dictum of Ecclesiastes that there will never be anything entirely new.

10 The original expression "the twelve disciples" does not show any particular concern for numbering, since this was a conventional epithet, like "the twelve tribes", used sometimes for poetical effect as an alternative to the prosaic "disciples" or "tribes". But to specify "eleven" is to show an anxiety to state the right number, and this is best explained not by the narrative context but by the exigencies of editing.

11 Vogler (1983), p. 128.

12 See Klauck (1987), p. 131.

13 The date of composition of this work is not known; it may have been written at any time between 500 and 1000 CE. It is in fact a compilation, being partly based on the Protevangelium of James and the Gospel of Thomas. Large portions consist of imaginative stories reminding one of the Arabian Nights or the *Golden Ass* of Apuleius. The compiler was evidently an Oriental. It was translated from Arabic into Latin and published in 1697.

14 The name Joses is taken from the list of Jesus's brothers in Matthew 13:55. It is a Grecized form of the Hebrew name Jose (an abbreviation of Joseph) very commonly found in the rabbinic literature.

15 Klauck (1987), p. 133.

16 James (1953), pp. 166–186.

17 An even earlier idea was to identify the featureless Bartholemew with Nathanael (see John 1:45–51), about whom some interesting details are given.

18 For fuller discussion, see Maccoby (1991).

19 This type of argument is known as *tendenz*-theory, based on the general *tendenz*, or bias, of the author. If a statement appears that is unpalatable to the author, as judged by his general bias, it is likely to be historically true, or at least early, since it probably survives from an earlier stage of the narrative, and cannot have been added at a late stage by the author himself. This is an offshoot of the general principle in textual criticism, *lectio difficilis melior* ("the difficult reading is better")—i.e. when we have two readings (in separate manuscripts) one easy and one difficult, it is more likely that the difficult reading was changed to an easy one than the reverse.

20 It may possibly have influenced the Christian picture of Judas by making it even more negative. In the medieval *Narrative of Joseph of Arimathaea*, Judas is represented as having deliberately joined Jesus's band for the purpose of betraying him, playing the role of spy for two years. This alteration of the Gospel story may derive from *Toledot Yeshu*. Other features of *Narrative of Joseph of Armimathaea* also suggest that its author may have had some knowledge of the Jewish version of the story.

21 See Catchpole (1971).

22 In fact, there is no penalty in Jewish law for someone merely declaring himself to be God, which would be regarded as evidence of lunacy. The precise charges against Jesus in the Jewish saga were (1) persuading other people to worship him as God ("seducing to idolatry", Hebrew *mesit*, see Deuteronomy 13:6–10); (2) sorcery, i.e. performing real or pretended miracles in support of idolatrous claims (Deuteronomy 13:1–2).

CHAPTER SEVEN

1 See *In Ps.* 108 (*PL*, 26, 1224). "St. Jerome, for whom Judas is the image of Judaism ... " (Simon, 1986, p. 230).

2 John Chrysostom *De proditione Judae homiliae 1–2*. Migne (1857), vol. 49, pp. 373–392.

3 St. John Chrysostom, *Homilies against the Jews*. See especially Homilies 1 and 6.

4 The situation was very different in the Byzantine Empire, which never suffered cultural breakdown. Here periods of toleration alternated with massacres and forced conversions. Judaism, as in Europe, was in theory a permitted religion, but outbreaks of hostility were common. Information about the history of Byzantine Jewry, however, is too scanty to contribute significantly to our theme, though a new scholarly interest in the subject is beginning to unearth some interesting material.

5 The *Legenda Aurea* (Golden Legend) was written by Jacobus de Voragine (*c.* 1230–*c.* 1298), Archbishop of Genoa. It contains legendary lives of saints and other figures, and was one of the most popular works of the Middle Ages.

6 Adapted from the summary by P.F. Baum (Baum, 1916, pp. 482–483).

7 See Verard.

8 For example, in the Passion Play performed in Alsfed (Bavaria), the scene of the Crucifixion is prolonged for over seven hundred lines, with a wealth of realistically portrayed and ingeniously varied sufferings inflicted on Jesus by executioners egged on by the Jews.

9 It should be noted that there is a certain savage humour about the portrayal of Jews (including Judas and Herod) in the Passion Plays. It should not be thought, however, that this humour mitigates the hatred and contempt expressed. Satan too was treated with the same kind of humour.

10 For a full analysis see Heinz Pflaum, "Les scènes de juifs dans la littérature dramatique du moyen-age", *REJ*, 89 (1930), pp. 111–134.

11 Examples of the Passion Plays in Germany are the two Frankfurt Passions (mid-14th century and 1493), the Alsfeld Passion (1501) and the Donaueschinger Passion (last half of fifteenth century). An example of a secular play employing the theme of ritual murder is *Das Endinger Judenspiel* (manuscript 1616, copy of an older manuscript). See Cohen (1989).

12 See Gasparro (1985), pp. 56–64.

13 Reider, p. 93.

14 Zafran (1973).

15 Shachar (1975).

16 Linthicum (1936), p. 47. Zafran (1973), p. 11.

17 For further discussion of Shylock as Pharisee, see Maccoby (1970), where the notion that Shakespeare's Shylock was intended as a sympathetic picture of a Jew is criticized, and the play is analysed as a contest between the allegedly Jewish doctrine of justice and the Christian doctrine of mercy. What is beyond doubt is that before the nineteenth century, no production of the *Merchant* portrayed Shylock with any sympathy. This was the most popular of Shakespeare's plays, and the audiences that hissed and jeered at Shylock were hardly distinguishable from their forebears who attended the Passion Plays. A further medieval element in both *The Jew of Malta* and *The Merchant of Venice* is the motif of "the Jew's Beautiful Daughter". This derives from the "exempla" or moral tales, which featured an old and ugly Jewish miser and sorcerer who is robbed of both his treasure and his daughter by a Christian. The story often ends with the conversion of the old Jew to Christianity. See Maccoby, November, 1970.

18 For Origen's friendship with Jewish scholars, see Nicholas de Lange, *Origen and the Jews*, Cambridge, 1976. Jerome, too, frequently consulted Jewish scholars while preparing his translation of the Bible.

19 See E.E. Stoll, "Shylock", *Shakespeare Studies* (New York, 1927).

20 For an excellent account and discussion, see Wilson (1982).

21 Maurras himself later became a collaborator with the Nazis in their transportation of French Jews to the death-camps.

22 *La Libre Parole*, 3 Nov. 1894, p. 31.

23 Simon Deutz allegedly betrayed the Duchesse de Berry in 1832. See Z. Szajkowski, "Simon Deutz: Traitor or French Patriot?" *Journal of Jewish Studies*, 16 (1965), pp. 53–65.

24 Bloy (1892), p. 38.

25 *La Civiltà Cattolica*, February, 1898.

26 de La Tour de Pin *Vers un ordre social chrétien*. Cit. Lovsky, *L'Antisémitism chrétien*, p. 288.

27 Blum (1935), pp. 64–65.

28 Act IV, scene iv, 167–68.

29 Celeste Wright, *Studies in Philology*, XXXI, p. 190.

30 Article, "Israël", in the journal *La Rénovation*.

31 In Charles Fourier, *Publications des manuscripts*.

32 In the periodical *The Answer*, no. 5, Dec. 1972, p. 25.

33 Charles Y. Glock and Rodney Stark, *Christian Beliefs and Antisemitism*, New York, 1969, p. 49.

34 Robert Wilton, *The Last Days of the Romanovs*, London, 1920, p. 148.

CHAPTER EIGHT

1 Joshua 15:25, Jeremiah 48:24, Amos 2:2.

2 Even the occurrences of *keriyot* in connection with Moab do not unequivocally establish the word as a place-name, for the Septuagint (while treating it as a place-name in Jeremiah) translates it as "cities" in Amos.

3 Reading of D in John 12:4; 13:2, 26; 14:22.

4 For example, Nahum, a man of Gimzo, and Eleazar, a man of Bartota.

5 It has been suggested that there is a parallel case in Josephus in the name Istobus (*Antiquities* vii. 121) which is a transliteration of the name Ishtob (II Sam 10:6, 8). But this is very different, for here the word *ish* actually forms part of the name, and the second element *tob* is not a place-name but an adjective meaning "good", so that the whole name means "good man". A plausible Hebrew name beginning with *ish* has to be of this kind. Another example in the Bible is Ishbosheth (II Sam. 2:8), an alternative form of Ishbaal (see I Chron. 8:33), meaning "man of Baal", i.e. worshipper of Baal, where the phrase "man of . . ." is integral to the meaning of the name. On the other hand, the objection sometimes made to the "man of Kerioth" theory on the ground that "man of . . ." ought to be in Aramaic, not in Hebrew, is not compelling. Hebrew was far more frequently used in the time of Jesus, even in ordinary speech, than scholars of the last generation realized, as, indeed, the rabbinic parallels to the "man of . . ." style demonstrate.

6 It should be noted, however, that there can be no objection to this theory on the ground that "Iscariot" begins with an "I" which is not present in the word *scortea*. For there are many examples to show that speakers of Aramaic or Hebrew found it difficult to cope with Greek or Latin words beginning with a double consonant, and tended to make pronunciation easier by adding a short vowel, frequently "i", before the double consonant. An example of this is the word *ispaqlaria*, which appears in Aramaic as a derivative of the Latin word *specularia* ("window-glass"). This is an important point to bear in mind in further discussion of the derivation of "Iscariot".

7 Genesis 48:22, where the word translated "portion" is in Hebrew *shechem*, and the reference is to the land bought by Jacob in Shechem, Gen. 33:19.

8 These forms beginning with "s" also present a difficulty for the "man of Kerioth" theory. If the first syllable of Iscariot represents the Hebrew *ish*, such a shortening would be most unlikely.

9 For a further confirmation of the early existence of a designation Judas

the Zealot in the writings of the important witness John Chrysostom, see Appendix.

10 There is also evidence of the existence of the name "Judas the Zealot" in the Coptic and the Ethiopic *Epistola Apostolorum*, ed. C. Schmidt and Wajnberg, *TU* 43 (1919), 26 c.2. See also Hennecke-Schneemelcher, *Neutestamentliche Apokryphen*, 4th ed., 1968, 1,192 and 2, 31f.

11 For a previous attempt to argue a connection between "Iscariot" and *sicarius* see O. Cullmann, *The State in the New Testament*, 15. He was anticipated by F. Schulthess (1917) pp. 54 ff, who however regarded the Sicarii as non-Jewish. See also E. Klostermann (1950), p. 35, and Hengel (1990), pp. 47–48, saying that the theory is "not convincing".

12 A frequent argument is that the Zealot movement did not exist at this time, and that therefore the term "zealot" (as in Simon the Zealot) had only a religious connotation, meaning "one zealous for the Torah". Confirmation for this purely religious use is found in Paul's description of himself as "zealous of the traditions of my fathers" (Galatians 1:14), and the description of members of the Jerusalem Church as "zealous of the law" (Acts 21:20). See also Acts 22:3, 2 Maccabees 4:2 and Josephus *Antiquities*, 12.271. The argument is that scrutiny of Josephus shows that the term Zealots was not used as a political term until a later period. This argument has been comprehensively refuted by Martin Hengel, who shows that the term when used alone (without an ensuing phrase such as " ... of the Law") always has a political reference, and that the Zealots did exist as a political movement in the time of Jesus (Hengel, 1990, pp. 70ff).

13 A prominent early supporter of the theory was Thomas de Quincey (*Works* 6, pp. 21ff.). Among scholars supporting it have been Neander and Volkmar (*Jesus Nazarenus*, 1882, p. 121). Fictional examples are Klopstock's poem "Messias", Cecil Roth's *Iskarioth*, London, 1929, the film, "Jesus of Nazareth", scripted by Anthony Burgess (1982), and the rock opera, "Jesus Christ Superstar".

14 Form criticism is able to discount the evidence of Jesus's firm adherence to Judaism by the concept of "re-judaization", i.e. that the Gospels evidence a tendency of the early Church to return to Judaism, and that Jewish traits were therefore unhistorically attributed to Jesus. This theory is part of an overall conception that the Gospels contain very little material of historical value, but only materials that had a function in the liturgy and faith-system of the early Church. All material that appears to show Jesus as a believing Jew should therefore be regarded as having its *sitz im leben* in the needs of early judaizing Christian communities. This theory can therefore present itself as very sceptical, hard-headed and scientific, while in fact bolstering conventional Chris-

tian belief. That this was the main aim of form criticism was more openly acknowledged by its earliest practitioners, such as Max Müller.
15 Tarachov (1960).
16 See Wright (1916), A.T. Robertson (1917), Harris (1917).

CHAPTER NINE

1 Martin Hengel has argued (against J. Klausner) that "Canaanite" would be rendered *chananaios*, not *kananaios*. He suggests that the latter word is derived from Aramaic *qanana*, a variant form of *qanai*. This is doubtful, because the *-aios* ending is a typical tribal or national adjectival ending, and therefore most readers would take this to be a form of "Canaanite". The same can be said about the textual variation *kananites*, found in these texts (Hengel admits that this variation provides some evidence for Klausner's view, but says it is "a secondary reading"). In any case, even accepting Hengel's case, the shift from the intelligible Greek *zelotes* to the unintelligible Aramaic would have to be regarded as a cover-up device. (Hengel, 1990, p. 70). Hengel rightly rejects the view (stemming from Jerome) that the word means "man from Cana".

2 This name may be a curious exception, because in manuscripts of Matthew it appears as "Jesus Barabbas", which has been accepted by most modern scholars as the correct reading (see NEB translation of Matthew 27:17). If so, this could be the only NT parallel to "Simon Bar-Jonah" in having "son of" in Aramaic. But this is on the assumption that Jesus Barabbas means "Jesus son of Abba". Other explanations of the name, however, are possible: Jesus Berabbi ("Jesus the Teacher"), or "Jesus son of God". For the theory that Jesus of Nazareth and Jesus Barabbas were the same person, see Maccoby (1968) and Maccoby (1980).

3 In recent times, the interpretation of Bar-Jonah as "Zealot" (advocated earlier by Robert Eisler) has been supported by Cullman, but opposed by Hengel. See Cullman (1970), pp. 22f, Hengel (1990), p. 55ff. Hengel's argument is that the word *bariona* is not found in early sources, and that in some sources it means merely "bad, indisciplined people". These arguments, however, are of little weight. It is hardly likely that a word would be coined at a late period as the designation of a movement of an earlier period; and words frequently have more than one meaning. The expression "Abba Sicarius, captain of the Barions" has a technical ring, reflecting a conscious recalling of the nomenclature of an earlier period. A further argument of Hengel's is that the context in which

186

Jesus addresses Peter as "Simon Bar-Jonah" is inappropriate for the meaning "Zealot", being the occasion of Peter's salutation of Jesus as "Christ". This argument depends on the notion that the "spiritual" Christ is meant at this point; but it is very doubtful whether the kind of otherworldly Christ worshipped in the later Pauline Church would have been accepted either by Jesus or by Peter. If Peter was hailing Jesus as Christ (Messiah) in the Jewish sense (i.e. Davidic king), then Peter was raising the standard of revolt against Rome, and a reply by Jesus addressing Peter by a title expressing his valour would be quite appropriate (see Maccoby, 1980, pp. 95–96).

4 It has been suggested that the name has an apocalyptic reference, being an allusion to the prophecy, "I will shake (Hebrew, *mar'ish*) the heavens and the earth" (Haggai 2:6). On this theory, Jesus bestowed this name on John and James to mark their role in the new dispensation. It is not clear why two apostles out of the twelve should be singled out in this way; and, in any case, the usual Christian interpretation of the verse from Haggai is that it prophesies the world-shattering disturbances accompanying the Second Coming of Christ, hardly relevant to apostleship during Jesus's lifetime.

5 For example, "We had been hoping that he was the man to liberate Israel" (Luke 24:21). Even in the account of Jesus's Resurrection appearance, the apostles ask him, "Lord, is this the time when you are to establish once again the sovereignty of Israel?" (Acts 1:6). That the apostles' understanding of Jesus's mission was that he would free the Jewish people from the Roman Occupation has been obscured by the later belief that the word "Israel" denotes the Christian Church.

6 The three views about the brothers of Jesus are known as the Helvidian view (that they were full brothers, being born of Joseph and Mary), the Epiphanian view (that they were half-brothers, being sons of Joseph by a previous marriage), and the Hieronymian view (that they were cousins). Most modern scholars take the commonsensical Helvidian view; even some Catholic scholars agree with it. The Eastern Church followed Epiphanius, the Western Church, Jerome. See Bauckham (1990) for a full discussion. Helvidius was a fourth-century theologian who argued against the perpetual virginity of Mary. His work has been lost, and his views are preserved only in the work of St. Jerome attacking him (*De perpetua virginitate B. Mariae adversus Helvidium*). Jerome argued that the brothers of Jesus were the sons of another Mary, the wife of Alphaeus, and sister of the Virgin Mary. That there were two sisters, both called Mary, is somewhat hard to believe, and the view of Helvidius, about whom, unfortunately, nothing more is known, nowadays seems far more acceptable.

7 It is clear from the lists of Jesus's brothers in Mark 6:3 and Matthew 13:55 that James was the oldest brother after Jesus.

8 See Isaiah 22:19–23. Here the appointment of Eliakim to the position of Chief Minister to King Hezekiah is described in these terms: "And the key of the house of David will I lay upon his shoulder; so he shall open, and none shall shut; and he shall shut and none shall open." Compare this with Jesus's charge to Peter: "And I will give unto thee the keys of the kingdom of heaven; and whatsoever thou shalt bind on earth shall be bound in heaven; and whatsoever thou shalt loose on earth shall be loosed in heaven." (Matthew 16:19). The Hebrew term for "binding" or "shutting" (*issur*) means "declaring forbidden", and the Hebrew term for "loosing" or "opening" (*heter*) means "declaring permitted".

9 A case can be made for the proposition that Peter too was Jesus's brother. Peter's real name was Simon, and one of Jesus's brothers was also called Simon (Mark 6:3, Matthew 13:55). As we saw in the last chapter (p. 144), three Simons can be discerned in the Gospel narrative: Simon Peter, also called "Bariona" (meaning "Zealot"), Simon the Zealot, and Simon Iscariot (meaning "Zealot"). It would certainly be in the interests of theoretical economy if all three, all called Simon, and all having a nickname equivalent to Zealot, were the same person. Simon Iscariot was probably the brother of Judas Iscariot, which, again, would make him Jesus's brother. It is interesting that Ephraem, the fourth-century Syrian commentator on the Bible, identifies Simon the Zealot with Simon the brother of Jesus. He also identifies the apostle Judas of James (understood as Judas the brother of James) with Judas the brother of Jesus. (Ephraem on Acts 1:13, preserved in Armenian, quoted in Harris, 1894, pp. 37–38).

10 See Maccoby (1980), pp. 139–149.

11 It might be argued that the apostle Thomas, known in East Syrian circles as Judas Thomas or Didymus Judas Thomas, is the same person as the apostle Jude, and that therefore the considerable literature, mostly legendary, about Thomas is part of the Judas-saga. Indeed, there were some ancient traditions (the Book of Thomas and the Acts of Thomas) identifying Thomas with Jude, and some modern scholars have argued in favour of these traditions and associated the authorship of the Epistle of Jude with Thomas (Koester, 1965, pp. 296–297, Layton, 1987, p. 359). In particular, the legends about Thomas call him not only the brother but the twin-brother of Jesus. It seems, however, that though Thomas's real name was indeed probably Judas, he was not, historically, a brother of Jesus. His nickname "Thomas" does mean "twin" in Hebrew, but he was the twin of someone else, not Jesus, and he was known by this nickname for the specific purpose of distin-

guishing him from the other Judas, the apostle and brother of Jesus (see Bauckham, 1990, pp. 32–36). In the lists of Jesus's brothers, Judas is either the youngest or second youngest of the four, and the Gospel narratives hardly leave room for the supposition that Jesus had a twin brother. On the other hand, from a mythological standpoint, it is interesting that the legend of Jesus's twin brother arose, and that it was associated with a disciple called Judas. In the East Syrian literature, the twin-motif appears somewhat lacking in depth, and may be a secondary development, serving a Gnostic purpose. There is substance in the suggestion of Gunther (1980, p. 117) that the legend was originally influenced by Greek myth, especially that of the Dioscuri, Castor and Pollux. If so, it is altogether possible that the twin-motif arose at some stage of the development of the Judas-as-Betrayer myth. For the Betrayal stories in mythology often involve a pair of twins, one of whom betrays or murders the other, for a salvific purpose. Examples are the story of Romulus and Remus, Jacob and Esau. The twin-brother relationship expresses the identity of victim and slayer, found in an even more ideal form in stories of divine self-immolation, such as the self-hanging of Odin. I would suggest, therefore, that the notion that Jesus had a twin-brother called Judas arose first in the context of the Judas-as-Betrayer myth, but was erased from this by the needs of the Mary-as-Perpetual-Virgin myth (demanding that Jesus should have no brothers at all). It lingered, however, in Gnostic circles, attached to Judas Thomas (Judas the Twin), as a symbol of the spiritual identity of every true Gnostic with Jesus.

12 See Bauckham (1990), pp. 354–365.

13 The abundant evidence of dynastic succession in the history of the Jerusalem Church has led to a theory, put forward by several authors, of a Christian "Caliphate". This theory differs from that put forward in the present book, for a Caliphate implies that, as in the case of Islam, a new religion had been founded, the leadership of which passed in dynastic succession. My argument, on the contrary, is that the Jerusalem "Church" regarded itself as part of the Jewish religion, its distinctiveness consisting only in its belief that the promised king-Messiah had come and would come again shortly. The succession of relatives was not exactly monarchic, because it was believed that the true King was Jesus himself, and therefore the dynasty always had the character of a Regency. The "Caliphate" theory was earlier advocated by Harnack, Schoeps and others. For more recent discussion, see von Campenhausen (1950–51), Stauffer (1952) and Bauckham (1990), pp. 125–130. The main objection to the Caliphate theory is that the Jerusalem Church never gave up its allegiance to the Jewish Temple and its

priesthood. They could not, therefore, have set up a rival priesthood of their own. Also, the Eucharist, which was the central sacrament administered by the priesthood of the Pauline Christian Church, was not practised by the Jerusalem Church, and could not have been so long as they retained loyalty to the sacraments of the Jewish Temple. The "wine and bread" ceremony practised by the Jerusalem Church is preserved in the Didache, and it has no sacramental reference to the "body and blood of Jesus". It is simply the well-known Jewish *qiddush* ceremony, observed by all Jews on Sabbaths and festivals. It is distinguished from the Pauline Eucharist, too, by a wine-bread order (as in the *qiddush*), as opposed to the bread-wine order of the Eucharist. (See Maccoby, 1991.) The leader of the Jerusalem Church, therefore, was not a hereditary priest or "Bishop" of a new religion, but essentially a political leader of a messianic movement within Judaism.

14 Bauckham (1990), pp. 171–178. One of the main questions to be answered about the Epistle of Jude is "Who are the opponents whom the author is criticizing?" The famous scholar Ernest Renan thought that the opponent is none other than Paul (Renan, *Saint Paul*, Paris, 1869, pp. 300–303). F.C. Baur and other authors of the Tübingen school thought that the Epistle is anti-Paulinist, but belongs to the second century. Bauckham thinks that the opponents are first-century Paulinists of an extreme, libertarian kind. The moral concern of the Epistle is certainly consistent with authorship by Judas the Apostle, and the arguments for second-century authorship are not convincing. The Christology has no obvious Paulinist features, and certain passages could be anti-Paulinist. The concern with angelology is somewhat puzzling, however, and I do not think that Bauckham has solved this problem. He thinks that the author regards the angels as the givers of the Torah, but such an opinion is inconsistent with Judaism (see Maccoby, 1986, p. 220). An interesting pointer to authenticity, offered by Bauckham, is that the author gives Jesus the title *despotes* (Jude 4), unique in the New Testament writings. But it is known (from Julius Africanus, quoted in Eusebius, *HE* 1:7:14) that those members of the Jerusalem Church who had special rank as relatives of Jesus had the title *desposunoi*, meaning "those belonging to the Lord". It seems then that *despotes* was a special title of Jesus (expressing his royalty) used by his relatives.

15 See Brandon (1951), pp. 168–73, and Lüdemann (1980).

16 See Maccoby (1986), ch. 15, "The Evidence of the Ebionites".

CHAPTER TEN

1 Crista Wolff, the German novelist, wrote that she learnt to despise and hate the Jews not because of anything explicit that was said to her, but because of a certain glint that came into the eyes of adults whenever they used the word "Jew".

2 It should be mentioned that Judas Iscariot plays no part in Muslim mythology. The only Muslim work that attempts to give an account of Judas's treachery is the so-called Gospel of Barnabas, which was probably composed in Italy in the fifteenth century by a renegade from Christianity to Islam (see M.R. James, *The Apocryphal New Testament*, p. xxvi). In this Muslim version of the Gospel story, Judas is foiled by a miracle. He is transformed into the exact likeness of Jesus, and is crucified in his place. Jesus ascends to heaven without dying. The concept that Jesus's place on the cross was taken by another is found in the Koran (Sura IV), which, however, does not mention Judas. The story that Jesus did not die on the cross derives ultimately from Gnosticism, from which Islam also derived the concept of the Jews as contemptible incompetents rather than hateful murderers. For discussion of modern virulent Islamic antisemitism (contrasting with the earlier milder version) see p. 17.

3 This optimistic vision of a *Judenrein* world characterized not only Hitler but also the left-wing theorists who looked forward to a world without Jews through the abolition of class-conflict. It may seem strange to include Hitler, in this context, among the rationalists, but it should be remembered that he prided himself on his freedom from religious dogma and on the scientific basis of his racialist theories.

Appendix

St. John Chrysostom on Judas Iscariot

1. From *De Proditione Judae:* Homily 1.

"Judas who was called Iscariot" (Matthew 26:14).

"Why do you name his city? There was another disciple Judas, who had the surname 'Zelotes'. Lest, therefore, some error should arise from the identity of names, he distinguished this one from that one. And that one indeed he named Judas the Zealot according to his virtue, but this one he did not name according to his sinfulness: for he did not say, 'Judas the Traitor'."

NOTE. Chrysostom evidently regards the name "Iscariot" as denoting Judas's place of origin, perhaps seeing the name as equivalent to "man of Keriyot". But what is especially interesting in this comment is Chrysostom's statement that the other Judas had the cognomen "Zelotes". The name "Judas the Zealot" is found in the New Testament only in certain manuscripts of the Old Latin (Itala) Version of Matthew 10:3 (instead of "Thaddaeus"). Chrysostom is thus an important witness for the designation "Judas the Zealot" (see p. 133 and p. 134 for the relevance of this designation). In the corresponding passage in Chrysostom's second Homily on Judas Iscariot, "Judas the Zealot" is not found; instead, Chrysostom substituted "Judas of James" (from Luke 6:16), thus omitting the argument that "Zealot" indicates "virtuous". The Second Homily is a revised version of the First, and it seems that Chrysostom came to the conclusion that the reading "Judas the Zealot" was untrustworthy and altered his argument accordingly. The reading, however, must have been quite well supported in the Greek manuscripts available to him at that time, or he would not have used it in the First Homily. For the designation "Judas the Canaanite" (equivalent to "Judas the Zealot") see p. 133.

2. From *De Proditione Judae*, Homily 1.

"Do you see how impure is this unleavened bread? how unlawful the feast? how this is not really the Jewish Passover? There was once a Jewish Passover, but now it is abolished. The spiritual Passover has arrived, which Christ gave us. While they were eating and drinking, he took bread, broke it and said, 'This is my body, which is broken for you for the remission of sins.' They who are initiated know the things that are said; and again, taking the cup, he said, 'This is my blood, which is shed for many, for the remission of sins.' Judas was present when Christ was saying these things. This is the body, Judas, which you sold for thirty pieces of silver! this is the blood for which you insolently entered into a contract recently with the wicked Pharisees!"

NOTE. Chrysostom here weaves together a condemnation of the Jewish Passover with a lament over the crime of Judas. The Jews are condemned for continuing to celebrate their Passover with unleavened bread, for this is to reject the new dispensation, in which the Eucharist takes the place of the Passover. Similarly Judas rejected the new dispensation, even though he was present when it was instituted. Instead he conspired with the "wicked Pharisees" to sin against the body and blood of Christ. This passage of Chrysostom has a sombre ring when read in the light of later Christian persecutions of the Jews arising from the accusation that they blasphemed by stealing the Host and puncturing it with pins, thereby causing it to exude miraculous blood. Thousands of Jews were tortured to death on the basis of this kind of accusation. It is noteworthy that Chrysostom fails to read the Gospels accurately; it was not the Pharisees, but the priests, with whom Judas allegedly plotted. But the Pharisees, being the main religious representatives and leaders of the Jewish people, are more suitable for Chrysostom's purpose.

3. From Homily III on Acts of the Apostles 1:15–22

"God compelled them to call the field in Hebrew 'Aceldama'" (Matthew 26:24). "By this also the evils which were to come upon the Jews were declared: and Peter shows the prophecy to have been so far in part fulfilled, which says, 'It had been good for that man if he had not been born.' We may with propriety apply this same to the Jews likewise; for if he who was guide suffered thus, much more they. Thus far however Peter says nothing of this. Then, showing that the term, 'Aceldama' might well be applied to his fate, he introduces the prophet, saying, 'Let his habitation be desolate.' For what can be worse desolation than to become a place of burial? And the field may well be called *his*. For he who cast down the price, although others were the buyers, has a right to be himself reckoned owner of a great desolation. This desolation was the prelude to that of the Jews, as will appear on looking closely into the facts. For indeed they destroyed themselves by famine, and killed many, and the city became a burial-place of strangers, of soldiers, for as to those, they would not even have let them be buried, for in fact they were not deemed worthy of sepulture."

NOTE. St. John Chrysostom here points plainly to the affinity between Judas and the Jews. Judas, he says, was merely the "guide" to those who arrested Jesus (Acts 1:16), and was thus less guilty than the Jews who arrested him and brought about his death. The punishment of Judas, he argues, prefigures that of the Jews, for Aceldama ("the field of blood"), where Judas died, prefigures the destruction of Jerusalem, where the Jews suffered their national defeat in punishment for killing Jesus. Most sinister of all is Chrysostom's application to the Jews of the saying about Judas: "It had been good for that man if he had not been born." The sufferings of the Jews in Christendom are thus regarded as ordained by God.

Bibliography

Bauckham, R., *Jude and the Relatives of Jesus in the Early Church*, Edinburgh, 1990.

Baum, P.F., "Judas's Red Hair", *JEGP* 21 (1922), pp. 520–9.

Baum, P.F., "The Medieval Legend of Judas Iscariot", *PMLA* 31 (1916), pp. 481–632.

Baum, P.F., "Judas's Sunday Rest", *MLR* 18 (1923), pp. 168–82.

Baum, P.F., "The English Ballad of Judas Iscariot", *Publications of the Modern Language Association*, 31 (1916), pp. 181–9.

Baur, F.C., *Paulus, der Apostel Jesu Christi, Sein Leben und Wirken, seine Briefe und seine Lehre. Ein Beitrag su einer kritischen Geschichte des Urchristenthums*, Stuttgart, 1845.

Benoit, P., "La mort de Judas" in *Synoptische Studien (A. Wikenhauser Festschrift)*, 1953, pp. 1–19.

Berlin, I., *Against the Current: Essays in the History of Ideas*, London, 1979.

Besnard, A.M., "Judas bouc émissaire des apôtres? Un compagnon dangereusement semblable", *BTS* 158 (1974), p. 8f.

Billings, J.S., "Judas Iscariot in the Fourth Gospel", *ET* 51 (1939–40), pp. 156f.

Blinzler, J., *Die Brüder und Schwestern Jesu*, SBS 21, Stuttgart, 1967.

Bloy, L., *Le Salut par les Juifs*, Paris, 1892.

Blum, L., *Souvenirs sur l'Affaire*, Paris, 1935.

Blumenkrantz, B., *Juden und Judentum in der mittelalterlichen Kunst*, Stuttgart, 1965.

Bousset, W., *The Antichrist Legend*, London, 1896.

Brandon, S.G.F., *The Trial of Jesus of Nazareth*, London, 1968.

Brandon, S.G.F., *The Fall of Jerusalem and the Christian Church*, London, 1951.

Brandon, S.G.F., *Jesus and the Zealots*, Manchester, 1967.

Buhl, F., *Geographie des Alten Palästina*, Freiburg and Leipzig, 1896.

Bultmann, R., *History of the Synoptic Tradition*, Oxford, 1958.

Bultmann, R., *Primitive Christianity in its Contemporary Setting*, London, 1956.

Burkert, W., *Homo Necans: the Anthropology of Ancient Greek Sacrificial Ritual and Myth*, Berkeley, 1983.

Campbell, J., *The Masks of God*, 3 vols., New York, 1959–64.

Catchpole, D., *The Trial of Jesus in Jewish Historiography*, Leiden, 1971.

Cohen, F. G., "Jewish Images in Late Medieval German Popular Plays", *Midstream*, Aug/Sept. 1989.

Cohn, N., *Warrant for Genocide: the Myth of the Jewish World-conspiracy and the Protocols of the Elders of Zion*, London and New York, 1967.

Cohn, N., *The Pursuit of the Millennium*, London, 1957.

Constant, Rev. Father, *Les Juifs devant l'Eglise et l'histoire*, Paris, 1897.

Creizenach, W., "Judas Ischarioth in Legende und Sage des Mittelalters", *BGDS* 2 (1876) pp. 177–207.

Cullmann, O., *The State in the New Testament*, 15.

Daudet, L., *Au Temps de Judas*, Paris, 1933.

Davies, A.T. (ed.), *Antisemitism and the Foundations of Christianity*, New York, 1979.

Derrett, J.D.M., "Miscellanea: a Pauline pun and Judas's punishment", *ZNW* 72 (1981), pp. 131–3.

Dickey, H.B., *Judas Iscariot*, New York, 1970.

Drews, A., *Das Markus-Evangelium als Zeugnis gegen die Geschichtlichkeit Jesu*, Jena, 1921.

Dronke, P., *The Medieval Lyric*, New York, 1969.

Drumont, E., *La France juive devant l'opinion*, Paris, 1886.

Eckardt, R., *Elder and Younger Brothers: the Encounter of Jews and Christians*, New York, 1973.

Ehrman, A., "Judas Iscariot and Abba Saqqara", *JBL* 97 (1978), pp. 572f.

Eisler, R., *The Messiah Jesus and John the Baptist*, London, 1931.

Enslin, M.S., "How the Story Grew: Judas in Fact and Fiction", *Festschrift to Honor F. Wilbur Gingrich*, Leiden, 1972, pp. 123–41.

Epiphanius, *Panarion (Refutation of All Heresies)*, in Migne, 1857–66, xlii–xliii.

Eusebius, *Ecclesiastical History*, tr. K. Lake (Loeb Classical Library), London/Harvard, 1926.

Feigel, F.K., *Der Einfluss des Weissagungsbeweises und anderer Motive auf die Leidensgeschichte. Ein Beitrag zur Evangelienkritik*, Tübingen, 1910.

Foakes-Jackson, F.J. and Lake, K. (ed.), *The Beginnings of Christianity*, V, London, 1933.

Frazer, Sir J.G., *The Golden Bough*, abr. ed. in 2 vols., London, 1957.

Freud, S., *Moses and Monotheism*, London, 1939.

Friedman, S.S., *The Oberammergau Passion Play: A Lance against Civilization*, Carbondale, Ill., 1984.

Gager, J.G., *The Origins of Anti-Semitism*, New York/Oxford, 1983.

Gärtner, B., *Die Ratselhaften Termini Nazoräer und Iskariot* (Horae Soederblomianae, IV, 1957).

Gasparro, G.S., *Soteriology and Mystic Aspects in the Cult of Cybele and Attis*, Leiden, 1985.

Girard, R., *Violence and the Sacred* (Eng. tr.), Baltimore and London, 1977.

Glasson, T.E., "Davidic Links with the Betrayal of Jesus", *ET* 85 (1973/4), p. 118f.

Glock, C.Y., and Stark, R., *Christian Beliefs and Anti-Semitism*, New York, 1969.

Goldschmidt, H.L., "Das Judasbild in Neuen Testament aus jüdischer Sicht", in *Judas im Neuen Testament*, eds. H.L. Goldschmidt and M. Limbeck, Stuttgart, 1976, pp. 9–36.

Griffin, C.S., *Judas Iscariot, the Author of the Fourth Gospel*, Boston, 1892.

Gunther, J.J., "The Meaning and Origin of the Name Judas Thomas", *La Muséon* 93 (1980), pp. 113–48.

Guttmann, J., "Judas", *EJ* IX, pp. 526–8.

Halas, R.B., *Judas Iscariot. A Scriptural and Theological Study of his Person, His Deeds and His Eternal Lot*, Washington, 1946.

Hand, W.D., *A Dictionary of Words and Idioms Associated with Judas Iscariot. A Compilation Based Mainly on Material Found in the Germanic Languages*, (UCP. Modern Philology 24/3), Berkeley, 1942, pp. 289–356.

Harris, J.R., "Did Judas Really Commit Suicide?" *AJT*, IV (1900), pp. 490–513.

199

Harris, J.R., *Four Letters on the Western Text of the New Testament*, London, 1894.

Harrison, J.E., *Prolegomena to the Study of Greek Religion*, 3rd ed. London, 1922.

Haugg, D, *Judas Iskarioth in den neutestamentlichen Berichten*, Leipzig, 1930.

Hay, M., *The Foot of Pride*, Boston, 1950.

Heer, F., *God's First Love*, London, 1967.

Heller, B., "Über Judas Ischariotes in der jüdischen Legende", *MGWJ* 77 (1933), pp. 198–210.

Hengel, M., *The Zealots*, London, 1990.

Hiltebeitel, A., *Criminal Gods and Demon Devotees*, New York, 1989.

Horkheimer, M. and Adorno, T.W., *Dialectic of Enlightenment* (Eng. tr.), London, 1973.

Imbach, J., "'Judas hat tausend Gesichter'. Zum Judas bild in der Gegenwartsliteratur", in Wagner, 1985, pp. 91–142.

Ingholt, H., "The Surname of Judas Iscariot", in *Studia orientalia joanni Pedersen dicata*, Kopenhagen, 1953, pp. 152–62.

Irenaeus, *Against Heresies*, in *Early Christian Fathers*, tr. and ed. C.C. Richardson, London, 1953.

James, M.R. (ed.), *The Apocryphal New Testament*, Oxford, 1953.

Jonas, H., *The Gnostic Religion*, 2nd ed., Boston, 1963.

Jursch, H., "Das Bild des Judas Ischarioth im Wandel der Zeiten", *Akten des VII. Internationalen Kongresses für Christliche Archäologie, Trier 1965*, SAC 27, Rome, 1969, pp. 565–73.

Jursch, H., "Judas Iskarioth in der Kunst", *WZ(J).GS* 5 (1952), pp. 101–5.

Kazantzakis, N., *The Last Temptation*, trans. P.A. Bien, London, 1975.

Kermode, F., *The Genesis of Secrecy*, Cambridge, Mass./London, 1979.

Klauck, H.-J., *Judas—ein Jünger des Herrn*, Quaestiones Disputatae, 111, Herder, Freiburg/Basel/Wien, 1987.

Klostermann, E., *Das Markusevangelium*, HNT 3, 4th ed. 1950, 35.

Kluckhohn, C., "Recurrent Themes in Myths and Mythmaking", in *Myths and Mythmaking*, ed. Henry A. Murray, Boston, 1968, p. 52.

Körtner, U.H.J., *Papias von Hierapolis. Ein Beitrag zur Geschichte des frühen Christentums*, Göttingen, 1983.

Köster, H., "GNOMAI DIAPHORAI: The Origin and Nature of Diversification in the History of Early Christianity", *Harvard Theological Review* 58 (1965), pp. 279–318.

Krauss, S., *Das Leben Jesus nach juedischen Quellen*, Berlin, 1902.

Kümmel, W.G., *Introduction to the New Testament*, London, 1975.

Kürzinger, J., *Papias von Hieropolis und die Evangelien des Neuen Testaments* (Eichstätter Materialen 4), Regensburg, 1983.

La Tour de Pin, René, Marquis de, *Vers un ordre social chrétien*, Paris, 1907.

Lake, K., "The Death of Judas", in Foakes-Jackson and Lake, 1933, pp. 22–30.

Layton, B., *The Gnostic Scriptures*, London, 1987.

Leach, E., *Genesis as Myth*, London, 1969.

Lévy, L.G., "Que Judas Iscariote n'a jamais existé", *Grande Revue* 55 (1909), pp. 533–9.

Lévi-Strauss, C., *The Raw and the Cooked*, London, New York, 1969.

Linthicum, M.C., *Costume in the Drama of Shakespeare and his Contemporaries*, Oxford, 1936.

Lovsky, F. (ed.), *L'antisémitisme chrétien*, Paris, 1970.

Lublinski, S., *Das werdende Dogma vom Leben Jesu*, Jena, 1910.

Lüdemann, G., "The Successors of Pre–70 Jerusalem Christianity: A Critical Evaluation of the Pella-Tradition", in Sanders, 1980, pp. 161–73.

Lüthi, K., *Judas Iskarioth in der Geschichte der Auslegung von der Reformation bis zur Gegenwart*, Leipzig, 1955.

Lüthi, K., "Das Problem des Judas Iskariot—neu untersucht", *Evangelische Theologie*, 16, 1956, pp. 98–144.

Maccoby, H., "Jesus and Barabbas", *New Testament Studies*, 16, 1968, pp. 55–60.

Maccoby, H., "The Antisemitism of Ezra Pound", *Midstream*, 22, March, 1976.

Maccoby, H., "The Delectable Daughter", *Midstream*, 16, Nov., 1970.

Maccoby, H., "The Figure of Shylock", *Midstream*, 16, Feb., 1970.

Maccoby, H., *Judaism in the First Century*, London, 1989.

Maccoby, H., *Paul and Hellenism*, London/Philadelphia, 1991.

Maccoby, H., "Gospel and Midrash", *Commentary*, 69: 4 (April, 1980), pp. 69–72.

Maccoby, H., *Revolution in Judaea*, New York, 1980.

Maccoby, H., *The Mythmaker: Paul and the Invention of Christianity*, London, New York, 1986.

Maccoby, H., *The Sacred Executioner*, Thames & Hudson, London, 1982.

Maier, J., *Jesus von Nazareth in der talmüdischen Überlieferung*, Darmstadt, 1978.

Mellinkoff, R., "Judas's Red Hair and the Jews," in *Journal of Jewish Art*, vol. IX, 1989.

Migne, J.P. (ed.), *Patrologia Graeca*, Paris, 1857–66.

Migne, J.P. (ed.), *Patrologia Latina*, Paris, 1844–64.

Montefiore, C.G., *The Synoptic Gospels*, 2 vols. Macmillan, London, 1927 (2nd ed.)

Pearson, B.A., "I Thessalonians 2:13–16: A Deutero-Pauline Interpolation", *Harvard Theological Review* 64 (1971), pp. 79–94.

Péguy, C., *Oeuvres en prose 1898–1908*, Paris, 1959.

Pflaum, H., "Les Scènes de Juifs dans la littérature dramatique du Moyen-âge," in *Revue des études Juives*, vol. lxxxix (1930), pp. 111–34.

Pierrard, P., *Juifs et catholiques français: De Drumont à Jules Isaac (1886–1945)*, Paris, 1970.

Poliakov, L., *The History of Antisemitism*, 4 vols. London, 1974–1980.

Porte, W., *Judas Ischarioth in der bildenden Kunst*, Diss. Jena, Berlin 1833.

Propp, V., *Morphology of Folktale*, Bloomington, 1958.

Quinn, R.M., *Fernando Gallego and the Retablo of Ciudad Rodrigo*, Tuscon, 1961.

Rand, E.K. "Medieval Lives of Judas Iscariot", in *Anniversary Papers by Colleagues and Pupils of George Lyman Kittredge*, Boston, 1913, pp. 305–16.

Réau, L., *Iconographie de l'art chrétien*, Paris, 1957.

Reider, J., "Jews in Medieval Art", in Pinson, Koppel S., (ed.) *Essays in Antisemitism*, New York, 1946.

Reider, N., "Medieval Oedipal Legends about Judas", in *Psychoanalytic Quarterly*, 29 (1960), pp. 515–27.

Reik, T., *Ritual: Psychoanalytic Studies*, New York, 1957.

Reitzenstein, R., *Die hellenistische Mysterienreligionen*, 3rd ed., Leipzig/Berlin, 1927.

Renan, E., *Saint Paul*, Paris, 1869.

Robertson, A.T., "The Primacy of Judas Iscariot", in *Exp*, VIII/13 (1917), pp. 278–86.

Robertson, J.M., *Jesus and Judas: a Textual and Historical Investigation*, London, 1927.

Robertson, J.M., *Die Evangelienmythen*, Jena, 1910.

Robinson, J.M. (ed.), *The Nag Hammadi Library in English*, 2nd ed., Leiden, 1984.

Rosenberg, E., *From Shylock to Svengali: Jewish Stereotypes in English Fiction*, Peter Owen, London, 1961.

Roth, C., *The Jewish Contribution to Civilisation*, 2nd ed., Oxford, 1943.

Ruether, R., *Faith and Fratricide*, New York, 1974.

Sanders, E.P. (ed.), *Jewish and Christian Self-definition*, vol. 1: *The Shaping of Christianity in the Second and Third Centuries*, London, 1980.

Sanders, J.T, *The Jews in Luke-Acts*, SCM Press, London, 1987.

Schiller, G., *Iconography of Christian Art*, London, 1972, 2 vols.

Schläger, G., "Die Ungeschichtlichkeit des Verräters Judas", *ZNW* 15 (1914), pp. 50–59.

Schoeps, H.J., *Theologie und Geschichte des Judenchristentums*, Tübingen, 1949.

Schueler, D.G., "The Middle English *Judas*: An Interpretation", *PMLA*, 91 (1976), pp. 840–45.

Schulthess, F., *Das Problem der Sprache Jesu*, Berlin, 1917.

Shachar, I., *The Emergence of the Modern Pictorial Stereotype of "the Jew" in England*, (Studies in the Cultural Life of the Jews in England, no. 5.) 1975.

Simon, M., *Verus Israel: A Study of the relations between Christians and Jews in the Roman Empire (135–425)*, Oxford, 1986 (first pub. in French, 1964).

Smith, W.B., "Judas Iscariot", *HibJ* 9 (1911), pp. 529–44.

Stauffer, E., "Zum Kalifat des Jacobus", *ZRGG* 4 (1952), pp. 192–214.

Steiner, G., *Bluebeard's Castle*, London, 1971.

Talmon, J.L., *Political Messianism: the Romantic Phase*, London, 1960.

Tarachov, S., "Judas the Beloved Executioner", in *Psychoanalytical Quarterly* 29 (1960), pp. 528–54.

Thompson, S., *Motif-Index of Folk-Literature*, 6 vols, Bloomington, 1989.

Tierney, P., *The Highest Altar*, New York, 1989.

Torrey, C.C., "The Name 'Iscariot'", *HTR*, XXXVI (1943), pp. 51–62.

Trachtenberg, J., *The Devil and the Jews*, New York, 1966.

Verard, A. (ed.), *Mistere de la Resurrection de Notre-Seigneur, Jésus-Crist*, Paris, Classification Res. y f.15 of the Bibliothèque Nationale.

Vermaseren, M.J., *Cybele and Attis: the Myth and the Cult*, London, 1977.

Vogler, W., *Judas Iskarioth. Untersuchungen su Tradition und Redaktion von Texten des Neuen Testaments und ausserkanonischer Schriften* (ThA 42), Berlin, 1983.

Visuvalingam, S., "The Transgressive Sacrality of the Diksita", in Hiltebeitel, 1989, pp. 427–63.

von Campenhausen, H., "Die Nachfolge des Jakobus; Zur Frage eines urchristlichen Kalifats", *ZKG* 63 (1950–51), pp. 133–44.

Wagner, H., *Judas Iskariot. Menschliches oder heilsgeschichtliches Drama?* Frankfurt, 1985.

Weber, P., *Geistliches Schauspiel und kirchliche Kunst*, Stuttgart, 1894.

Wells, G.A., *The Jesus of the Early Christians*, London, 1971.

Williams, A.L., *Adversus Judaeos*, Cambridge, 1935.

Wilson, S., *Ideology and Experience: Antisemitism in France at the Time of the Dreyfus Affair*, London, 1982.

Wright, A., "Was Judas Iskarioth the First of the Twelve?", *Interpreter* 13 (1916), pp. 18–25.

Yerkes, R.K., *Sacrifice in Greek and Roman Religions and Early Judaism*, London, 1953.

Zafran, E.M., *The Iconography of Antisemitism: a Study of the Representation of the Jews in the Visual Arts of Europe 1400–1600*, Ph.D. thesis (unpublished), New York University, 1973.

Index